GW00535567

Race in the Making

Learning, Development, and Conceptual Change

Lila Gleitman, Susan Carey, Elissa Newport, and Elizabeth Spelke, editors

John Macnamara, *Names for Things: A Study in Human Learning* (1982)

Susan Carey, *Conceptual Change in Childhood* (1985)

David Premack, *"Gavagai!" or the Future History of the Animal Language Controversy* (1986)

Daniel N. Osherson, *Systems That Learn: An Introduction to Learning Theory for Cognitive and Computer Scientists* (1986)

James L. Morgan, *From Simple Input to Complex Grammar* (1986)

Frank C. Keil, *Concepts, Kinds, and Cognitive Development* (1989)

Steven Pinker, *Learnability and Cognition: The Acquisition of Argument Structure* (1989)

Kurt VanLehn, *Mind Bugs: The Origins of Procedural Misconception* (1990)

Ellen M. Markman, *Categorization and Naming in Children: Problems of Induction* (1990)

Henry M. Wellman, *The Child's Theory of Mind* (1990)

Charles R. Gallistel, *The Organization of Learning* (1990)

Josef Perner, *Understanding the Representational Mind* (1991)

Eleanor J. Gibson, *An Odyssey in Learning and Perception* (1991)

Simon Baron-Cohen, *Mindblindness: An Essay on Autism and Theory of Mind* (1995)

Alvin M. Liberman, *Speech: A Special Code* (1995)

Barbara Koslowski, *Theory and Evidence: The Development of Scientific Reasoning* (1995)

Lawrence A. Hirschfeld, *Race in the Making: Cognition, Culture, and the Child's Construction of Human Kinds* (1996)

Race in the Making

Cognition, Culture, and the Child's Construction of Human Kinds

Lawrence A. Hirschfeld

To Isaac, to meals + talks in Provence, particularly to talking

best, L.

A Bradford Book

The MIT Press
Cambridge, Massachusetts
London, England

Set in Palatino by The MIT Press.
Printed and bound in the United States of America.

Library of Congress Cataloging-in-Publication Data

Hirschfeld, Lawrence
Race in the making : cognition, culture, and the child's construction of human kinds / Lawrence A. Hirschfeld.
p. cm. — (Learning, development, and conceptual change)
"A Bradford book."
Includes bibligraphical references and index.
ISBN 0-262-08247-0 (hardcover : alk. paper)
1. Cognition and culture. 2. Racism. 3. Ethnopsychology. 4. Cognition in children. 5. Child psychology. 6. Prejudices in children. I. Title. II. Series.
BF311.H54 1996
155.8'2—dc20 95-40230
CIP

Contents

Series Foreword

This series will include state-of-the-art reference works, seminal monographs, and texts on the development of concepts and mental structures. It will span domains of knowledge from syntax to geometry to the social world, and it will be concerned with all phases of development, from infancy through adulthood. The series intends to engage these fundamental questions:

> the nature and limits of learning and maturation: the influence of the environment, of initial structures, and of maturational changes in the nervous system on human development; learnability theory; the problem of induction; domain-specific constraints on development
>
> the nature of conceptual change: conceptual organization and conceptual change in child development, in the acquisition of expertise, and in the history of science.

Lila Gleitman
Susan Carey
Elissa Newport
Elizabeth Spelke

Preface

I don't remember "discovering" race as a child. I actually have a clearer memory of race's discovering me. My family lived in Father Charles Coughlin's parish, near Detroit. Readers with a memory for pre–World War II radio will recall Father Coughlin as an extreme populist with a wide following and markedly anti-Semitic politics. I was in early elementary school, perhaps first or second grade, and someone called me a kike. I didn't understand. So I asked my older brother what "kike" meant. For whatever reason, he told me that it was a house of legislature, "like the Congress." I remember being confused.

Later, when kids began beating me up when they called me kike, I figured out that my brother had been joking with me. "Kike," I realized, was a nasty name for my kind of people. The taunts and the attacks suddenly became explicable, virtually the "natural" consequence of my having a racial identity. (When I was 7 years old, in 1954, Jews were still a race in many people's minds.) The noteworthy discovery for me was not that people disliked me because of my racial identity but that I had one. Other people—blacks especially, to a youngster growing up in my neighborhood—had racial identities. Not me, though. I had believed that I was part of the great unhyphenated-white move to the suburbs.

Although I thought a lot about race and racism after that, not until I went to college was I again shaken about my racial beliefs. I was profoundly impressed by a course I took on race and anthropology. The professor, Frank Livingstone, explained that race is not real, not natural. Socially designated races, he told the class, have no biological basis. I was fascinated (and I remain so today) that something so obviously real could be contrived. This was news.

It would be both satisfying and tidy if these events had prompted me to do the research I report in this book. It would provide both epistemic and personal motivations for working on what is after all a marginal topic in both anthropology and cognitive science. But that isn't how my interest developed. Obviously it was not the case that these events had little impact on me. They were tremendously influential. The issue was whether I imagined these sorts of practices and beliefs to be amenable to scientific scrutiny. I was convinced that they were not. To me, and to many others with my political and academic affiliations, race and racial politics were culturally contingent and historically constructed. They were the kinds of things that lent themselves to political action, not scientific explanation. Ironically, I was as convinced then as I am now of the book's central claim—that race is easy to think but difficult to think about, that it is experienced as a self-evidently natural part of the modern world, and that it is contrived in the extreme but in ways that people hardly notice. At the time I took this as evidence that race raised interesting political and cultural but not psychological questions.

Indeed, it was a number of years later that I thought to examine as a matter of science why it is that we so firmly believe that race is real. I ended up doing so not so much because of an intellectual interest in race itself as because I was concerned with how humans conceptualize the groups with which they affiliate. I was struck by a psychological gap in our anthropological understanding and an anthropological gap in our psychological understanding. Filling these gaps turned on finding an adequate psychological description of the causal forces that anthropologists appeal to in explaining and describing social experience and making these causal forces relevant to psychologists. Anthropologists take as self-evident that enduring, diffuse, yet corporate aggregates of people are the stuff around which social life is organized and social structure coalesces. Particularly in the small communities that anthropologists frequent, understanding corporate aggregates of tribe and kin is crucial to understanding local existence. Yet we have remarkably little knowledge of how people mentally represent these sorts of groups or of the social and political consequences such mental representations might have.

Thus, when I set off to do my dissertation fieldwork among a highland tribal group in Sumatra, the problem that interested me was how social categories—particularly those of kinship—are conceptualized. I thought that I could explore the question by traditional anthropological means: through the collection of ethnographic data, particularly the explications that adults offered of their own actions and motivations. After I left the field I realized that this would not do. The material I had gathered simply did not speak to the questions I wanted to answer. I found that in the existing literature there was a good deal of data, mostly experimental and mostly meant to answer other sorts of questions, that did permit speculation on how social categories are cognized. Most of this work proceeded from the assumption that social categories are cognized much as other object categories are cognized. Yet a second look at these studies invariably lent support to the argument that social categories—particularly those that capture the sorts of enduring corporate collectivities that anthropologists are convinced have such causal force—are mentally represented in their own unique way.

It was during this time that I began to seriously engage race as a object of scientific study. My initial intent was not to study race but to study the enduring corporate collectivities that have traditionally been of interest to anthropologists, particularly those of kinship. It turns out that, although we don't know a great deal about how kinship is psychologically represented, there is a considerable body of literature on how this other corporate collectivity, race, is psychologically fixed. So I turned my attention to race. I began to conjecture on what race's cognitive foundations are, how it is learned, and how belief in it is sustained over time and space. My intellectual concern at the time was not with race's relationship to power—an issue that had hardly begun to catch anthropological attention then and still hasn't caught the attention of many in psychology. Still, it became evident that it is not possible to study race and be unconcerned with its role in the regulation, distribution, and explanation of power, authority, and wealth.

After almost 15 years of working on the mental representation of race, the conclusions I've come to are in many respects disquieting. Strikingly, the basis for this is cognitive. Race is not simply a bad idea; it is a deeply rooted bad idea. This is not an appealing thought. It implies that race may be as firmly grounded in our minds as it is in the politics of our day. Many people, perhaps understandably, prefer to believe that this is not the case. Many prefer to believe that race is an accident of how we happen to categorize the world. I suppose that this preference alone accounts for why so many people continue to believe that race is not only a bad idea but a superficial one—one that could be "set straight" by simply correcting the misinformation that we receive as children, by extolling the virtues of our diverse world. As comforting as this view may be, children, I will show in this book, are more than aware of diversity; they are driven by an endogenous curiosity to uncover it. Children, I will also show, do not believe race to be a superficial quality of the world. Multicultural curricula aside, few people believe that race is only skin deep. Certainly few 3-year-olds do. They believe that race is an intrinsic, immutable, and essential aspect of a person's identity. Moreover, they seem to come to this conclusion on their own. They do not need to be taught that race is a deep property, they know it themselves already.

If race is a deep belief, does that mean that it is genetically determined? If it is, does that mean that it is an evolved adaptation? One could deny both out of hand, and I suspect most do. But doing science by ruling out possibilities because we are uncomfortable with them is not a good strategy. I hope to convince the reader that the answers are more complex and more informative than we might have expected. Race—the idea of race—isn't biologically determined. Nor is the idea of race an evolved adaptation. But the abstract principles that give rise to the idea probably are both biologically determined and products of an evolved adaptation. In short, race is something for which we have a prepared susceptibility.

This does not mean that racial ideas are incorrigible or that they are themselves biologically determined. Because something emerges out of an inborn susceptibility does not mean that we have no control over it or that the thing itself is innate. For example, we now know that infants are born with a susceptibility to develop certain expectations about the behavior of physical objects. Yet it is obvious that humans come to hold alternative models of (and expectations about) the physical world (models, like quantum physics, that are less tied to objects within the unaided perceptual field of human beings). We acknowledge, however, that acquiring such models is hard work. They are learned only with elaborate institutional support (like college instruction). Another apt analogy is to disease states that have been widely distributed among humans. Virtually all humans are born with susceptibilities to contract smallpox and tuberculosis. The diseases themselves are not innate; the susceptibilities to contract them are. We have discovered ways to alter our inborn susceptibilities to these diseases and hence change the possibility of actually contracting them. Race has some interesting parallels with both of these cases. With hard work we are able to rethink the commonsense commitment to the race concept, just as we are able to rethink the commonsense commitment to a certain model of the physical world. Doing this does not require eradicating that commonsense commitment; instead it involves loosening the hold one image of the world has on our cognition. Similarly, in arguing that we have an inborn susceptibility to race does not mean that race (or racism) is innate. Rather, like smallpox or tuberculosis, race emerges out of the interaction of prepared inborn potentialities and a particular environment. By definition the notion of inborn susceptibility implies an interaction between the organism and the environment.

Nonetheless, there is a great reluctance to see things political as based on anything but systems of learning, systems of nurture. The notion that nature and nurture represent competing explanations is curious. No biologically based adaptation is immune to environmental influences. Indeed, no biologically based adaptation can even be realized without an environment that guides and constrains development.

As Lila Gleitman (1986) notes, to know that language is a special biological adaptation it is sufficient to observe that virtually all human children and none of their dogs acquire a language. To know that language is learned it is sufficient to observe that there is a "massive correlation" between living in France and learning French (ibid., p. 3).

Just above I used of smallpox and tuberculosis as examples of biologically grounded susceptibilities that we can alter. We do so by vaccinating our young against these diseases. Multicultural interventions aside, there is no reason to believe that we can similarly vaccinate our young against racism. In part this is because cognitive vaccinations have the unfortunate property of looking more like propaganda than anything else. They are attempts to convince people that something they know perfectly well is not the case. We don't get people to diet by telling them that they are not hungry. We won't get people to stop deeply cognizing race by telling them that they do not. It matters little whether we are talking to adult followers of Jean-Marie Le Pen or David Duke or to 5-year-olds. We are simply not likely to rid ourselves of racialist thinking by denying that racialism is deeply grounded in our conceptual endowment. The susceptibility to think in racial terms is genuinely within us, clearly in virtue of our cognitive endowment.

Thus, the enterprise in which I engage in this book stems from three kinds of reflection. As a cognitive scientist I am concerned with how everyday concepts about humans and human nature are formed. As a psychological anthropologist I am concerned with how cultural ideas are mentally represented and socially distributed. Finally, as someone who came of political age in the late 1960s I am concerned with how racialism and racism develop and are sustained. That my conclusions run counter to conventional wisdom from all three perspectives is perhaps not surprising. Cognitive scientists as a whole aren't interested in the messier categories of human affairs. The prevailing tendency within anthropology is a consistent skepticism about explaining cultural things in psychological terms. And, most important, almost everyone is uncomfortable with viewing race as fundamentally part of the human cognitive endowment. For one thing, such a view violates our image of the innocent child—a notion that, despite its relative recency, is close to a foundational belief of American culture. It animates our pedagogy, our pediatrics, and assuredly our politics of race. The notion that political and moral transgressions are the results of learned responses rather than of biologically determined susceptibilities is similarly foundational. Neither notion, I will argue here, is well founded. It is precisely because these questions are so disquieting that they demand our attention today.

Acknowledgements

I have incurred too many debts in conducting this research and in writing this book to thank properly all those who contributed. I am grateful for generous research support from the National Science Foundation grants SBR-9319796, INT-8814397, RCD-8751136. Various units of the University of Michigan, including the Office of the Vice President for Research (to whose Assistant Vice President for Research, Marvin Parnes, I owe a special debt), the Department of Anthropology, the Institute for Social Research, and the School of Social Work have all provided substantial support. I thank each.

Friends, students, and colleagues have read various manuscript drafts and generously given me thoughtful and detailed advice. I warmly thank Scott Atran, Fernando Coronil, Val Daniel, Guy Denhière, Susan Gelman, Rochel Gelman, Conrad Kottak, Frank Livingstone, Bruce Mannheim, Hazel Markus, Janet McIntosh, Richard Nisbett, Doug Medin, David Premack, Heidi Schweingruber, Ed Shoben, Ed Smith, Ken Springer, Henry Wellman, and Bob Zajonc for their comments. I am extremely grateful to Susan Carey for her patience, close reading, and comments on the manuscript as it approached completion. I thank my colleagues and students in the Culture and Cognition Program, particularly Dick Nisbett, who both individually and as a group engaged this work in extended and helpful discussion. My collaborators, Susan Gelman and Ken Springer, have graciously allowed me to report joint work as if it were mine alone. I acknowledge and thank them. I also am grateful to Rangka Bijeljac, Grace Carreon, John Coley, Mary Dwyer Dankoski, Corine Dubon, Lisa Duncan, Nicole Fleischman, Ada Haiman-Arena, Aimee Hiske, Leila Hudson, Kim Piontek, and Heidi Schweingruber for their help with the experiments, and to John Warner for his assistance with the analyses. Katie Heffernan has been an exceptionally hard-working and thoughtful assistant.

Even a most cursory reading will reveal the enormous debt I owe to Dan Sperber. For more than 20 years we have discussed, argued, and rethought this project, the very notion of which would be impossible without his work.

Finally, and most crucially, my family has provided an extraordinary level of support. My children, Tessa and Bruno, have patience for (and, not incidentally, an understanding of) my work far beyond anything I thought possible. I wish that the book had cost less of my time, energy, and enthusiasm. My children have given up much too much in order that it could be completed. I not only thank them with all my heart but apologize sincerely. There is no category of thanks that remotely expresses my gratitude to Ann Stoler. She has been with me at every step, suggesting, cautioning, and cajoling me about the political consequences, social implications, and cultural reverberation of my claims. I would not have completed it without her support and council. Perhaps most remarkably, and certainly a measure of her generousity, she and I have arrived at a book each on more or less the same topic—and with hardly a point of overlap between them. She is my most patient, thoughtful, and of course beloved colleague. I dedicate this book to her.

Race in the Making

Introduction

To people living in the contemporary world, racial thinking seems a conspicuous and ubiquitous aspect of everyday life. This doesn't seem all that surprising. It is widely believed that the notion of race derives directly from the spontaneous perception of physical variation that is diagnostic of the major partitions of humanity. It is also widely accepted that evidence of these major partitions is frequently encountered, given the rich diversity of modern societies. Thinking racially, then, seems to be directly tethered to unremarkable sensory experience. Still, the idea of race involves more than an awareness of surface difference. In particular, race is thought to capture less obvious variation in humanity. Racial thinking is not simply a catalogue of human difference; it also encompasses beliefs about the very *nature* of difference. When imaging the world in racial terms, people are also making judgments about the inner and the nonobvious. Some of these beliefs enjoy the cachet of modern science (e.g., the genetic basis of the distribution of sickle-cell anemia), but most lack any rigorous footing outside of common sense.

Race, of course, is more than a concept. It is a fundamental aspect of social life, one that plays a pivotal role in predicting differential access to resources. In a wide range of social formations—and under disparate conditions of social existence—wealth, power, and opportunity are distributed racially. Answers to questions about who is impoverished, in poor health, politically disenfranchised, or poorly motivated in school invariably mention race (at least in modern secular society). Crucially, race differences are seldom if ever the *cause* of impoverishment, ill health, political disenfranchisement, or poor academic motivation, nor are these social ills always consistently distributed along racial lines. Other aspects of socio-economic structure (e.g., class, labor position, economic status, and cultural affiliation) often more appropriately specify the dimension along which such disadvantage lies—and differences in an individual's or a group's position with regard to these dimensions clearly are often the basis for it.

Thus, race does not explain disadvantage so much as explain it away by "distorting" our perception of other material relations (Winant 1994). Expectations about differences in human nature stand in a complex relation to the structural consequences attributed to them. Beliefs about inner racial qualities perpetuate discrimination. They also create compelling (though misguided) explanations for it. That is to say, racial thinking serves both to legitimize and to misrepresent the way power is wielded and opportunity apportioned. To some extent this means that race is a closed system of practice and thought: racial thinking serves as a rationalization for inequitable distribution associated with racial status.

Not surprisingly, an idea that warrants so broad a range of expectations is complex. In addition, it incorporates some contradictory aspects. On the one hand, racial thinking often involves contrived taxonomies of difference directly linked to specific cultural, political, and economic traditions. At the same time, racial thinking also involves robust, seemingly self-evident, widely rehearsed, and highly shared beliefs about the meaning and nature of human difference. In this regard, the concept of race appears to vary little by time and place. A distinct disciplinary approach can be identified with each of these contradictory characteristics. Psychologists have examined the way in which the organization of human mental life both captures and creates racial thought. Anthropologists, historians, and other comparative scholars have tracked the emergence and the evolution of racial thinking as a principal political and economic fact of the modern world. These two disciplinary traditions remain largely independent of each other and are often mutually uninformative.

This book has two principal goals: to reinterpret the tension between the universal and the specific in race and to provide an account of racial thinking that adequately captures both of these characteristic qualities. This enterprise takes two forms: specifying a model of racial thinking that is consistent with the insights of both disciplinary traditions and empirically exploring how culture and cognition shape the development of racial thinking in the child. I can recast this project as an attempt to answer several questions: Why is it so easy to racialize explanations of human behavior and potential? Why are failings (and successes) in human arenas as varied as the commercial, the cognitive, and the athletic so readily attributed to racial causes? Why is it difficult to see past racial accounts to more structural (e.g., political, economic, and even cultural) descriptions? Why does racial thinking stabilize so quickly and seemingly effortlessly in the minds of children? This book ventures, sometimes indirectly, to provide a framework in which to answer these questions. It is a first step in a jointly psychological and cultural account of why racial ideas come to be widely distributed, easily transmitted, and predictably transformed. In short, it represents the first moves toward an epidemiology of racial representations.[1]

Whence Race?

In view of the remarkable capability of racial thinking to reconcile, explain, and obscure disadvantage, it is no surprise that there has been a major effort by social and biological scientists to understand its psychological, social, and biological sources. It is important, however, to keep in mind that this effort consists in explaining two distinct phenomena. On the one hand, there is *racialist* thinking—the conviction that human beings (and perhaps other species) can be partitioned into discrete kinds whose reproduction turns on natural processes such as inheritance. On the other hand, there is *racist* thinking—the widely shared belief that the value and potential of individuals follows from their membership in the various races of humankind. Despite the fact that this latter mode is clearly contingent on the racialist one, it is the tenacity and ubiquity of racism—typically registered and expressed through racial stereotypes and prejudice—that has drawn the sustained and intense interest of social scientists.

Somewhat ironically, we now know that one thing that cannot explain a racialist mode of thought is the phenomenon of race itself. Humans are not discriminable into discrete, self-evident biological kinds. Race is "an ideological analysis of social relationships" (Guillaumin 1980, p. 59), not a category of the biological world. It is an artifact of human culture, not a reading of the natural environment. Nor does the natural environment provide reliable evidence for the ideological analysis that is ascribed to it. The *idea* that race has a natural basis cannot be inferred from human biological variation. Although there is now a considerable body of literature in biological anthropology demonstrating that race lacks a scientific basis (Marks 1995; Molnar 1992; Alland 1971; Brace 1964), at first blush the idea may seem counterintuitive. It is accordingly worth examining the claim in more detail.

The strength of our intuitions aside, the human races of both common sense and science simply do not designate biologically interesting populations. Genetic variation between races (to the extent that there is

1. Sperber (1985, 1990, 1994) has outlined the general theoretical program for an epidemiology of representations. He proposes interpreting beliefs, particularly the widespread beliefs typically associated with culture, as the precipitate of cognitive endowment and constraints on communication and meaning. It may be that social structure and institutions can be recast as part of the distribution of ideas, thereby doing away with an ontology that includes them as elemental parts. I remain agnostic on the question, at least as regards the structural and institutional aspects of racial thinking.

a systematic way to determine racial membership—a tenuous assumption at best) is small compared to variation within racial categories (Nei and Roychoudhury 1983; Latter 1980; Lewontin 1972). To claim that racial categories lack a scientific basis is not to say that there are no biological differences among humans, nor is it to claim that there are no biologically grounded differences in human external anatomy. It is merely to say that races as socially defined do not (even loosely) capture *interesting clusters* of these differences. In large part this follows from the fact that the races as socially defined do not pick out genuine reproductive populations.

Difficulties arise even if the racialist claim is restricted to one about continuities in outward appearance (as opposed to a cluster of inner and outer qualities). At least since Boas, most anthropologists have accepted that, whereas racial *talk* is about patterned variation in immutable external traits, racial *classification* tends to be both context specific and task specific. Summing up decades of anthropological research, Molnar (1992, p. 21) concludes: "The number of races and their boundaries remains a subject of [scientific] dispute partially because of the lack of agreement on which traits identify a person's racial identity. Just what constitutes a race is a difficult question to answer, because one's classification usually depends on the purpose of classification." Nor is this realization limited to anthropologists. In psychology, Klineberg (1935, p. 20) made much the same point six decades earlier: "Granting that physical traits are important, it remains to be decided which trait is most important for purposes of classification; it is clear that the classifications will not be the same if, let us say, skin color is selected by one anthropologist and the shape of the head by another. Since there appears to be no objective way of deciding which trait is preferred, there are a great many different racial classifications, all of them equally subjective and equally arbitrary."

To complicate matters, commonsense systems of racial classification encompass beliefs about inner nature as well as outward appearance. In fact, race is commonsensically interesting precisely because putative physical resemblances are supposed to be emblematic of a host of other, often nonobvious attributes, properties, and competencies. Frequently these involve beliefs about morally laden and valuative characteristics. Although scientists have speculated on the relationship between racial-category membership and such characteristics, more often formal accounts of race have attempted to ground the notion in less charged traits. Perhaps the most widely studied of the supposedly race-relevant biological traits are genetic differences in the agglutinative reaction of blood, the various ABO blood types. The discovery of these types at the turn of the century led many to believe that a scientific foundation for racial classification was at hand: to the extent that the relationship between specific local races (i.e., populations typically defined by some shared geographic origin) and certain blood types was determinable, a scientifically reliable measure of race was possible (Hirszfeld and Hirszfeld 1919; Snyder 1947). Ultimately, however, this line of speculation did not pan out. For one thing, there turns out to be little correlation between blood type and other racially relevant characteristics, such as skin color (Molnar 1992). In fact, there is little correlation between supposedly racially relevant blood types and racial categories. When scientists examined how the ABO blood-group allele is distributed across a large number of populations, it became evident that serum types tend to pick out groups that are racially incoherent (e.g., one cluster consists of an African population, three Asian populations, and one European population) (Lewontin 1987). Moreover, there is little reason to believe that the different blood-group genes typically associated with a particular "racial" population form a coherent marker. At least this appears to be the case under conditions of hybridization. Loehlin et al. (1973) assessed blood-group genes among U.S. blacks to determine levels of admixture of European genes. They wanted to know whether variations in admixture correlated with different levels of performance on intelligence tests. They found that they did not. But they also found that the various blood-group genes typically associated with particular racial populations were not inherited as a unit. That is to say, there is little intercorrelation among the blood-group genes even within a single population. Thus, in sharp contrast to the folk notion of racial "blood" (i.e., a unitary physical manifestation of racial heritage), racially relevant properties of blood are independently recombined in reproduction.

There is no reason to believe that other traits or qualities putatively linked to race would be any more likely to cluster in inheritance or to map onto the culturally specified populations called races. There are several reasons for this. First, the notion of racial type has never been tied to a particular *level* of classification in zoology (e.g., species or variety) (Banton 1987), let alone a particular phenomenon. Consequently, it is difficult to imagine how it could be reliably mapped to any biologically grounded property. Second, although the folk notion of race brings to mind images of great genetic differences and great natural distance between groups, the reservoir of genetic variability in any species is actually small compared with what conspecifics share. The sexual reproduction of species-typical architecture could hardly occur otherwise (Tooby and Cosmides 1992). Third, as Loring Brace has long asserted, the argument that distinct human types emerged as responses to adaptive pressures makes little sense:

> It has become apparent that the assumption that there is something significant in the association of traits in a single group of people is an assumption which obscures the factors influencing the occurrence and distribution of any single trait. *The most important thing for the analysis of human variation is the appreciation of the selective pressures which have operated to influence the expression of each trait separately.* Since in many important cases the crucial selective factors have no reference to ethnic or population boundaries, obviously an approach which takes population as its unit for study will fail to produce an understanding of whatever is influencing the distribution of the characteristics in question. (Brace 1964, p. 107)

When nonbiological factors influence the distribution of a particular property, attribute, or competence, the problem is even more intractable. Consider the long debate about race and intelligence. In later chapters I will discuss the issue in some detail, but for the moment it is worth pointing out that mental ability, although significantly influenced by genetic factors, is clearly sensitive to environmental factors that disproportionately affect members of minority groups.[2] These include factors directly linked to minority status (e.g., lower levels of academic preparation due to enforced racial segregation) as well as factors indirectly related to racial status (e.g., poorer health and lower birth weight, which are linked to race via poverty). Most dramatic, even when membership in a racial group *is* the most important influence, evidence shows that biological arguments simply do not hold. Ogbu (1990) has found that poor school achievement is associated less with minority status itself than with the particular cultural meaning that minority status has. The latter, he argues, derives not from the nature of the group but from the initial terms of the minority's incorporation into the host society. The same ethnic or racial group may excel or do poorly in school depending on the particular meaning group membership has in a particular cultural context. For example, in Japan Buraku ethnics (whose conditions of incorporation in Japanese society parallel those of blacks in North America in important respects) do poorly in school relative to other Japanese. When members of the same group immigrate to the United States and are viewed essentially as undifferentiated Asians, they do better in school than their majority counterparts.[3]

2. The idea that intelligence is inherited is often associated with the notion that there is some unitary phenomenon corresponding to mental ability. There is little reason to believe that this is the case. It is more accurate to say that what is at issue is differences in performance on standardized tests.

3. Race not only lacks the biological basis common sense invests it with; it often lacks the

Studying Race

In short, a simple bottom-up approach to the race concept will not do. The idea of race as a complex of beliefs about physical appearance and inner qualities cannot derive from perceptual analysis alone. All this renders race all the *more* interesting as a widely shared concept. If race is not a genuinely natural phenomenon (i.e., if races as they are socially defined do not pick out biologically interesting or even physically discrete populations), the question "Whence racial beliefs?" demands even more explanation. If people do not discern race, how is it that they come to think about it as they do? Researchers from a remarkably wide range of disciplines—anthropology, biology, history, literary criticism, paleontology, philosophy, political science, and sociology—have all made substantial contributions toward answering this question. Despite this diversity in scholarship, virtually all existing work on race falls under one of two approaches: an avowedly universalist one that interiorizes the source of racial beliefs and a decidedly comparative one that seeks to ground such beliefs in structural features of sociocultural formations. The first approach, adopted principally by psychologists, explores the underlying mental processes that give rise to

---

sociological basis too. According to North American common sense, humans are segmentable into discrete groups on the basis of differences in phenotype. Inasmuch as the racially relevant aspects of phenotype are immutable, membership in these groups should not change during an individual's lifetime. However, racial identity is often more labile than this model implies. Researchers in health statistics, who otherwise are committed to the notion that racial categories represent distinct populations, have noted considerable inconsistency in racial identification. For instance, Hahn et al. (1992) found that individuals often are identified as belonging to one race at birth and another at death. Similarly, census followups have found that a nontrivial portion of the population identify as members of one racial group on the initial census report but as members of another racial group on subsequent interviews (Hahn and Stroup 1994). In part this follows from the fact that the processes involved in *self*-identification are quite different from (and often produce less "stable" categorizations than) those underlying *other*-identification. The data-collection techniques used in the census and in other federal research generally do not take this into account. But inconsistencies in racial identification also result from the fact that race and racial identity are often less about membership in distinct groups (based either on common biology or sociology) than about how identity is fundamentally conceptualized and socially enacted. Race is less about groups in the world than about groups in individuals' minds. These conceptual representations underlie a range of practices and discourses. There are differences in the degree to which these practices and discourses are racialized; that is, differences in the degree to which practices and discourse are interpreted in racial terms. To some extent, then, it is incorrect to talk about race at all, even in quotation marks, if we intend by the term distinct and corporate groups of people. Rather we should talk about the way conduct and cognition are racialized. Still, that we can talk about race as a thing is a deeply held notion—indeed, it is almost impossible not to talk about it that way. For this reason, I will continue to use the term in nominal form throughout the book.

racial cognitions and biases. The second, favored by scholars in the comparative and interpretive disciplines (history, anthropology, historical sociology, philosophy, literature), approaches race as the product of specific social and historical forces.[4] Each tradition of research provides plausible arguments about the conditions that underlie a belief about the existence of races. Each offers sound explanations for why these beliefs are highly salient. However, each presents claims that directly contradict those of the other. To illustrate these contradictions, let me sketch each approach.

The Psychology of Racial Ideas

The prevalent point of view in psychology is that racialist thought is a by-product of the way information is organized and processed. In contrast to the comparativists' emphasis on the specific content of racial thought, the psychological approach stresses the consequences of information processing for the way we make sense of intrahuman differences. The generic universalist story has two parts, one situated in the way object categories are generally formed and one situated in the way social categories gain substance.

Object categories The signature property of human information processing is a well-developed capacity to sort objects into categories. Not only do these categories facilitate thought by reducing the sheer amount of information to which people need to attend; natural categories (i.e., those that bring together natural objects, such as cats, water, or gold) extend our knowledge of the world by capturing nonobvious similarities between their members. Once we recognize that a particular creature is a dog, we can infer that it shares with other dogs certain food preferences, certain sleeping habits, and an aversion to cats, even in the absence of opportunities to observe this particular dog eat, sleep,

4. In large measure both views evolved in response to an endemic racism permeating both scholarly and folk thinking. In academic thought this has taken two allied forms: an attempt to "scientifically" systematize commonsense intuitions about racial difference and a eugenicist impulse to theorize reproductive strategies with an eye toward "improving" racial stock. Although cloaked in the guise of natural science, both efforts served to justify the prevailing racial hierarchies of nineteenth- and twentieth-century Europe and North America. These were not isolated research activities, taking place on the fringes of the academy. Any attempt to deny that racism has powerfully shaped the evolution of both psychology and anthropology risks missing the source and the significance of the countercurrents embodied in modern psychological and cultural theory. For the most part, however, I will not be concerned with this heritage of racism. Instead, I am interested in showing that, in contrast to this third (explicitly racist) view, which made (and continues to make) incredible claims about the innate inferiority (typically) of non-Europeans, both the psychological approach and comparative approach have considerable merit.

or interact with any feline. In recent years cognitive psychologists have shown that such category-based knowledge plays a fundamental role in the way we gain and organize knowledge about the natural environment.

Social categories In view of the compelling interest we humans have in other humans, it is not surprising that people also possess a remarkable capacity to categorize and reason about others. A rich and attention-demanding quality of other humans is their elaborate mental life. Thus, it is unremarkable that we recognize commonalities derived from shared mental states and proclivities. There are friendly individuals, angry individuals, depressed individuals, and so on. In short, we classify and label people in terms of transient beliefs and emotions as well as in terms of more stable traits and dispositions.[5] This capacity allows both children and adults to extend explanations of human behavior to unknown instances in unfamiliar circumstances. Knowing that humans are psychological creatures—that they act in accord with their beliefs and desires—allows us to predict what individuals will do in virtue of what we can infer about their beliefs and desires independent of the specific situations in which they find themselves.

Humans also form knowledge of human types on the basis of outward appearance. Two sorts of appearance, gender and race, have been found to be particularly salient. Psychologists typically attribute this salience to two factors: the propensity to classify together objects that share conspicuous physical similarities and the fact that gender and race have prominent physical correlates. Like other natural categories, gender and racial categories seem to capture nonobvious similarities that can be recruited to extend knowledge. However, in contrast to the benign way other natural categories promote inference, these cognitive simplifications—usually called stereotypes—create patterns of belief that have undesirable social and political effects.

Consider how one of these processes, *illusory correlation*, contributes to the formation of social prejudice. Hamilton and Gifford (1976) describe illusory correlation as erroneous inference about the relationship between two classes of events. According to their model, people overestimate the frequency with which distinctive events co-occur because infrequent events may demand more attention than frequent events, and therefore the conjunction of two infrequent events is even more noteworthy. It is plausible that a process of this sort underlies the formation of racial prejudice. When two things share a distinctive feature

5. Although there is dispute as to whether all peoples equally use this capacity to organize trait and disposition knowledge in order to *explain* everyday behavior, there is no evidence that would provide doubt that everyone can *form* such categories.

(such as being rare), people tend to perceive a correlation between them. Negative events are rarer than neutral or positive events, and minority individuals are rarer than majority individuals. Thus, people tend to attribute negative events or descriptions more frequently to minority-group members than to majority-group members. The content of the events and the specific nature of the minority status is unimportant. What counts is the relative frequency with which a particular type of event is encountered and the prevalence of a particular status in the social environment. Cultural, political, and other social factors influence the formation of racial prejudice by determining which events are rare and which are not. However, the motor that drives prejudice is psychological: it is the impulse to form categories and to calibrate their occurrence with other salient dimensions of the world.

The Comparative Study of Race

In contrast to psychologists' concern with the mental processes that give rise to racial thinking, historians and other comparativists have turned their attention to the social-structural antecedents of such thinking. Instead of focusing on mental and private embodiment, comparativists have been largely interested in public representations of and doctrines about race. Typically this means an examination of the discursive practices in which European states (and especially their colonial administrations) engaged (and continue to engage) when enumerating and controlling peoples of non-European descent. Race, on this view, is not the inadvertent by-product of the way information is processed; it is the contrived application of a post-Enlightenment impulse to systematize knowledge of natural phenomena in the service of the imperial enterprise. As such, race is not a discovery about the structure of nature but an invention inscribed onto it. Comparativists acknowledge that non-Europeans also think racially, but they interpret such practices as the adoption by colonized and formerly colonized peoples of a historically unique and European ideology about the nature of human difference.

Scholars in this tradition do not deny that before the European imperial enterprise humans conceived of themselves and others as belonging to specific groups whose members shared a range of common and fundamental properties. They claim, however, that racial ideology stands apart from these antecedent forms because of the special power relationship with which the modern idea is invested and the special kind of commonality that supposedly is shared among members of the same race. The idea of race is a historically unique phenomenon, arising out of a singular confluence of cultural, political, and economic events and practices that defined a particular set of political relations (generally but not always involving colonized and colonizer). This range of relationships was justified in terms of inborn differences in moral, temperamental, and other essential potentials. Because systems of power differ and notions of potential vary, one of the fundamental lessons of historical and other comparative accounts is that racial thinking is not the same in all contexts. Instead it depends on the particular way domination is defined and the context in which is it transacted. Consequently, rather than a single entity "racial thinking," there are the various and contingent systems that have developed in different cultures and historical epochs.

This emphasis on aggregate populations and systems of domination does not mean that comparativists have failed to recognize that racial relations of power are lived by individuals in the context of everyday practice. Nor does it deny that these power relations are interiorized in the individual's psychological experience. In fact, several influential works point out the crucial importance that interiorization plays in imperial racism (Mannoni 1964; Fanon 1968). But these studies differ from the psychological accounts described above in two respects. First, although historically specific systems of racial thinking are sometimes associated with specific mental experiences, such systems are seldom *explained* by psychological (and particularly cognitive) causes. Second, in comparison with psychological researchers who attribute the development of ideas about race and racism to biases in information processing, interpretive scholars who engage questions of interior states are much more likely to turn to the theories and the vocabulary of psychoanalysis than to those of cognitive psychology. In part this follows from the role that interiorization is supposed to play. For most comparativists, even those concerned with the psychological, the interior landscape provides an understanding of the motives and emotional consequences of racial thinking, not an account of how racial thinking came to exist (see, e.g., Adorno et al. 1950).

An Alternative View: Race as a Specialized Belief System

Clearly, attention to both information processing and historical factors contributes to our understanding of how it is that people understand race in the way they do. But by itself neither the historical approach nor the psychological approach adequately captures the complexity of racial thinking. Of particular interest is that neither approach alone is capable of answering one fundamental question about racial thought: Why is it that people so readily move from visual categories to inner nature? General psychological processes do not entail this, nor does the instrumental application of race in the service of unequal power and authority. I will argue that only by reconciling the study of mental and structural (i.e. economic, political, and cultural) factors can we advance an adequate answer to this question.

Students of both approaches have provided important insights into the nature of racial thinking, and I acknowledge the wisdom of both traditions. However, I propose to rethink the two approaches in the following way: Race is indeed a unique sort of belief, in significant measure unlike any other commonsense notion. This uniqueness is due in part to the interaction of historical and cultural particulars, as comparative scholars have long contended. Nonetheless, as psychologists have long maintained, race is an extraordinarily widely encountered notion whose recurrence across varied cultural and historical landscapes derives from deep-rooted psychological processes. I will argue that the two crucial shortcomings of this previous work are the following:

> The specificity of racial thinking derives as much from the unique manner in which our conceptual system creates and harnesses knowledge of intrinsic human kinds as from historical and cultural conditions.
>
> The human conceptual system contributes to the creation of knowledge of human kinds less through the operation of general classifying skills bound to raw sensory perception than through the operation of a special-purpose conceptual device: a domain-specific competence for creating knowledge of and reasoning about human kinds.

I will have considerably more to say about domain specificity in chapter 3. Briefly, a domain-specific competence is a cognitive structure dedicated to gaining, organizing, and using knowledge about a particular content area. Traditionally the mind has been conceived as a general-purpose problem solver whose operation can be studied largely independent of particular content. In recent years a sustained challenge to this view has emerged that proposes that the mind is a collection of more special-purpose tools, each targeting a specific problem or content. Commonsense knowledge of the physical world, of the biological world, and of the psychological world have all been interpreted as the products of domain-specific competences. Although each competence is the basis for a distinct body of knowledge, all domain-specific competences share common structural features. Each directs attention to certain sorts of data, specifies the existence of certain kinds of entities, and guides the formation of a certain range of hypotheses. Such devices perform two crucial functions: they simplify the task of imposing order on an often disorderly world and they provide the means to enrich and extend otherwise limited knowledge.

I argue that racial knowledge too emerges out of the operation of a special-purpose device. But it is important to underscore what I am *not* proposing. I am not suggesting that humans possess a special-purpose cognitive competence that targets a *racial* domain or that is dedicated to the creation of *racial* cognition. In short, I am *not* suggesting that race is an innate concept. It would be curious if I were to make such a claim. As I remarked earlier, races are not genuine categories of the natural environment, so the idea that humans have a special-purpose device that targets a racial domain would be bizarre. Humans create races, they don't discover them. It remains an open question how long they have been creating them. It could be that human cognition is prepared to create specifically racial categories. Evolution has prepared humans to believe in the existence of a range of contrived categories, ranging from highly abstract ones, such as the language-specific categories of noun phrase and verb phrase (Pinker and Bloom 1990), to very concrete ones, such as folk species (Atran 1990; Berlin 1992). It is unlikely, however, that humans evolved to pick out what might be called pseudo-races because the historical conditions for discerning pseudo-races (if there are such things) are a fairly modern phenomenon and were absent for most of human history. Indeed, until relatively recently, with the advent of long-distance sea exploration, humans simply did not encounter groups of other humans who differed abruptly in their external race relevant physical anatomy (van den Berghe 1981).

Rather, humans appear to be ready to conceptualize the human world as composed of distinct types—what I call *human kinds*. A range of human kinds are possible. There are kinds based on common behavioral features, kinds predicated on common physical features, kinds predicated on common emotional characteristics, and so forth. The race concept, I suggest, emerges out of a notion of human kinds *predicated on the attribution of common inherent or intrinsic features.* Like other domain-specific devices, the human-kind competence is comprehensive. People not only create human kinds (in the sense of sorting individuals into relevant sorts), they assume that category members who might otherwise be dissimilar are fundamentally alike in their nonobvious and basic natures. As we will see, this is a crucial point.

The human-kind-creating competence delivers categories that do not embody difference; they interpret it. This feature contributes significantly to the structural consequences of race. Historical and cultural forces do not so much make race essential to the distribution of power and authority as they *enlist* race to legitimize that distribution. It is widely accepted that race legitimizes the inequitable distribution of resources by essentializing and naturalizing both similitude and difference. Paradoxically, race relations are seldom about race *per se*; usually they are about the social organization of labor and commodities expressed through and justified by supposedly genuine and "natural" human kinds (Fields 1990). Race "discovers what other ideologies have to construct: an apparently 'natural' and universal basis in nature itself" (Hall 1980, p. 342).

The notion of the naturalness of embodied difference provides race with one of its most powerful conceptual features: race is both material and hidden. As a considerable body of literature by historians and other comparativists has demonstrated, a hallmark feature of beliefs about the nature of race is the expectation of commonalities that are not obvious from visual inspection alone. This turn of thought—that things that are physical may not be as they appear—makes it easy to think about race as fundamental, essential, and basic, on the one hand, and concrete, on the other.

In significant measure, this book is about how cognition and culture intersect to construct this apparently natural, universal, and perceptual basis.

Children and the Comparative Study of Human Kinds

A cultural psychological or universal constructivist account (I use both terms loosely to describe my project) would seem to rise or fall on comparative data. Of course, there is no logical requirement that work of this sort be comparative. Cultural psychological or universal constructivist research requires that we study the way culture and cognition intersect and articulate. It does not require that we employ a comparative perspective, only that we attend closely to the cultural environment's relationship to thought—and vice versa. And, of course, there is as much culture in North America and Northern Europe as in other parts of the world. Through necessity or not, I propose here to rely on studies that are at their base comparative. I will present evidence about the way European and American children come to racial thinking, and I will compare their systems of racial thinking to those of the adults with whom they live.

At first blush this strategy does not seem to turn on truly comparative data, since it is not cross-cultural. It is, however, comparative in the sense that it contrasts two systems of thought; the child's and the adult's. Again, at first blush this may seem an odd way to approach comparative research. After all, differences between the ways children and adults think about social categories may be attributable to the simplest processes of knowledge accrual. Children start off knowing very little about the social environment. What they eventually come to know they acquire largely in virtue of the ample opportunities they have to learn from their parents and other important adults. I will show, however, that direct learning has less to do with the way racial thinking develops than is often imagined. Substantial aspects of children's racial cognitions do not appear to be derived from adult culture. Rather, they represent interpretations of the social world that children come to on their own. In particular, the impulse to naturalize the social world is grounded less in historically or culturally specific causes than in the way the human mind makes sense of the world.

The paradoxes and specificities of children's thinking, though interesting to students of development, do not necessarily provide insights (comparative or otherwise) into adult belief—particularly adult belief in cultures distant in time and space from those in which these children live. Nonetheless, it is plausible to see children's and adults' thought in a comparative light, in the anthropological sense. By this I mean the commonplace observation that children's thought and adults' thought are related yet different—the basic quality one looks for in a comparative enterprise. Children do not quite talk like, behave like, or think like the adults who share their life space. These differences are not simply quantitative; it is not that children have a smaller set of adult knowledge or a smaller set of adult skills. Children hold beliefs and employ modes of reasoning—i.e., develop representations of the world and rules for manipulating these representations—that are clearly not exemplified in adult practice. Some of these are trivial from a conceptual perspective: whereas few English-speaking adults form the past tense of "go" as "goed," virtually all English-speaking children do so at some point in language development. Children also develop *cultural* forms that are related to but distinct from adult forms (Corsaro and Eder 1990; Mead 1932).

Still, adults' and children's beliefs and behaviors stand in a special relationship: juvenile forms tend to evolve toward adult ones, but the converse seldom occurs. Today's children are tomorrow's adults. Although every cohort of adults maintain cultural vestiges of their childhood (the music that triggers nostalgia in me is hardly the same as the music that sets off wistful reminiscence in my parents), adult traditions invariably look more like those of the preceding adult generation than those of their child selves. Thus, children's systems of belief evolve predictably toward an adult endpoint in a manner not unlike the way systems of cultural knowledge invested with unequal power predictably converge: hegemonically, with noncoercive changes in a subordinate population's beliefs toward those of a dominant population.

To be sure, I am not proposing that historically earlier forms of thought are more childlike than contemporary ones. Although this is an enduring and compelling folk and scientific belief, there is no reason to imagine it is the case.[6] Rather, what I am suggesting is that changes in thought during childhood afford a window on the ways in which endogenous conceptual organization and context contrive to fix belief. It matters little whether those changes occur during childhood or across historical epochs. Conceptual endowment may well guide change in ontogenesis and history in distinct ways, if for no other reason than that adults and children have distinct capacities to process, store, and recall information (Carey 1990).

There is precedent for treating child–adult differences in a comparative perspective. For example, an intracultural comparative question that has attracted considerable attention involves the relationship between common sense and scientific theory (Atran 1994). Children's versus adults' belief has figured in this through exploration of the relationship between children's common sense and formal scientific theories (Brewer and Samarapungavan 1991; Wellman and Gelman 1992; Gopnik and Wellman 1994). Further, we know that the structure of theory change in childhood in some ways closely follows the structure of theory change in the history of science (Wiser and Carey 1983; Gopnik and Wellman 1994). Remarkably, what is perhaps the most sustained study of how theory change in childhood might inform our understanding of cultural variation in common sense was written more than 60 years ago (Mead 1932).[7]

The empirical goal of this book is to provide a sustained exploration of continuity and change in the child's notion of race. Implicit in this project is the claim that common to both ontogenetic and historical changes in racial thinking is a skeletal conceptual model. I propose that a commonsense theory that uniquely targets human kinds constrains the way change in racial thinking occurs, whether it is in historical time or during childhood. This commonsense theory impinges on change in development in modally specific ways: during childhood the skeletal model provides the basis for acquiring and elaborating the culturally ambient model, producing a rather stable system of belief; in historical change, the skeletal model articulates with conditions of political, economic, legal, and cultural relations to transform one system of adult

6. For an excellent review of the issue, see Shweder (1982) on Hallpike (1979).

7. The bulk of existing studies that look at cultural variation in common sense and at age-dependent changes in children's thought have been so ethnocentric as to be of little value. Demonstrations that adults in Pago Pago do less well on conservation tasks than pre-adolescent Genevan children tell us a great deal more about Western common sense than about anything else.

belief into another. In both instances the skeletal model places limits on the versions of race that ultimately emerge. The relevant point is that changes in racial thinking are situated in—and guided by—the distinct ways in which humans organize knowledge of the social world. What follows is an attempt to theoretically model and empirically document the organization of that knowledge.

A Note on Organization

The first part of the book, comprising chapters 1–3, explores the existing literature relevant to the development of a cultural psychology of race. Chapter 1 introduces the psychological and comparativist approaches to race. Chapter 2 suggests a way to reconcile these opposing traditions—or at least a way to allow them to provide converging insights. Specifically, I review claims made about the singular character of varied historical and cultural versions of race with an eye toward finding a comprehensive psychological description that does not overlook this specificity. It is possible to do this, I suggest, precisely because the idea of race is as psychologically singular as it is historically specific. Chapter 3 examines the principal theoretical construct animating this argument: domain specificity.

The second part, comprising chapters 4–7, gives substance to the argument by exploring the way children make—and make sense of—racial thinking. The idea is to sketch how a jointly cultural and psychological approach to race might proceed, and in particular to show how this approach permits new insights into the emergence and the elaboration of racial thinking during childhood. These chapters document change and continuity in the child's thoughts about race—change and continuity that accord well with the claim that children's racial representations are shaped by a special-purpose conceptual device dedicated to understanding and representing human kinds. Topically, the studies reviewed in chapters 4–7 focus on European and American children's beliefs about racial and other social difference. Chapters 4 and 5 look at the sorts of things children believe about racial difference. I show that children's thinking is more sophisticated, more theory-laden, and more adult-like than previous research would suggest. Chapter 6 examines the sorts of data children rely on when building racial and other social categories, in particular it explores whether visual information is a central part of early racial concepts. Together these studies reveal the existence of a body of knowledge that cannot be attributed to simple perceptual learning or derived directly from adult belief. This knowledge is better understood as the output of a domain-specific mental device that creates knowledge of intrinsic human difference. In chapter 7 I present evidence of how this process unfolds culturally by exploring how representations unique to racial categorization in the United States come to be held by older children and how socio-cultural factors affect what children come to believe. Chapter 7 is perhaps the most important of the empirical studies, because it demonstrates how the mental module makes contact with a culturally specific system of racial thinking. Here, as throughout, I am concerned to show that the creation and the distribution of cultural knowledge are best explained by taking into account forces that produce both conceptual salience and institutional significance.

Chapter 1

Representing Race: Universal and Comparative Perspectives

Both universalist and comparativist accounts have provided fundamental insights into the way racial concepts emerge and are sustained over historical time and cultural space. In this chapter I pursue the ways in which these accounts diverge and converge, particularly with respect to the assumptions they make.

On the Notion of Human Kinds

Like most things in the world, humans vary one to the other. As with other variation, we take some but not all of this diversity to be meaningful. Relevant to theories of everyday reasoning in both anthropology and psychology is variation diagnostic of the types of humans there are—what might be called *human kinds*. People everywhere and at all times appear to recognize human-kind variation. The notion of kind is of course a vague one, admitting all sorts of stable differences. There are tall (kinds of) people, grumpy (kinds of) people, and Italian (kinds of) people. It is uncontroversial that all humans recognize human kinds of the tall sort. It is likely, although disputed, that all humans recognize human kinds of the grumpy (or nervous, or generous) sort.[1] In this chapter I am concerned with the third sort of human kind: Italian (kinds of) people, or kinds that specify that an individual is fundamentally a certain sort of person.

Hacking (1995) has been skeptical of the universal recognition of human kinds. Our notions of kindhood, however, are somewhat different. He defines human kinds as classifications predicated on specific

1. The dispute is twofold. First, anthropologists and a few psychologists have noted that in many (perhaps most) cultures we find little of the discourse that explains human behavior in terms of the trans-situationally stable traits and dispositions favored by European and American lay folk and psychologists alike (Geertz 1973; Lutz 1988; Markus and Kitayama 1991). This does not, however, raise doubt that humans everywhere recognize different personal moods, or that all humans are capable of categorizing others in virtue of being in a particular mood. This is all I am suggesting here.

sorts of behaviors, propensities, or temperaments—the sort of systematic, general, and accurate knowledge nation states like to have and the modern social sciences like to provide. Such knowledge is sought, Hacking points out, because of a desire to formulate explicit and general truths about people. Hacking notes that this version of human kindhood is a fairly recent phenomenon, rising out of the conjunction of the enumerating state and the application of statistical reasoning to questions of human behavior. I concur. Still, I am not sure that Hacking's sort of human kind is really patterned after the notion of natural kind, as Hacking also suggests. Natural kindhood is about what causes something to *be* a certain sort of thing; the kindhood that concerns Hacking is about what causes something to *behave* in a certain sort of way. Although the two causalities are clearly related (some things behave in certain ways because they are certain sorts of things), I have argued that we should keep the psychological descriptions of these causalities distinct (Hirschfeld 1995a).[2]

In contrast to Hacking's point of departure, the notion of human kindhood that interests me here is not a construction of modern science or of the centralized state; rather, it is the familiar and eminently commonsense notion of what at times has been called a "primordial group." I mean by this any diffuse group of individuals that a person recognizes as being like him or her in some fundamental and enduring way but whose similarity is not historically traceable to local events (e.g., immediate relations of kinship). Such groups are not organized around specific properties or states of affairs (e.g., a common activity or instrumental function) or shared sentiment (e.g., a common political or moral perspective). Rather, the level at which this cut is made is determined by a commonsense partitive logic or social ontology that picks out the "natural" kinds of people that exist in the world. People

2. Dupré (1987, p. 342) suggests another interpretation of human kinds as "cultural species," the paradigmatic case being "the relatively isolated tribal groups that are the classical subject matter of anthropology." Dupré argues that it is over cultural rather than biological species that evolution operates in the case of humans. Cultural species are analogous to biological species in that the extent "to which an organism belongs [to a particular cultural species] will be an excellent and indispensable predictor of its susceptibility to the various environmental forces that impinge on it" (ibid., p. 338). Several things distinguish Dupré's use of the term "human kinds" from mine. First, to the extent that evolution is operating over cultural species, these are real objects of the world. I make no parallel realist claim about human kinds. Second, I do not believe that human kinds fall into relatively isolated groups whose membership can be readily discriminated one from the other—I am skeptical that there are such tribal groups outside the minds of colonialists and anthropologists. However, I concur that people *believe* that there are real groups in the world whose membership is systematically enumerable. Third, by identifying a cultural species at the level of tribe or class, Dupré's cut on human variation is at a more specific level than concerns me here.

of this kind are relevant because they are relevant to what it is like to be you *and* yours. Members of this kind are not all known to you, nor are they all directly or biographically related—in short, they are neither kinsfolk nor what Geertz (1973), following Schutz, called *consociates.* They are people whose identity turns on a higher-than-local level of inclusion. In order to avoid loading this notion unreasonably, for the moment I will call borrow Goldberg's (1993) term *ethnorace.*

How universal is the awareness of ethnoraces?[3] How universal are Italian kinds of people? Clearly, if we intend by this the recognition of a human kind based on citizenship in a nation state, the notion is fairly modern. However, if we mean a recognition that people perceive themselves as belonging to "deeply" constituted and primordial populations, then the notion may be less tied to a particular historical period. Members of all human societies appear to be capable of discriminating between the members of their own and other ethnoraces, because all humans apparently display a tendency to favor members of their own ethnorace over others (LeVine and Campbell 1972).

More important, people the world over appear to discriminate between members of their own and other ethnoraces in a unique way: they naturalize the difference. "Naturalization" here involves the practice of conceptually identifying social differences with natural ones. Evidence that the social world is naturalized is both varied and widespread. Anthropologists have demonstrated that cultures the world over link systems of naming social collectivities with systems of naming natural groupings, typically folk species (Lévi-Strauss 1962; Leach 1964; Crocker 1977; Turner 1989). Totemism is a good example. Indigenous naming practices in traditional societies also appear to give expression to a naturalizing view of human variation. Many traditional tribal names originate in native words for "people," "real humans," or "men." As a consequence, they bear a not-so-subtle implication that peoples to whom the label does not apply are something less than (or at least different from) human (Fried 1975; Shanklin 1994). The notion

3. It is important to distinguish between *awareness* of ethnoraces—in the sense that they figure in one's commonsense ontology—and their *prominence* in commonsense theories of action. For example, a number of scholars, including Jordan (1968), Morgan (1975), and Fields (1990), have observed that in the American colonies blacks and whites (particularly indentured whites) initially interacted fairly freely, in what is sometimes called a color-blind manner. From this Jordan, Morgan, and Fields conclude that awareness of racial difference was lower than in later historical periods. This conclusion confuses the awareness of (ethno)racial differences with the degree to which they organize social relations. There is little reason to believe that colonists in colonial Virginia were any less aware that blacks and whites were supposedly racially distinct (after all, a distinct term was applied to each population), even if the racial politics did not distinguish between them markedly.

of primordial groups is closely linked to relations of power, and other indigenous names reflect this: many tribal appellations are pejoratives, etymologically derived from a neighboring and dominant population's term for "beast" (Dole 1967). Nor is this sort of naming solely the practice of non-Western and localized populations. Initial contact between Europeans and the newly encountered peoples of Africa and the New World provoked speculation about cultural and racial variation; it also provoked conjecture among Europeans that non-Europeans were subhuman—i.e., naturally different from Europeans. Both scientific and popular writers of the sixteenth century debated whether Africans (and the Irish) represented an intermediate population between ape and man (read "real Europeans") in the "great chain of being" (Banton 1987; van den Boogaart 1980; Curtin 1964; Mosse 1978). Finally, there was considerable discussion as to whether the indigenous populations of the New World had redeemable souls and accordingly could be considered fully human (Guillaumin 1980).

On its face, this seems compelling evidence of a premodern naturalized notion of human kinds. Yet there is reason to be skeptical. Despite the fact that many of these naming and reasoning practices involve premodern populations (i.e., traditional societies or European populations in premodern periods), it is not clear that the *practices* themselves are truly premodern. The relatively remote highland Sumatran village in which I did fieldwork has many hallmarks of a traditional society—kinship-based social organization, swidden agriculture, aboriginal religious system, etc. It also has motorcycles and plastic buckets and is serviced by a modern postal system. Generally the meanings and practices associated with the motorcycles, the plastic buckets, and the modern postal system assume a local and distinct flavor, so that the behaviors and beliefs attendant on these things are clearly influenced by indigenous culture. Still, they are decidedly not *of* traditional culture. For the present argument, the relevant "plastic bucket" may well be the notion of tribe itself, the unit named with this naturalizing vocabulary. Fried (1975) has argued, and many now agree, that the classical notion of a tribe as a politically and culturally bounded unit is modern, and that, hence, many of these pejorative (and "traditional") linguistic practices may be rooted in the political economy of colonialism.[4]

4. The argument that tribes are of the modern and not the premodern world receives support from more cognitively and biologically minded theorists, too. Tooby and Cosmides (1992) point out that, with the possible exception of language, the various subsystems of cultural life that are typically associated with a single "tribal" entity (e.g., systems of kinship, marriage, economy, and polity) are in fact often distributed in distinct and orthogonal patterns. In the absence of an intervening force—like a colonial empire—there is little reason to believe that the subsystems of belief and regulation that used to make up the chapter headings of traditional ethnographies (kinship, economy, polity,

The Psychological Study of Race

By contrasting psychological and comparative treatments of race, I have implied that psychologists have a theory (or theories) of race, and that this theory (or theories) differs from the theory (or theories) of race that comparative scholars favor. Actually, I do not intend such an implication. The fact is, psychologists have not really developed theories about race. Instead they have elaborated theories about mental processes that produce beliefs about categories of things that include, but are not restricted to, race. Psychologists do not theorize race; they theorize operations (e.g., prejudice, stereotypy, ingroup bias) that act on racial and other categories. Take as an illustration of this the cross-cultural evidence for a pervasive ethnocentrism that LeVine and Campbell (1972) document. The fact that people invariably favor members of their own ethnorace does not necessarily have anything directly to do with race or ethnicity. The tendency to favor members of one's own human kind may simply reflect a propensity to form asymmetrical "us versus them" identities which are independent of any particular contrast. Tajfel (1981) and his colleagues have found that ingroup biases depend neither on perceptions of potential group conflict nor on a consolidated notion of group. Simply telling subjects that they have been assigned to certain groups is sufficient to trigger ingroup favoritism. This is no less true when people are aware that the basis for group assignment is arbitrary (e.g., based on the last digit of one's Social Security number) or when they are aware that their "group" has no existence outside the experimental context. To the extent that this is the case, the empirical finding that race is a particularly salient dimension on which to sort people and distribute power would not be attributable to our psychological endowment *tout court*. Instead it would emerge out of an undifferentiating intergroup bias given substance by specific political and economic conditions. That is, human psychological endowment would provide a cognitive bias to favor members of any ingroup, while the politics of group relations would direct ingroup/outgroup judgments to race (cf. Hirschfeld 1988).[5]

---

etc.) would be tightly clustered in their distributions. There is thus little reason to believe that the umbrella concept for such clustered subsystems—i.e., the "tribe"—prevailed in the absence of an intervening force.

5. Another intuition that lends credence to the naturalness of ethnoraces is the "they all look alike" phenomenon. A large body of experimental research has found that people are better at distinguishing between members of their own race than they are at distinguishing between members of other races (Lindsay et al. 1991; Barkowitz and Brigham 1982; Goldstein and Chance 1981). However, Chance et al. (1982) found that this "natural" ability appears to be learned: preadolescent children were as accurate in recognizing previously seen faces of another race as their own race. They found that it is only in adolescence that better recognition of own-race faces emerge. Thus, for younger children all people look more or less alike.

Under this interpretation, the phenomena worthy of *psychological* study—the phenomena of interest—are prejudice, stereotyping, and ingroup favoritism, not racial prejudice, racial stereotyping, and racial ingroup favoritism. Indeed, Hamilton and Trolier (1986, p. 152) are explicit about this: ". . . the cognitive approach assumes that the fundamental nature and functioning of all stereotypes is the same. As cognitive categories, all stereotypes are assumed to have the same basic structural properties and influence information processing in the same ways. . . . The cognitive mechanisms involved in stereotyping are assumed to be general across all stereotypes." The reasoning behind this is that social categories (and the stereotypes attached to them) have the same basic structure regardless of whether the social category stereotyped is a race, a gender, an occupation, or some other status. Arguably, even the notions of prejudice and stereotypy (i.e., biases about a social object) may overstate the specificity of the phenomenon to be explained. Prejudice and stereotypy are simply examples of category biases: ". . . if there is a *social psychology* of intergroup relations, it should not be altogether different when we consider small groups, ethnic groups, labor and management groups, or nationalities. What may be different, of course, are the sets of factors to be included in our analysis. In the rivalry between two churches, economic considerations may be very slight, whereas they may dominate labor-management negotiations." (Sherif and Sherif 1969, p. 223) The target category has little consequence for how this bias is played out. According to Taylor (1981, p. 84), stereotypes are "no more or less inaccurate, biased, or logically faulty than are any other kinds of cognitive generalizations." (See also McCauley et al. 1980.)

Theories about racial difference are thus no more motivated than theories about other sorts of difference, say, those based on personality type, on occupation, or on sexual orientation. Racial categories stand out, relative to these other social dimensions, to the extent that their physical correlates are clearly marked (Taylor et al. 1978)—and presumably to the extent that significant economic, social, and other structural consequences are associated with them. The same logic underlies many legal measures against discrimination. These laws are meant to protect a range of groups (including groups based on race, gender, sexual orientation, and disability) from discriminatory treatment, and it is the existence of group discrimination, not the basis on which group membership is made, that is critical. In part, this move to disengage definitions of discriminatory behavior from particular targets of discrimination may reflect a particular political theory. Starr (1987) points out that, although the liberal state often accords groups special protection, this protection is not permanent, guaranteed, or fixed by special constitutional status.

What is regulated in liberal states such as the U.S. is discrimination itself, not discrimination against a particular target group.

Such attempts to decontextualize collectivities are not without difficulties, as we can see from the recent controversy surrounding efforts to identify the gay rights movement with the civil rights movement of the 1960s. Even if both blacks and homosexuals are targets of public and institutional prejudice, and even if both groups may seek the state's protection against discrimination, many civil rights activists have heatedly rejected the parallel, arguing that the structural consequences of race seem greater than those of sexual orientation. Gates (1993) points out that there is an interaction in the contrast between the structural (e.g., political and economic) and the psychological dimensions of race versus sexual orientation. "Most people think of racial identity as a matter of (racial) status, but they respond to it as behavior. Most people think of sexual identity as a matter of (sexual) behavior, but they respond to it as status." Implicit in Gates's argument is the claim that the causal relations in the two cases are not the same. In the case of racial prejudice, the category identity has a considerably greater mantle of naturalness. The "noxious" behavior is produced in virtue of an attribution of hidden, internal causal forces associated with the identity. In the case of sexual orientation, the category identity is simply a shorthand description for the behavior. The identity results from the behavior, not vice versa. In this sense, the identity simply names the behavior, rather than explaining it, in much the same (epistemic) way that occupational categories are descriptions of habitual instrumental behaviors.

Actually, the intersection of psychological and structural (i.e., historical and political) factors may be more interesting than Gates notes. In particular, Gates may have underestimated the causal story captured by the category "homosexual," especially its historical specificity. The relationship between same-sex sexual behavior and the notion of a specialized homosexual category identity has been much explored, particularly the extent to which it is a natural identity (say, with respect to whether it has a genetic basis—see Bailey et al. 1993; Byrne and Parsons 1993; McConaghy 1994). Clearly the idea that anti-gay and anti-black prejudice bear a special parallel relationship is facilitated by the contemporary willingness to naturalize and essentialize both homosexuals and blacks—the structural differences between gays and blacks in American society aside. It is important to keep in mind that this naturalness is not a pancultural given; the essentialization of gays is a fairly recent and culture-bound turn of thought (Plummer 1981; Whitehead 1981).

We can better appreciate the relationship between essentialized categories and historically specific conditions by looking at a less politicized domain. Americans tend, I suspect, to underestimate the natural affinities of many common behavioral categories that other cultural groups stress. For example, according to American common sense, occupational categories do not *cause* the behaviors; they are labels for them. But in other systems of common sense occupation *is* a naturalized category, linked to a causally potent politics of identity. In much of South Asia there is no principled way to distinguish the type of person inhabiting an occupational category from the occupational category itself. Put another way: Symbolic relations embedded in a profession are inseparable from symbolic relations embedded in a caste. Both are mediated by the same system of religious belief (Dumont 1970). Specific occupations adhere intrinsically to specific castes—and to specific caste homelands. As Daniel (1984) points out, this is another way of saying that occupation adheres intrinsically to a specific kind of person. The naturalness of this relationship is underscored by the ambiguity in the term for caste itself, "jati," which is also the term for genus.

Thus, it should be evident that the psychological processes that apply to social categories cannot be fully understood outside the cultural frame of reference in which the categories are embedded. Imagining that all categories, whatever their content and whatever the context in which they occur, are processed in the same way is problematic, perhaps in the extreme.

Psychology, Race, and Causality

As was remarked above, psychologists generally do not theorize race or racism. Rather they offer theories of group categorization and intergroup relations. I will argue that this flows from the way psychologists have viewed the models of folk causality in which race is embedded. In particular, race is seen not as a set of beliefs about folk collectivities but as a set of beliefs about aspects of individual persons. Race is not a way of defining major human groupings, nor is it a way of defining the way human groupings are related to one another. Rather, it has been taken to be an aspect of person perception. Let me explore the basis for this position.

Psychological treatments typically do not construe folk causality to be as fluid or as contingent as culturalized and historicized models imply. Part of the reason for this is that notions of folk causality have been fairly rigidly taxonomized in cognitive and social psychology. The dominant view is that common sense distinguishes between two quite distinct kinds of causality, and that these causal principles are determined by the domain of events, very broadly conceived, to be explained. The first kind of causality involves the transmission of energy and is typically seen as having an external origin. One object (the agent) causes something to happen to another object. The action of billiard balls is a good example. The second sort of causality involves the enactment of intentions, and is usually seen as internal. Human action is a good example. For better or worse, psychologists have come to refer to these as *physical causality* and *social causality* (Shultz 1982).

Social psychologists have further distinguished between two sorts of social causes. On the one hand, there are psychological causes (in the sense that theorizing about theory of mind entails psychological causality. These typically involve transient beliefs and desires. For example, John wants a cookie; John knows that the cookies are in the cookie jar; hence, John opens the cookie jar in order to satisfy his desire. On the other hand, there are social causes. These tend to involve trans-situationally stable internal constructs (e.g., generosity). For example, John helps an old woman cross the street because he recognizes that crossing the street can be difficult for the elderly and he is generally sensitive to others' feelings and needs. Social causes tend to be seen as attribute-based rather than belief-based. The attribute (which is the trans-situationally invariant element) causes the belief to come into existence. In other words, the attribute provides the motivation for taking action, holding a belief, or forming a specific attitude. Further, the primary function of attribute-based causal reasoning seems to be to individuate people, inasmuch as the paradigm case of this sort of stable construct is a personality trait or a disposition. These traits and dispositions can be complex (as with an authoritarian personality), or they can be discrete elements of a person's intrinsic character (e.g., the degree to which a person is self-monitoring).[6]

Attribute-based causal reasoning is further seen to be embedded in those processes of person perception that emerge principally out of self-identity processes. That is to say, attribute-based reasoning is viewed as a fundamental part of the way people formulate self-images and orient those images to others (Fiske and Taylor 1991). These images are overwhelmingly interpreted as being made up of *internal* (i.e., mental) attributes: "The model that underlies virtually all current social [psychology] views the self as an entity that (a) comprises . . . internal attributes (e.g., preferences, traits, abilities, motives, values, and rights) and (b) behaves primarily as a consequence of these internal attributes" (Markus and Kitayama 1994, p. 569). Other-identity processes, in

6. Psychological (transient) and social (stable trait/disposition) causalities may be related in that the latter may be derived from (and describable in terms of) beliefs and desires. Thus, a particular personality type is the stable embodiment of a constellation of beliefs and desires, and a particular trait is representable as a stable propensity to believe or desire (Wellman 1990).

turn, are viewed as derivative of self-identity processes. Consider the common representation of social cognition as concentric circles beginning with "self" at the centermost position. We see this clearly in much of the work on the development of identity, in which the child's discovery of the other is seen as contingent on the discovery and exploration of self (e.g., Piaget 1967; Rosenberg 1979; Ross 1981).

The concept of race has been incorporated—rather awkwardly—into this perspective by treating it as one individuating trait or attribute among many. Race is simply one of the salient dimensions along which an individual might form an image of himself or of another individual. As such, the notion is integrated into the cognitive depiction of individuals rather than groups. Group membership is conceived as an aspect of an individual's identity—as a part of the repertoire of characteristics that make a particular individual distinct—rather than as an aspect of an individual's beliefs about collectivities *per se* (for exceptions see Brewer 1988 and Hewstone et al. 1991). Even when category-based processes are stressed (see, e.g., Taylor et al. 1978; Fiske and Neuberg 1990), the emphasis is on information that allows the perceiver to designate an individual's category membership as an attribute of that person (rather than the person becoming a marker for the category). Race becomes a quality of a person, not a means for defining major human groupings and their interrelationships.

In view of this tradition, and despite the important role that categories targeting collectivities play in the regulation and organization of social life, it is not surprising that psychology has told us relatively little about how human *groups*, as opposed to individuals, are mentally represented (Hamilton 1981; Steiner 1974). What we do know raises doubt about conventional wisdom with regard to the relationship between individual and group identity processes. For example, there is reason to believe that self-identity and other-identity are fundamentally distinct cognitive tasks (which is not implausible, since *reasoning* about the self and about the other is fundamentally distinct, as work on the fundamental attribution error demonstrates).[7] Cross (1985, 1991) has convincingly argued that reference group identity and personal identity involve quite separate mechanisms. For example, minority children's preference for representations of majority identity were long interpreted as evidence of black self-hatred. Cross argued that this makes little sense, if for no other reason than that black children do not display evidence of the personal identity pathology (e.g., low self-

7. For example, Jones and Nisbett (1972) found that people reason about the causes of their own behavior differently than they reason about the causes of others' behavior. Specifically, they tend to attribute their actions to situational factors, whereas they attribute the same actions by others to personal dispositions.

esteem) that pervasive self-hatred would entail. Children's preferences for representations of majority identity reflect, Cross suggests, issues having to do with *reference-group* identity, not *personal* identity. Previous work that conflates these two distinct cognitive spheres misinterprets the domain in which identity conflict and tension occur. Other research suggests that information about groups is actually stored in memory independent of information about individual group members, particularly traits associated with individuals (Wyer and Martin 1986; see also Brewer 1988 and Pryor and Ostom 1981). Milner (1984) suggests that different kinds of learning are involved in acquiring knowledge of individuals and knowledge of groups. My work indicates that people distinguish between social properties (i.e., attributes that are true of an actor) and social kinds (i.e., the sorts of actors there are) (Hirschfeld 1988).

In construing racial-group identity principally as an element of an individual's personal identity, standard views of race in social psychology shed little light on why some group identities are more important and bear more causal weight than other identities. Different kinds of individuals are differentially salient, depending both on how salience is construed and on the context in which it is played out. Thus, some human kinds are considerably more important than other kinds, both structurally (in terms of economic, political, and cultural salience) and psychologically (in terms of memorability, attention, and reasoning). Despite the importance in American culture of reasoning about personality traits and/or dispositions, it is widely accepted that, under certain conditions, we are much more likely to remember an individual's racial identity and more likely to use it as the basis for explaining that individual's behavior than his or her personality. In particular, race explains why some people do what they do in ways that personality does not. The reason is that race is conceived as a more natural way to group individuals than personality type is.

What conditions produce this effect? The answers are straightforward: race becomes central in contexts in which membership in a group is highlighted. Virtually by definition it is minority race that is highlighted. Race is not an attribute of an individual; it is the attribute of a *minority* individual. "Majority race," while strictly speaking not an oxymoron, captures a transparent event—something so ordinary as not to be noticed. Minority status, in contrast, is noteworthy. And minority status is defined by the relationship between *groups*, not individuals. This is not a novel observation—several studies have found that children acquire knowledge about minority races before knowledge of majority races (Radke et al. 1949; Proshansky 1966). Because most theorizing in social psychology is about commonsense attributions *within* groups, not across them, psychologists tend not to grasp what this evidence implies: race cannot be about individuals; it has to be about groups. The pervasive tendency to opt for personality-trait and/or disposition explanations in this context (at least among members of Western secular cultures) is well documented. But this sort of mentalistic explanation tends to overemphasize trait-based and disposition-based explanations of behavior and to obscure the societal and corporate aspects of identity that anthropological accounts stress. When used to characterize race, this theory (really an ethnotheory) about the masterful, bounded, and individuating self paradoxically becomes a theory (or ethnotheory) of society that ignores and effaces the corporate and collective nature of social thought, particularly the role played by social-category identity.

Psychology and the Reality of Racial Categories

To summarize: According to a range of psychological theories, racial thinking is a by-product of the human propensity to construct categories in the face of any identifiable difference (Fiske and Taylor 1991; Hamilton and Trolier 1986; Ashmore and Del Boca 1981; Allport 1954). Under one interpretation—and, as was noted above, this is a dominant interpretation in the field—there is nothing unique to racial differences themselves (in comparison to, say, gender, disability, or other physicalized dimensions). Strictly speaking, however, the perspective adopted by virtually all psychologists entails that racial differences are distinctive in at least one respect: they are real. That is, with strikingly few exceptions (Betancourt and Lopez 1993; Jones 1991; Zuckerman 1990), psychologists are inclined to construe race not only as concrete but as a real part of the natural environment. According to the bottom-up model that animates social-category theorizing, a conceptual representation of difference is consistent and coherent to the extent that the difference encountered is consistent and coherent. Most psychologists, certainly, treat racial categories as both consistent and coherent.

Actually, the evidence that most psychologists accept the realist interpretation is more persuasive, albeit indirect, than I suggest. Consider how putative racial differences in mental ability have been treated. The fact that differences in performance are regularly reported and interpreted in terms of racial-group affiliation implies a commitment to the realist interpretation. As intuitive as such comparisons often seem, recall that if racial groupings are arbitrary and contrived it is bizarre to expect racial comparisons in performance to yield interesting results. Clearly those who propose that intellectual potential is biologically linked to race—i.e., who believe that race somehow causes differences in intellectual potential—necessarily have adopted a realist view. What is more striking is that the bulk of the work *challenging* the claim that race biologically regulates mental ability also proceeds from the same realist assumption. Critics of the racial-intelligence claim have approached the problem largely by seeking alternative explanations for differences in test performance, arguing that previous researchers have taken too little account of bias in testing and inequities in educational opportunity (see, e.g., Klineberg 1975).

In many respects, this is a curious strategy. A more direct attack would involve questioning whether race *could* regulate the biological distribution of psychological traits like intelligence (leaving aside whether intelligence is a sensible concept in itself). Obviously, if race lacks biological coherence it could hardly control the inheritance of *any* property not specifically tied to the category's definition.[8] As straightforward as this seems, the rejection of the racialist claim in psychology has never included a sustained challenge to the notion of racial classification itself (Guillaumin 1980). That this challenge did not emerge earlier in the twentieth century, when the debate initially surfaced, is perhaps not surprising. Remarkably, however, the lack of any questioning of the realist claim is no less evident today than it was five decades ago. For instance, in the flurry of attention surrounding the publication of Herrnstein and Murray's (1994) rehearsal of the old canard about race and intelligence, virtually no psychologist has publicly suggested that their claims about a racialized or biologically cognitive underclass are implausible in the extreme. The one collaborative and putatively "mainstream" appraisal of current wisdom in psychometrics about race and intelligence, signed by 52 leading and not-so-leading scholars, never doubts that racial comparisons are a sensible way to explore *biological* differences (Arvey et al. 1994).[9]

8. Unless the criterion for category selection was the presence of a heritable trait, of course. Thus, for example, if general intelligence exists and is heritable and if there were a social category whose members were selected because their low intelligence led them to intermarry, then subsequent members of the social category might have consistently lower intelligence. But intelligence is not a criterion for membership in a racial category, even if relatively lower scores on standardized measures of intelligence appear to be a consequence of membership in some racial categories.

9. This despite the fact that one of the signers has conducted studies purporting to show that race does not govern the distribution of intellectual potential. Scarr et al. (1977) argued that on the basis of blood-group evidence there is no relationship between a black child's proportion of white and African heritage and the child's intellectual skills. Interestingly, the issue of race's scientific basis never arose when Scarr later (1988) discussed the virtues and problems attendant to using it as a psychological variable.

On the Historical Specificity of Race

In view of the foregoing, it is hardly astounding that nonpsychologists have generally found psychological accounts of race lacking. Consider the following comments, one by an anthropologist and two by historians.[10]

> [Race cannot be explained] by reference to psychological processes that we speculate may be taking place within individuals. (Smedley 1993, p. 24)

> Subliminal and deeply rooted psychological factors were undoubtedly present [in early forms of racial thinking in North America], but they can hardly explain the extent to which racial feeling and ideology have been developing and changing, subject to situational variations in intensity and character. (Fredrickson 1988, p. 205)

> Race is neither the reflex of primordial attitudes nor a tragically recurring central theme . . . [but is] the ideological medium through which Americans confronted questions of sovereignty and power. (Fields 1982, p. 168)

Over the past three decades, a broad consensus has emerged (outside of psychology) that race is a historically and culturally specific notion, embedded in a constellation of economic, political, and cultural discourses and uniquely linked to specific relations of power and authority. Further, race is widely believed to be a modern concept, traceable to the Enlightenment impulse to classify the natural world and naturalize the human one. This does not mean that historically race was an abruptly new concept. Racial thinking has antecedents in earlier ideological forms. It is even acknowledged that underlying varied forms of racial thinking may be a stable core concept, an enabling frame of reference (Goldberg 1993). What is widely rejected (outside of psychology) is the idea that this underlying frame of reference is interestingly mediated by mental processes. The argument runs like this:

(i) Race is about relations of power.

(ii) Power is about aggregate structural (e.g., political, economic, or cultural) relations, not mental ones.

10. Part of the problem here is that historians and other comparative scholars often do not consistently distinguish the idea of race from race itself. Too frequently the implied contrast is between race as a social institution and race as an aspect of the biological environment. But the question here is whence the *idea* of race. That race is not a biological fact is irrelevant to racial studies, since race (the concept) and race (the natural clustering of human types) have little to do with each other.

(iii) Structural relations are mental only incidentally, in that domination and subordination as lived practices minimally have to be both represented and representable (typically in some hegemonic guise).

(iv) Hence, a society's race *concept* is shaped by actually existing race *relations*, not vice versa.

Although there is agreement about these four points, it is important not to overstate the unanimity among comparativists. Scholars have overwhelmingly converged on a metastrategy for studying race, namely that it should be grounded in particular historical and cultural contexts. There is considerably less accord about which cultural and historical contexts played the most important role in shaping the modern concept.

Consider the following range of influential opinions:

- Gossett (1963, p. 3), citing ancient Biblical, South Asian, Chinese, and Egyptian descriptions of "the tendency to seize upon physical differences as the badge of innate mental and temperamental differences," argues that the race concept can be traced to widely distributed premodern xenophobic beliefs.
- Banton (1978, 1987), among others, grounds the concept in the sixteenth century, in originary systems of natural classification (Ray, Linneaeus, Buffon, et al.) and in French historical accounts that interpreted intra-European historical rivalries (e.g., the Franks vs. the Gauls or the Teutons vs. the Latins) in racial terms.[11]
- Anderson (1983) derives race from eighteenth-century European class relations, specifically the need of aristocracies to legitimate their rule in virtue of an inborn superiority.
- Jordan (1968) and van den Boogaart (1980) claim that racial consciousness is a discovery of the British Age of Exploration. The notion of race, on this view, developed out of sixteenth- and seventeenth-century overseas encounters between Northern Europeans and peoples of African descent as "one of the fairest-skinned nations suddenly came face to face with one of the darkest peoples on earth" (Jordan 1968, p. 6).
- Takaki (1992) contends that a nonracial image of (educable and redeemable) savagery became racialized (i.e., invested with the

11. The point here is not that Franks and Gauls saw their relations in racial terms (though they might have) but that historians of a given period interpreted them as racialized. The direct evidence is hence about sixteenth-, seventeenth-, and eighteenth-century historians and the customary wisdom of the cultural context in which they lived. Guillaumin (1980) observes that many intergroup relationships have been described as racial by outside observers—particularly during the nineteenth century—although those directly involved interpreted them in terms of other social dynamics (e.g., nationalism, class, religion).

notion of an innate, unchanging, and physicalized savage character) in the convergence of competition between settlers and Indians over land and the religious demonization of the indigenous population by colonists in the seventeenth-century Massachusetts Bay Colony.

• Morgan (1975, p. 328) traces the notion to colonial Virginia and the separation of "dangerous free whites from dangerous slave blacks by a screen of racial contempt."

• Harris (1964) and Fields (1990) argue that race consciousness is a New World, eighteenth-century invention that arose from the need to justify and explain slavery.

• Guillaumin (1980) and Smedley (1993) see race as a later-emerging concept, directly bound up with the social elaboration of nineteenth-century science (particularly biology).

Why is there such controversy about chronology and site in the advent of racial consciousness? In significant measure, the diversity of opinion can be traced to three problems. All three have to do with the way the race concept is embedded in systems of cultural and political belief and with the complexity of the concept itself. First, as I have already noted, race was not a *de novo* discovery but a subtle modulation of preexisting beliefs. Second, race is often identified with the use to which it is put, and in view of the range of plausible functions that race and race-like cognitions have served it is unsurprising that scholars have had difficulty linking the notion to a single type of instrumentality (Hall 1980). Third, most traditional approaches have equated the race concept (or race theory) with racial thinking (or racial consciousness). To the contrary, I will argue that the race concept underdetermines racial thinking, and that racial thinking can be explained only by reference to the instantiation of the race concept in a particular cultural environment.

The Modernity of Race

Consider the possibility that modern notions of race are closely tied to earlier conceptualizations of human difference. It has been widely argued—even by the scholars just cited—that humans everywhere and in all historical epochs view one another in terms of primordial human kinds that bear a striking resemblance to more modern notions of race. It is this often confusing resemblance between premodern and modern concepts that makes a chronology of racial thinking a contentious issue. The question is further clouded by the fact that even if the race concept emerges only *in* the modern era, it is not *of* modernity. Social theorists in the nineteenth century predicted, incorrectly as it turned out, that racial bonds were "remnants of a preindustrial order which would decline in significance in the modern period" (Omi and Winant 1994, p. 9). What distinguishes race as a modern concept is not so much the idea of primordial contrast—which few would deny is premodern in origin—as the singular way ethnoracial contrasts are naturalized in comparison to earlier forms.

It is widely accepted that race in its modern guise is framed by nineteenth-century biology:

> A distinctively modern understanding of what it was to be a people—an understanding in terms of our modern notion of race—was beginning to be forged: that notion had at its heart [the mid-nineteenth-century] scientific conception of biological heredity. (Appiah 1990b, p. 276)

> Theories of racial relationships rest on the postulate that there are biologically specific groups within the human race, and that these are separate from one another and recognizable by somatic, physical, genetic and physiological criteria. (Guillaumin 1980, pp. 56–57)

Goldberg (1993, p. 81) raises an important caution about this argument:

> The minimal significance race bears itself *does not concern biological but naturalized group relations*. Race serves to naturalize the groupings it identifies in its own name. In articulating as natural ways of being in the world and the institutional structures in and through which such ways of being are expressed, race both establishes and rationalizes the order of difference as a law of nature. . . . In this way, race gives to social relations the veneer of fixedness, of long duration, and invokes—even silently—the tendency to characterize assent relations in the language of descent. As such, group formation seems destined as eternal, fated as unchanging and unchangeable. [emphasis added]

What sets race off, according to Goldberg, is not so much its relationship to nineteenth-century systems of biological classification as its relationship to formal systems of classification. It is this link with science—the empirical, rational, and systematic investigation of natural phenomena—that distinguishes race from other forms of ethnoracial or primordial groupings. I will argue that the distinction goes beyond questions of science and systematic modes of gaining knowledge. The natural and the biological are not the same things. To naturalize (attribute to natural causes) and to biologize (attribute to biological causes) are not the same processes, inasmuch as biology is only one of many systems of natural causation. It is the former idea—that race is natural—that underlies virtually all systems of racial belief (including, I will argue, premodern ones).

Race and Instrumentality

Most agree, however, that there are more than epistemic constraints on the modern concept of race. If the idea had not figured so prominently in justifying regimes of power and authority, race would likely have remained an intellectual curiosity—like phlogiston, a quaint reminder of the limits of earlier scientific traditions to explain the natural world. Much of the potency of race as a concept follows from the historical uses to which it has been put. Surely one of the most important of these has been to justify systems of domination and subordination.

As with the chronology of the race concept, there is both agreement and dispute about how best to define race in instrumental terms. The fact that race serves to organize and obscure relations of power is widely accepted. What it is that race actually justifies is less clear. Fields (1990, p. 101), for example, argues that race emerged out of the unique circumstances of North American slavery, in which a social ideology "founded on radical doctrines of liberty and natural rights" had to be reconciled with the enslavement of blacks (see also Harris 1964). Others suggest that racial consciousness and slavery are "equally cause and effect" (Jordan 1968, p. 80; see also Fredrickson 1988). In contrast, Banton (1987) rejects the claim that race was initially tied either to slavery or to relations between Europeans and peoples of African descent. Instead, he grounds the concept in the appeals to common lineage that were embedded in the originary accounts of a range of European identities.

A number of scholars have linked the concept of race to class politics. Guillaumin (1980, p. 49), like Harris and Fields, grounds race in explanations for material relations but suggests a broader relationship, one that (paradoxically, in view of the nature of slavery) derives more from capitalism's need to annex labor power rather than the physical body *per se*: "The more the methods of appropriating people's bodies or labor came to be rationalized and systematized, the more, at the same time, the ideologists sought for a natural explanation of social groups." Goldberg (1993) also predicates race on an evolving systematization of discipline and power, but he ties the concept to post-seventeenth-century assumptions about mechanical bodies. Anderson (1983), by deriving racial thinking from ideologies of class that justified domination and authority, inverts the causal relationship between race and class. Moreover, unlike those who root the race concept in colonial discourse, Anderson links racial thinking to the putatively inherent and inborn superiority of the European aristocracies relative to their subordinate classes. Stoler (1995), in turn, suggests that race at times provides the conceptual template for class. For Omi and Winant (1994, p. 55) the instrumentality of race is more general: it is "a concept which signifies and symbolizes social conflicts and interests by referring to different types of human bodies."

Racial Thinking and Racial Theories

Although racial thinking clearly figures in the interpretation, the representation, and the explanation of social conflict, it may not always be useful to infuse the race *concept* with the uses to which it is put. For one thing, the concept does not always change with perturbations in the uses to which it is put. If conditions of political, economic, and cultural existence fundamentally shape racial ideology, why does racial thinking often remain unchanged when there are shifts in the underlying material basis and cultural context of the theory? Indeed, there is ample evidence for a lack of contingency between systems of racial thought and conditions of political and economic existence. Fields (1982, p. 153) provides a prime example. She argues that racial ideology is rooted in the historically specific conditions of slavery in the British North American colonies. Yet, contrary to what one would expect, she finds that racial ideology changed little after slavery was abolished. "There would be no great problem," she writes, "if, when things changed, the vocabulary died away as well. But far the more common situation in the history of ideologies is that instead of dying, the same vocabulary attaches itself, unnoticed, to new things. It is not that ideas have a life of their own, but rather that they have a boundless facility for usurping the lives of men and women." Where does this "boundless facility" come from? Fields, following in a long tradition of interpretive scholars, is sure that it is *not* the result of psychological process acting on history "from outside" (ibid., p. 149).

By now it should be evident that it requires considerable effort *not* to conceive of this boundless facility in psychological terms. Everyday thinking about race engages a complex of elements: a theory of intrinsic difference, a system for classifying such differences, and the instrumental purposes to which this knowledge is put. Relative to other systems of racial thinking—and relative to historical changes in any given system—each system of racial classification focuses on a particular set of characteristics, picks out a peculiar set of individuals, and fulfills a specific set of goals. There is no *a priori* reason to imagine that these three elements are contingent. The idea of race—the notion that there are intrinsic differences between groups of humans—may well be independent of any specific system of racial thinking (Appiah 1990a; Goldberg 1993).

Different scholars, adopting differing perspectives, have emphasized contradictory aspects of racial thinking, sometimes laying stress on the ways in which it is concrete, referential, and bounded (and thus capable of regulating a broad range of political, economic, and other power relations) and at other times drawing attention to the ways in which it is "fluid" (Goldberg 1993), "promiscuous" (Fields 1982), "protean" (Stoler 1992), and "uncertain" (Omi and Winant 1994). That race is at once concrete and immutable yet fluid and changing is paradoxical only if racial *thinking* and the race *concept* are taken to be the same thing. I suggest that they are not. The race concept is a property of mentation. Racial thinking, in contrast, is an aspect of cultural formations, derived in part from aggregate relations of power. Peoples the world over hold a very similar race concept that includes beliefs about primordial identities. This concept is embedded in a commonsense theory that holds that humans can be partitioned into enduring types on the basis of highly correlated clusters of naturally grounded properties. This theory, in turn, figures in widely varying systems of racial referencing that pick out, name, and coordinate relations among these supposedly distinct human types.[12]

The idea that racial discourse can be characterized in terms of theory is of course not new; a number of scholars have proposed it. Typically, however, little effort has been made to distinguish between the theoretical basis for racial thinking and racial thinking itself. Indeed, the two are usually taken to be one and the same thing. For example, in Banton's (1987) influential book *Racial Theories* the theories of the title are part of formal public discourse not individual mental life. These explicit and systematic theories are often construed as embedded within scientific theories of biology. Banton's analytic strategy involves describing and examining the implications of changes in racial theories over time and space. This means analyzing patterns of social relations as a way of *explaining* the racial theory. Omi and Winant (1994, p. 11) make much the same argument: "Racial theory is shaped by actually existing race relations in any given historical period. Within any given historical period, a particular racial theory is dominant—despite often high levels of contestation. The dominant racial theory provides society with 'common sense' about race, and with categories for the identification of individuals and groups in racial terms." To the

12. By theory I mean here a largely unreflexive, intuitive system of commonsense explanation that serves to account for folk perceptions of the world—in this case, variation in the human world. Considerable work in cognitive psychology has explored what such theories encompass. In chapter 3 I will discuss this research in greater detail. Here, suffice it to say that a broad consensus has emerged that everyday thought is theory-like when it displays at least the following characteristics: commitment to a specific ontology, attention to domain-specific causal principles, coherence of belief, and patterned resistance to counterevidence (Carey 1985; Wellman and Gelman 1992). All of these are apparent in virtually all systems of adult racial thinking.

contrary, I will suggest that there is a set of abstract principles that constrain the construction of particular theories of race (i.e., the conceptual basis for common sense) as distinct from the systems of racial referencing themselves (i.e., the systems of racial partitioning that have achieved cultural currency in a particular time and place). Further, I suggest that there is no reason to believe that the abstract principles derive from the particular theories. Indeed, it is plausible that the former not only constrain the latter but also constrain the uses to which the latter are put. I will try to show in the next chapter that compelling evidence for this position comes, ironically perhaps, from the findings meant to challenge such universalist speculation.

Chapter 2

Mining History for Psychological Wisdom: Rethinking Racial Thinking

Historians and anthropologists have documented tremendous variation in the way people think and talk about themselves and others, and particularly in the way people think and talk about the collectivities into which humans coalesce. Here I am concerned with a particular range of collectivities, ones that people believe arise out of the *inherent* and *intrinsic* nature of collectivity membership. A central question is whether these form a genuinely interesting cross-cultural and panhistorical class. Psychologists have been far more likely to answer Yes on universalist grounds; comparativists have been far more likely to answer No on constructivist grounds. In this chapter I will rethink which aspects of racial thinking are shared across cultures and historical epochs and which are culturally and historically distinct. I will propose an alternative model of racial thinking—one that can be thought of as encompassing a universal constructivism.

I make the following argument: (i) There is nontrivial variation in the sorts of inherent collectivities that members of different cultures imagine. (ii) One of the reasons for this variation is that the imagined range of intrinsic human collectivities is not tethered to real, intrinsic human variation—in this sense, these collectivities are constructions. (iii) However, this variation is nonetheless limited. Some kinds of intrinsic human collectivities are simply easier to think about than others. (iv) The easier-to-think-about collectivities are the ones that tend to recur across time and cultures. In investigating the nature of these collectivities, we will profit from examining the variation historians and anthropologists have found and distilling this against what is known of the way we think about human coalitions. By doing this, I hope to reveal a nontrivial recurrent cognitive core that underlies nontrivial socio-cultural variation.

Common Sense and Race: A Proposal

I begin by abandoning the canonical views of race proposed in psychology and in the interpretive disciplines. The experimental studies presented in chapters 4–7 were designed to examine conventional wisdom in psychology. In particular, these studies explore the possibility that race is not a simple induction from perceptual experience and the possibility that racial cognitions implicate mental processes more specific than a general impulse to categorize like objects.

In the remainder of this chapter I will revisit the conventional wisdom of historians, anthropologists, and other constructivists about the utility of a cognitive approach. Specifically, I will explore whether all systems of racial thinking can be nontrivially characterized in terms of a common conceptual framework. In order to do the latter, I must take a closer look at what racial theory encompasses. Toward this end, I offer the following as a description of the principal properties of a skeletal theory of race:

> Race theory is the recurrently encountered folk belief that humans can be partitioned into distinct types on the basis of their concrete, observable constitution. The notion of observable constitution captures the following features of racial thinking: racial differences are thought to be embodied, natural, and enduring, and are thought to encompass nonobvious or inner qualities (including moral and mental ones) as well as outward physical ones.

Clearly this characterization will be useful only if I can show that it is consistent with a range of racial beliefs, including familiar ones (such as "blacks and whites represent distinct races"), less current ones (such as "Jews and Italians are distinct races"), and even ones that today seem contradictory (such as "racial groups developed in articulation with environmental differences"). I will argue that a recurring problem in the comparative literature, ironically perhaps, is a tendency to read back in history from the present. That is, the contemporary version of racial thinking is often taken to be not only familiar but also paradigmatic. Other versions are thus seen as falling outside the genuine category of race because they do not share all the properties of the contemporary system of thought. I will argue that this strategy for interpretation grossly underestimates the scope of racial thinking, and particularly underestimates how recurrent a phenomenon it is.

Racial Differences Are Embodied

This belief includes the widely held physicalist criterion that members of different races differ in their external anatomy. In contemporary European-American cultures, differences in skin color, hair color and texture, and facial structure are all thought to signal differences in race.

The idea is so deeply rooted that some scholars have interpreted color consciousness as the same thing as racial awareness. Jordan

(1968) and Curtin (1964) identify color as the driving motivation behind the development of racial thinking (cf. van den Boogaart 1980). These and other scholars contend that major differences in the way colonial regimes were organized can be attributed to the distinct experiences that the English, on the one hand, and the Spanish and Portuguese, on the other, had with the peoples of Africa. Jordan (1968) argues that, in contrast to the English (who had been largely innocent of non-Caucasians before the Age of Exploration), the Portuguese and the Spanish had long had contact with Africa. Consequently there was less concern in the Iberian settler colonies with maintaining strict racial boundaries than in British North America, and this resulted in significant differences in racial policies (particularly with regard to mixed-blood individuals and miscegenation). Arguing along similar lines, Smedley (1993) suggests that, in view of the much greater rates of intermarriage in the Latin American colonies, race in fact was not an organizing factor there (the proliferation of named physical types being about social rank rather than race *per se*).

This is a fairly restrictive view of race, one in which a particularly strict physical criterion restricts the "genuine" notion of race to those populations in which phenotypic differences are both marked and bounded. According to this argument, parallel ideologies of domination that involve phenotypically similar groups are simply not racial:

> No one dreams of analyzing the struggle of the English against the Irish as a problem in race relations, even though the rationale that the English developed for suppressing the "barbarous" Irish later served nearly word for word as a rationale for suppressing Africans and indigenous American Indians. (Fields 1990, p. 99)

According to this view, a system of thought is racial when it captures (or posits) discretely distributed phenotypic differences. However, a cursory review of the historical literature suggests that race is also encoded and embodied in less visibly somatic ways. Moreover, racial categories do not always involve closely bounded groupings. A hallmark of racial thinking is that the physical characteristics of race are invariably linked to (and in fact cause the development of) other observable cultural and behavioral differences. Arguably, then, race is always thought to include behavioral proclivities. In contrast, race is not always associated with differences in external anatomy. For example, Banton (1978, 1987) traces the modern doctrine of race to sixteenth-century notions of "natural distinctiveness" that were part of historical accounts of conflicts and incursions between physically similar populations of Gauls and Franks, Norman and Saxons, and Teutons and Latins.

Fields's claim aside (that no one dreams of analyzing the struggle of the English against the Irish as a problem of race relations), Shanklin

(1994) has convincingly interpreted English discourse about the Irish as racial. Moreover, this sort of racialized but not physicalized interpretation is not restricted to distant historiography. During the first decades of the twentieth century in the United States, questions of race were more likely to contrast Northern Europeans of Protestant descent with Irish and Southern European Catholics than blacks with whites. In fact, as Alba (1985) notes, the racialization of what are now called "ethnicities" was so pervasive that in the early twentieth century most Americans denied that Italians were white. This was true not only of Italians but also of many other European groups:

> Many groups now commonly termed part of the "white" or "white ethnic" populations were in fact historically regarded as nonwhite, or of debatable racial heritage, by the host American citizenry. In the mid nineteenth century, the racial status of Catholic Irish incomers became the object of fierce, extended debate. . . . Later, sometimes darker, migrants from Southern and Eastern Europe were similarly cast as nonwhite. . . . Indeed, a 1987 Supreme Court decision used the record of Jews having been seen as a distinct race in the nineteenth century as a precedent to allow a Jewish group to sue under *racial* discrimination statutes. (Roediger 1994, p. 184)

Indeed, the language used to set off Southern European Catholic immigrants from "mainstream" American society is indistinguishable from the rhetoric used to describe blacks half a century later (Gordon 1990, 1994).[1] It is important to keep in mind that this racialization of what are now seen as white ethnics was not a function of lack of education or sophistication. The racializing agents in Gordon's work are bourgeois social workers—not uneducated folk, and certainly not the immigrant working class clients of these social workers. Higham (1955, p. 71) provides another example of this racialization of white ethnics, this time by some of the most educated Americans:

> Hardly had the new immigration begun to attract attention when race-conscious intellectuals discovered its hereditary taint. In 1890 the Brahmin president of the American Economic Association [in discussing Eastern European Jews] alerted his fel-

1. Gordon (1990) further observes that when racially mixed relationships were discussed during this period it typically was Protestant-Catholic unions, not black-white ones, that people had in mind. This does not deny that blacks were considered a race during this earlier period or that black/white differences were racialized. What it suggests is that the discourse on racialized social pathology elaborated in much of the northern United States, though familiar to modern readers, was not about blacks versus whites but about peoples of northern versus southern European origin. Among other things, the rural and southern concentration of blacks rendered their social existence "invisible to the influential experts" (Gordon 1994, p. 35).

> low scholars to the new tide of "races of . . . the very lowest stage of degradation." About the same time Henry Cabot Lodge noticed the shift away from northwestern Europe and began to bristle at its racial consequences.

This racialization of immigrants is well captured by Roediger's (1991) description of these groups as "not yet white." This portrayal vividly conveys the degree to which group differences were racialized, but it courts misunderstanding in that it suggests a transformation of race into color. As Fields (1982) notes, such a transformation is the "first fallacy" of racial studies. Although these discourses make vague reference to differences in external anatomy, when the issue of public emblems of race was raised during the early twentieth century it was behavioral (especially religious and cultural) cues rather than embodied ones that dominated most racial talk.

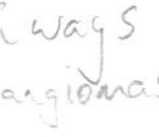

The caution that race drives perception (rather than vice versa) is well taken. It is an insight precisely because it violates commonsense (and sometimes scientific) versions of racial causality. Both lay folk and scientists have consistently conceptualized race as discernible to the naked eye. Intuitively, race always involves inborn, intrinsic, natural differences that can be seen and identified. Although modern views of race have tended to read this as predicting marked differences in body type corresponding to folk notions of species difference, racial thinking clearly admits less global and more subtle beliefs about embodiment. Again, if we bias our notion of what is "genuinely racial" to encompass only those things that are "genuinely racial" today, we miss what is recurrent in racial thinking.

Racial Differences Are Natural

The modern notion that identifies race with (some) biological type entails the presumption that racial differences are natural. Present-day readers tend to interpret this characterization as the claim that racial differences are natural *because* they are biologically grounded. Clearly this interpretation conflicts with earlier racial accounts. As we have just seen, race has frequently been applied to ethnic populations that, on folk belief, are neither distinct in phenotype nor (strictly speaking) biologically reproducing—for example, Italians or Irish around 1900, or Jews in fifteenth-century Spain. Thus, if we are to take Roediger's classification of European immigrants to the United States as nonwhite seriously—that is, if we are to infer that these groups were indeed viewed as distinct races—we have to take the racial discourse of the time at face value. We must acknowledge that when contemporaries used "race" to describe members of another group they actually meant race in a way that accords fundamentally with what we mean by it today.

On modern interpretation, this is problematic because biologically grounded racial groups and culturally grounded ethnic ones are now thought to differ fundamentally: ethnicity is "conditional, temporal, even volitional, and not amenable to biology or biological processes [whereas race] does not require the presences of empirically determinable cultural differences" (Smedley 1993, p. 32). Accordingly, many now view the use of racialized language to describe ethnic groups as figurative (Sollors 1986; Goldberg 1993), a way to emphasize the depth and importance of ethnic identity. The identification of the social (i.e., the ethnic) with the natural (i.e., the racial) evokes equation of "sections of the society with breeding lines of animals, even symbolically, [which suggests] a kind of permanency and immutability to their social qualities that are found only in biological transmission" (Smedley 1993, p. 66).

As intuitive as it might seem to interpret ethnicity as figurative race, there is no historically rigorous and principled means of distinguishing figurative uses of racial terms from literal ones. Criteria like those proposed by Smedley are problematic because they read back from contemporary usage to earlier forms—largely by tethering the idea of race to modern notions of biology. Yet there is no obvious justification for doing this. Some of the reasons for being skeptical of this move are general and semantic; some are specific ones and have to do with race.

Consider the general semantic problem first. Figurative language—say, the kind encountered in cultural symbolism—is distinguishable from nonfigurative language in virtue of the scope of the evocations produced by utterances containing that language. Sperber (1975a) has modeled this in terms of conceptual representations of interlocutors rather than in terms of the meaning of utterances *per se*. He argues that when a person uses any form of language that person provokes in others the construction of a particular range of conceptual representations. What sets symbolic and other figurative language apart from nonfigurative language is that the conceptual representations provoked by symbolic language are less stable than those provoked by nonfigurative language—that is, the probability that the speaker and the hearer share somewhat equivalent conceptual representations declines when the language is figurative. Because of this statements in which figurative language is used also are typically more limited in their implications than parallel statements in which literal language is used (Hirschfeld 1986). For example, it might be common usage to say that "Bill is a fox," meaning that he is shrewd. We know this is a figurative use of "fox" because most of the implications of being a fox do not hold for Bill (he is not covered in fur, he does not weigh the same as the average 6-year-old human child, he does not live in the wild, and so on). Apply the same logic to statements like "Jews are a race" (regardless of whether it is uttered by Quasimodo, Hermann Goering, or any of a number of the characters in *Gentlemen's Agreement*). It is not obvious that what follows from this statement differs fundamentally in scope from what follows from the proposition "Blacks are a race" (whether it is uttered by David Duke, A. R. Jensen, or the Census Bureau). In fact, the only difference (and this one *is* historically specific) involves assumptions about the mediating role biology supposedly plays in group reproduction.

Of course it does not follow that, because race and ethnicity are not rigorously distinguishable at the semantic level, they refer to the same phenomenon. It might be that the similarity in the inferential potential of racial and ethnic terms follows from the fact that the phenomena to which they refer are systematically related. One such semantic relation is inclusion. For example, there is considerable overlap in the meaning of "dog" and "mammal" because the concept DOG is included in the concept MAMMAL. A parallel semantic relationship between race and ethnicity has been proposed. Several researchers suggest that the concept of race is included in the concept of ethnicity. Race, on this model, would be a special kind of ethnicity (Sollors 1986; Goldberg 1993; van den Berghe 1981). According to this argument, the superordinate category, ethnicity, is predicated on boundaries constructed around many kinds of difference, including differences in language, lifeways, national origin, religion, and physical type. Race, in turn, is the form of ethnicity constructed around biological difference—a sort of "unmeltable" ethnicity, the most extreme form of social boundary (Sollors 1986).

Smedley (1993, pp. 66–67) makes a similar argument when discussing racialized description of Jews during the Spanish Inquisition:

> Spanish folk ideology and the practices of the Spanish church seemed to define Jewishness and Moorishness as something almost biological, using the idiom of "blood" ties. . . . And the Spanish use of the term "race," along with "casta," for both Jews and Moors bespeaks a potentially new kind of image of what were essentially ethnic (religious) differences. . . . But any idea of biologically hereditary social positions was contradicted by the more massive uses of conversion, essentially baptism, to eliminate the presence of Jews and Moors in Spanish society.

Does this argument read back historically from contemporary use? In particular, does it assume that what is specific about modern notions of race is paradigmatic of the concept? I suggest that the answer to both questions is Yes. First, Smedley's interpretation greatly discounts the extent to which the reproduction of group identities was thought to be mediated by natural processes and physicalized. In the case of Iberian Jews, she tends to render the conversion process into late-twentieth-century terms: conversion is a change in ideation and ritual behavior, and little more. This may both underestimate and overestimate conversion's role in fifteenth-century Spanish thought. It underestimates it in that conversion as a fifteenth-century cultural construct arguably signaled a *natural* transformation in identity as well as a change of religious practice (hence the close scrutiny of genealogies for "secret Jews"). It overestimates the consequences of conversion in that during the Inquisition Jewish converts to Catholicism were thought to maintain a distinct, literally embodied Jewish identity. Stringent laws identified as a Jew a person who had any traceable Jewish ancestry. Crucially, these laws turned on the notion of pure versus contaminated blood (a natural property), not on religious practice (a behavioral one); thus, like the one-drop rule for determining black identity in the United States (see chapter 7 below), they clearly naturalize identity (Shell 1993).

The idea that race is a specific form of ethnicity, like the idea that ethnicity is figurative race, entails that there is a principled way to distinguish race from ethnicity *independent of the ideological context in which the distinction is drawn*. Yet this is often not possible. Consider the difference between the categories "black" and "Hispanic" in the modern American context. As Fields (1982) points out, in contemporary American culture blacks are seen to constitute a race whereas Hispanics constitute an ethnicity. The rationale is that a category like Hispanic collapses several relevant group dimensions: culture, class, religion, and country of origin. The term aside, even language is not an inviolable criterion, since not all Hispanics speak Spanish. Members of this group simply are supposed to be descendants of a Spanish-speaking cultural group (ignoring the problems this poses for those who are descendants of former Portuguese colonies). The criteria are too varied to allow all Hispanics to be put under a single racial category, and the courts consequently have occasionally not afforded Hispanics standing under those affirmative action laws that were written to protect the rights of members of racial minorities (Haynes-Bautista 1980). Blacks, however, were initially perceived in much the same way (Fields 1982). As with the members of the contemporary category "Hispanic," considerable cultural, linguistic, and physical differences existed among the populations from which African slaves were drawn—and the slave-buying planters were aware of and concerned with these cultural and national differences. What eventually made peoples of African descent a single race was thus not a biological fact, or even a belief about a biological fact, but the social fact of slavery, which eventually "caused similarities to overwhelm the differences" (ibid., p. 145).

The notion that some groups should invariably be considered ethnicities and other groups invariably races is also curious in that it rests on a singular interpretation of the notion of natural connectivity. As observed above, the principle rationale for distinguishing ethnicities from races is to restrict the notion of natural connectivity to a strictly biological one. This move, however, puts inordinately great store in the nineteenth-century version of race by putting inordinately great store in the nineteenth-century notion of natural connectivity. In other historical and cultural contexts *both* common sense and scientific theory imagined a much wider range of natural commonality. Evidence for this is found in the historically recurring anxiety about intergroup contamination. Some of the fears implicate modes of biologically mediated pollution familiar to modern folk, as when colonial administrators showed concern about the appropriate category assignment of mixed-race children. Essentially the fear was that lower-class, minority, or enslaved women would manipulate biological ambiguity (i.e., racial hybridity) to produce social ambiguity. By having children with upper-class, white, or freeborn fathers, these women supposedly sought to improve the social status of their offspring (Morgan 1975; Stoler 1992).[2]

For the present discussion the relevant point is that these fears are embedded in and clearly facilitated by beliefs about a sort of natural connectivity implicit in group identity that is less directly familiar to modern readers. As with contemporary models, membership in certain groups was thought to provide a natural context in which natural contamination would occur. Fears about natural contamination were not restricted to groups that are markedly different physically, nor were they limited to relations mediated by biological inheritance. Over several centuries the French bourgeoisie voiced fairly constant concern about the influence of servants on their children, including fears of sexual corruption (Ariès 1962). At first glance this may seem more an occasion of behavioral than natural contamination (not unlike the hysteria

2. It is important to keep in mind that, although the anxiety is expressed in biological terms, it is about social status. For example, until racial identity served to assign class status (say, before the late 1600s in colonial America), little effort was made to regulate intermarriage between races, and little concern was shown about the category membership of racial hybrids (Morgan 1975). Before the 1690s, opposition to interracial marriage was motivated principally by a desire to regulate unions between individuals of different *social statuses*, not different races (Fredrickson 1988). As political and economic conditions changed, antimiscegenation sentiment was invested with a natural rationale: the fear that racial mixing leads to racial degeneration and infertility. This reflects more a concern about the social positioning of racial hybrids than a concern about their biological status. Although other interpretations of the meaning of miscegenation fears have been proposed (e.g., that they developed from concerns about maintaining racial boundaries after abolition (Kalmijn 1993; Myrdal 1944)), the underlying issue remains the same, viz., an attempt to keep the races separate for status considerations.

about "black influence" during the early days of rock and roll). However, it is important to bear in mind that the underlying mechanism of such contamination was in fact thought to be natural (although not biological). This is evinced in fears often expressed about the potential for transmitting undesirable class and racial properties to bourgeois children by using lower-class and minority race wet-nurses (Stoler 1995). Consider the following two seventeenth-century French speculations about natural contamination and the basis for the development of a natural similarity:

> The nursing relationship was seen as the more profoundly influential on the developing nature of the child than the pre-natal experience. The threshold of birth was not the decisive one. Intrauterine gestation and extrauterine parasitism were regarded as one continuous process in the formation of the child's *naturel.* (Marvick 1974, p. 264).

> It is an accepted thing that milk . . . has the power to make children resemble their nurses in mind and body, just as the seed makes them resemble their mother and father. (Jacques Guillemeau, seventeenth-century French physician, quoted in Fairchild 1984, p. 195)

Note the degree to which such beliefs evoke the language of racial identity—particularly the trope of racial blood. Contamination is described as the servants' degenerate essence transmigrating to the child not through intercourse but via breast milk: ". . . the blood of the lower-class wet-nurse entered the body of the upper-class baby, milk being thought to be blood frothed white." (deMause 1974, p. 536) There is no reason to believe that these class fears are a conceptual extension of racial ones, or a trope for racial anxieties. Instead, a single notion of contamination and natural connectivity is subsumed under both systems of belief. To distinguish race from ethnicity, or even race from class, as we tend to do today, may be to miss a fundamental continuity in thought about natural groupings.

The same logic appears to animate more recent North American concerns about group impurity, even ones that assume a more directly biological mode of contamination. As Sollors (1986), Banton (1987), and Williams (1980) point out, the belief that racial mixing produced biologically compromised offspring—e.g., that mixed-bloods are sterile—remained widespread in the United States through the early years of the twentieth century. The point is that sterility *necessarily* means that the two populations stand in a specific biological and natural relationship. Children of mixed unions were "inevitably tragic or horrifying" because people conceptualized the reproduction of racialized ethnicities as mediated by natural processes and subject to natural calamity (see also Mosse 1978). Granted, the specific nature of that natural calamity was uncertain. It might manifest itself in an insult to biological integrity (i.e., sterility) or to natural beauty (as when, in American fiction, intermarriage between gentile and Jew produced "a hooknosed brat" (Sollors 1986, p. 224)). The important point is that hybridity was thought to necessarily provoke group catastrophe.

In summary: Racial thinking is about natural explanations of primordial similitude, and this has as much to do with internal and hidden substances and essences as with external physical properties (Appiah 1990b). There is no reason to restrict the range of explanations to ones that fit modern notions of biologically transmitted similarity or to ones that target differences in external anatomy. Clearly, explanations couched in modern biology and focusing on external anatomy are encountered in racialized discourse. Just as clearly, however, there are many explanations for racial similarity that do not invoke modern biological constructs and that are still concerned with racial blood, substance, essence, and the like. Excluding these systems of thought from racial discourse on *a priori* grounds is motivated more by historicentrism than by history.

Race Is Enduring

According to current European-American thought, a person's race is fixed at birth. In virtue of biological grounding, racial features are considered immutable. Change of race is thus not possible. This model has animated European-American thought at least since the late eighteenth century. Nonetheless, the notion that race is enduring was widely accepted even before this period. On premodern versions, the mediating mechanism for racial persistence was less biological inheritance than shared contextual heritage. Earlier iterations of racial thinking were concerned more with common descent and ties of kinship than with whether race was heritable *per se* (Banton 1987). This does not exclude the possibility that racial identity was seen as incorrigible, as is evident (in what were popular cultural representations of race) in Shakespeare's treatment of Othello, Shylock, and particularly Caliban—who in Prospero's famous plaint is "a born devil, on whose nature/Nurture can never stick" (*The Tempest*, IV.i.188–189).

The explanation for racial immutability embedded in these representations is not biologistic, in that it is not thought to arise from the inheritance of racial properties. Frequently the causal mechanism is unspecified, although environmental explanations are sometimes encountered. In fact, such environmental explanations are quite ancient. In the fifth century B.C., Hippocrates attributed the superiority of

Greeks to the barren soils of their homeland (Appiah 1990b). Similar theories of race appear in the Bible—particularly the story of Ham, whose descendants were cursed with dark skin because Ham refused to avert his eyes to Noah's shame (Gossett 1963; van den Boogaart 1980). Environmental theories were an attempt to reconcile the evident physical diversity among humans with ideologies that claimed that all people could be traced to a single set of ancestors. These theories invest the environment with the power to produce physical and temperamental adaptations to local problems,[3] thus reconciling the contradiction that theories of monogenesis faced when encountering racial diversity.[4]

Unresolved in these theories is what happens when environmental conditions change—particularly when change is rapid. According to modern biological thought, environmentally induced changes in physical form are not heritable because they are not linked to any relevant genetic change. This has led some scholars to argue that environmental explanations of racial difference really target ethnic (or cultural), not racial (or natural) differences, since they leave open the possibility that descendants of an environmentally conditioned racial group "could change if they moved to new conditions" (Appiah 1990b, p. 275; see also Fredrickson 1988). Takaki (1992) suggests that the turn to a "deterministic" view of racial character—one that sees race as unredeemable and innate—was an early seventeenth-century phenomenon, precisely because it was at this historical moment that a cultural account of savagery was replaced by a racialized one. All these arguments resonate with current interpretations of both environmentally caused changes and the notions of race and ethnicity. It is not clear, however, that they accord with the interpretation that the environmental theory's original proponents held. For one thing, the notion that biological speciation results from the inheritance of acquired characteristics is an idea that has been widely entertained, well into twentieth century. In fact, it appears to be the favored interpretation for the emergence of new species by American children (Evans 1994).

Indeed, racial thinking is the arena in which the question as to whether environmentally induced physical changes are likely to endure has been most elaborated. Europeans regularly explained racial qualities of the Other in climatic terms, and they frequently expressed anxiety that their own racial identity was also sensitive to changes in environment: As Banton (1987, p. 8) notes, in the eighteenth century "it was widely believed that Europeans who migrated to North America were liable to degenerate because they were not suited to that climate." Nor did this sort of speculation disappear with the advent of a modern

3. Early accounts of racial difference tended to emphasize the apparently fantastic range of functional variation, such as heads shaped like umbrellas (Banton 1987).

4. Monogenesis is the doctrine that all people are descendants of a single original pair.

biologistic view of racial difference. Environmentalist explanations of racial diversity persisted at least until 1800.[5] Stepan (1985) documents continuing reservations throughout the nineteenth century about Europeans' capacity to adapt to tropical climates. Similarly, well into the late nineteenth century Europeans continued to believe that semi-permanent racial differences would develop from extended residence in inhospitable climates, as evidenced by the late-nineteenth-century Dutch colonial administration's view that European-born whites were particularly susceptible to cultural and physical environments and were liable to "metamorphize" into Javanese (Stoler 1992).[6]

Two points emerge from this. On the one hand, it is evident that the notion of a *stable* racial identity encompasses more than the notion of a *permanent* racial identity. On the other hand, the idea that race is enduring is not limited to the modern biologistic view. Clearly, premodern folk believed that natural human differences were transgenerationally stable. That these systems of thought often linked specific human types with environmental causes does not mean that these views of human types were conceptually unrelated to subsequent biologistic ones. Rather, it suggests that these views simply may have been more encompassing.[7] To hold that environmental explanations for physical differences are not racial is to read back from the present to explain the past. Such a reading incorrectly assumes that "race is enduring" means "race is permanent."

Race Encompasses Nonobvious and Inner Qualities as Well as Outward Physical Ones

According to contemporary European and American belief, racial groups are phenotypically distinct by definition. However, as I noted at the outset, the expectation that races differ in less physical qualities (including customary forms of conduct, culture, morality, and psychology) is equally part of the meaning of the race concept. This is one of the most malign aspects of folk theory, because it is so closely bound to (and enabling of) racial prejudice (i.e., the notion that corporeal differences in appearance signal differences in potential and value that, in turn, legitimize invidious distinctions between races). In fact, the relationship between race (as a system of classification) and racism (as system of invidious comparison) is so fundamental that many scholars see the two as inseparable (Omi and Winant 1994; Fields 1982).

5. See, e.g., Jordan's (1968) discussion of Charles Stanhope Smith's contention that climate, state of society, and manner of living caused racial changes.
6. Nor is this sort of belief restricted to Europeans. Nigerian Moors also believe that the environment has a drastic effect on racial features, including skin color (Popenoe 1994).
7. For a detailed account of a system of naturalized thought that links human types with various sorts of environmental types, see Daniel 1984.

Still, the idea that each race is characterized by a complex set of physical and nonphysical properties is neither new nor tied to any particular political or economic context (Gossett 1963). The notion is not simply that each race is associated with a specified set of properties. Rather, according to a frequently encountered view, this specified set of properties signals the existence in each race of a *distinguishing essence.*

It is important to note that scholars have understood essentialism (whether it targets race, biological species, or nonliving things) to pick out two distinct kinds of belief. One involves expectations about how people "properly" *sort* individuals into coherent categories, and hence implicates processes by which categories are defined. The other involves beliefs about how people "properly" *explain* the development of individual category members, and hence implicates processes underlying causal explanations.[8] The sortal notion of essence turns on the distinction between accidental and essential properties. In contrast to accidental properties, which co-occur regularly with a category but are not necessarily tied to it, essential properties are those properties in the absence of which something would not be a member of that category. The causal notion of essence is somewhat different. On this interpretation, a category essence does not consist of the properties that a category member must possess in order to be a certain sort of thing. Rather, a category essence is the underlying property (relationship, process, function, etc.) that *causes a category member to develop* into a certain sort of thing. Claims about causal essence are stories about what causes something to become what it is.

Both types of essentialist thinking have long been applied to race. Appiah (1990b, p. 276) describes a sortal version that was widely held during the Victorian period: ". . . human beings [can be divided] into a small number of groups, called 'races,' in such a way that all the members of these races shared certain fundamental, biologically heritable, moral and intellectual characteristics with each other that they did not share with members of any other race. The characteristics that each member of a race was supposed to share with every other were sometimes called the *essence* of that race." On this sortal account, racial essences are the concatenation of the basic (i.e., essential) qualities that figure in racist discourse, the putative incapacities that Fields described as underlying racist justifications for slavery.

During the same historic period, however, another interpretation of racial essence, closely resembling the pre-Darwinian notion of species

8. Dennett (1995, pp. 36–39) makes an argument that suggests that the two interpretations may be derived respectively from Aristotle's and Plato's different notions of essence.

essence, was also frequently invoked (see Banton 1987; Guillaumin 1980).[9] According to the pre-Darwinian view, variations in outward appearances reflect the existence of "constant, sharply delimited essences [that] are identical for all the members of a class or species" (Mayr 1988, p. 186). The important quality here is that all members of a category equally share in the species essence. A parallel notion of shared racial essence is elaborated in Gobineau's (1883–1885) racialist theory. In it, Gobineau acknowledges that not all members of a particular race equally share the properties legitimately associated with that race. Nonetheless, he argues, this does not vitiate their full membership in that race. On his view, members of a race, whether they are typical or atypical in their outward appearances or patterns of conduct, share a particular racial essence. All things being equal, that essence causes category members to develop in a particular way and into a particular sort of being. However, all things are sometimes not equal. Hence, not all members of a race develop in a particular way. They will nonetheless be a particular sort of being. As we will see in chapter 7, this model of racial identity plays a crucial role in the politics of race, and in their reproduction, because it permits racial identification to be made on genealogical rather than visual grounds.

Where do these various forms of essentialist reasoning come from? According to one influential view, the categories of nature (i.e., natural kinds) actually have essences, and our commonsense commitment to them reflects this (Putnam 1975). Obviously, since race does not pick out genuine biological populations, there can be no question of real racial essences. Racial essences and their source turn on questions of belief, not biology. They involve what Medin (1989, pp. 1476–1477) calls *psychological essentialism*, the notion that "people act as if things (e.g., objects) have essences or underlying natures that make them the thing that they are." Medin continues:

> It is important to note that psychological essentialism refers not to how the world is but rather to how people approach the world. . . . If psychological essentialism is bad metaphysics, why should people act as if things had essences? The reason is that it may prove to be good epistemology. One could say that people adopt an *essentialist heuristic*, namely, the hypothesis that things that

9. Guillaumin (1980) suggests that the notion of racial essence is derived from Darwinian rather than pre-Darwinian thought. She argues that essentialism in racial thinking was inaugurated by Gobineau's *Essai sur l'inégalité* and Darwin's *Origin of Species*. Her choice of the latter is somewhat curious, since Darwin represented a major break with thinkers who identified each species with a common, distinctive, and inherited essence (Banton 1987). Darwin's crucial contribution was the idea of individual variation and variable populations composed of unique individuals (Mayr 1988).

look alike tend to share deeper properties (similarities). Our perceptual and conceptual systems appear to have evolved such that the essentialist heuristic is very often correct.

Allport (1954, p. 173) anchors racial essentialism in a parallel cognitive instrumentality, which he calls the principle of least effort. Allport suggests that racial thinking is useful because it saves processing time: "To consider every member of a group as endowed with the same traits saves us the pains of dealing with them as individuals."

As I have already observed, many comparative scholars are skeptical of arguments that derive the notion of racial essences either from general psychological processes or from functional utility. Rather, Appiah (1990b) and Guillamin (1980), among others, have suggested that the notion of racial essence is an attribute of a specific historical version of race prevalent in the middle of the nineteenth century in Europe and North America. Although there is little doubt that the notion of racial essence was extensively and publicly elaborated during the nineteenth century, the idea is older than that. For example, Stoler (1995) describes a considerable anxiety about racial contamination that is closely documented in the colonial record, even before the nineteenth century. These contamination fears, she suggests, involve a notion of racial essence that is transferrable through a variety of physical contacts, including miscegenation. Indeed, Stoler notes that the question of how to interpret (i.e., envisage) the racial essences of mixed-race individuals was of major concern to virtually all colonial regimes.

The reason that interracial unions bring to the fore questions of racial essence is simple: racial categorization follows neither from physical identity nor from demonstrated capacity. Virtually all systems of racial belief entertain the possibility that one can be mistaken about a person's racial identity on the basis of visual inspection alone. Hence, any system of racial thinking must provide some strategy for resolving ambiguity. Typically, such a strategy involves the articulation of a conventional wisdom that specifies the potential each race has for defining an individual. Such conventions recruit beliefs about racial essence, because it is essence that defines who a person is. In chapter 7 I will return to the question of how racial essence is thought to condition identity judgments. For the present, the relevant issue is how various systems of racial thinking have dealt with the question of racial hybrids, and what these strategies tell us about belief in racial essences.

It is important to acknowledge that mixed-race children pose a significant problem for racial classification. As van den Berghe (1981) and Harris (1964) point out, racial mixing is not the exception but the norm. Early North American colonial records reflect this. There was a lively concern with the status of racial hybrids, and the fears often took the form of coherent belief systems about essences. Morgan (1975, p. 329) provides evidence of distinct beliefs about the innate potential of American Indian and black essences, noting that while "the offspring of a mixed Indian and white couple were defined as mulattoes . . . Indian blood was evidently considered less potent than that of blacks, since not only a black parent but even a black grandparent or great-grandparent was enough to make a person qualify as mulatto." This sort of belief demonstrates how in otherwise similar circumstances different regimes of racial thought could emerge. In the British North American colonies, mulattoes were recognized as a "biological" fact but not as a categorical fact. That is, it was recognized that racial hybrids appeared mixed, but they were nonetheless counted categorically as blacks (Jordan 1968). Morgan (1975, p. 336) documents the development of this strategy (the antecedent to the modern one-drop rule), noting that because mixed-race unions could blur "the distinction between slave and free, black and white" pains were taken *not* to recognize mulattoes as an intermediate class. Degler (1971), noting the recognition of intermediate, mulatto racial categories in the Portuguese settler colonies, argues that fundamental differences in the racial systems of the United States and Brazil can be traced to these practices. In a society in which racial hybrids are recognized as a distinct category, many aspects of racialist thinking—including slavery justified as a function of immutable essence—were foreclosed. Starr (1987) notes a similar regional variation in the United States. In the lower South before the Civil War, mulattoes, in virtue of their affluence, were treated by whites as belonging to a third intermediate racial and/or class category. Ironically, this three-tiered system collapsed after emancipation.[10]

The point for the present discussion of this talk about mixed-bloods is that belief in essences is recruited to render systems of racial classification coherent. This is due, in no small measure, to the fact that such systems can rely neither on biology nor on physicality for their coherence. That is, racial systems are neither biological systems nor inductions from the physical environment. In fact, as we will see in chapters 4 and 7, racial systems invariably *conflict* with both the biology of human reproduction and its consequences for the physical environment. A principal strategy for reconciling these conflicts is through the essentialization of race. Attempts to locate this essentialist bias in modern versions of race invariably underestimate how pervasive this mode of reasoning is. Of course, specific essentialist arguments are tied to

10. Kalmijn (1993) also appears to locate the emergence of the one-drop rule in post-Abolition Jim Crow laws.

specific historical and cultural conditions, but the impulse to essentialize is fundamental to all commonsense theories of race.

Conclusions: Causality, History, and Psychology

In a widely cited analysis, Beck and Tolnay (1990) document a link between racial violence and economic conditions in the southern United States during the late nineteenth century and the early twentieth century. As the price of cotton declined, the lynching of blacks increased. To interpret this pattern of mob violence, Beck and Tolnay opt largely for a combined economic and (somewhat psychodynamic) psychological causal model. They argue that as economic conditions deteriorated small-scale farmers were increasingly marginalized. This led to more and more frustration, which produced more mob violence.

Beck and Tolnay's story of economic causation underdetermines the lynching of blacks for at least two reasons, both of which Beck and Tolnay implicitly acknowledge. First, the interpretation underdetermines the activity of lynching. There are countless examples of economically caused frustration, yet typically these lead to neither mob nor racial violence. Beck and Tolnay's account relies on a special psychological interpretation: that pent-up frustration leads to explosive, violent aggression—a notion that probably owes more to popular hydraulic metaphors of emotion (Lakoff and Kövescses 1987) and to the combustion theory of revolution (Aya 1971) than to systematic affective or political psychology.[11] Second, Beck and Tolnay's account underdetermines who is lynched. Nothing in the conditions of economic life (or in the hydraulic theory of emotion) determines that the targets of mob violence will be blacks, women, local elites, lawyers, or people over six feet tall. Beck and Tolnay recognize this, noting that marginal whites "could direct their rage toward the powerful class of whites, . . . [but] given the Deep South's racial caste structure, whites could assault blacks with virtual impunity. Blacks were considered legitimate, and even deserving, objects for white wrath." (p. 537) This is important because the white elite plausibly *did* play a causal role in declining cotton prices, while poor blacks almost surely did not. What predicts that blacks will be the "legitimate, and even deserving" object of white wrath? Beck and Tolnay do not elaborate beyond the claim that whites could assault blacks "with virtual impunity" (p. 537).

It should be evident from this chapter that I would argue that it is racial thinking that predicts who violence is directed against. Recall

11. For a recent psychological discussion of violence that attends to the specific cultural construction of violence in the South, see Nisbett 1993.

that on my proposal racial thinking consists of a historically specific system of racial referencing and a commonsense theory of race. Consider how each contributes to explaining why blacks were a "legitimate, and even deserving" target of mob violence. First, the *politics of race* in the South around 1900—the ambient system of racial referencing—determined that the predominant dimension on which people were distributed was that of black versus white. Again, it could have been otherwise. It could have been whites vs. blacks vs. creoles, as it was in Louisiana (Domínguez 1986); or Catholics vs. Protestants or people of Northern European descent vs. people of Southern European descent, as it was in the Northeast (Roediger 1994); or even people of Mandingo vs. people of Ebo descent, as in principle it could have been during the early slave period (Fields 1982). Second, the *psychology of race* (or the commonsense theory of race) determined that white vs. black made more sense than marginal small farmers vs. local elites or some other class-based distinction.

In what sense does the psychology of race account for this? We display acute attention to social groups predicated on a wide range of properties. On the one hand, we discern groupings derived from the common activities that people engage in (typically categories like occupation, but social class may fall under this rubric as well). On the other hand, we create groups predicated on the intrinsic kinds of persons there are (races, genders, ethnicities, etc.). As Sartre (1948) suggests, violence and prejudice attach more readily to the second kind of social contrast than to the first. Sartre relates an encounter with a woman who intensely disliked Jews and who attributed this aversion to her disagreeable experiences with Jewish furriers. Sartre astutely wonders why she chose to hate Jews rather than furriers (see also Rothbart 1981). The answer is that it is more "natural" to hate Jews than furriers because prejudice adheres to the kinds of people an individual recognizes more easily than to the kinds of activities in which people engage (Hirschfeld 1988).

Consider another instance where both historical and cognitive factors play a crucial role in the construction of a system of belief. Much has been made of how bad an idea essentialism is, both as a biological doctrine (Mayr 1988) and when it is applied to human kinds such as race and gender (Fuss 1989). As I noted earlier, the essentialized image of race is often attributed to a specific historical moment, particularly the nineteenth century and first half of the twentieth. In fact, there is little historical evidence of variation in the extent to which race was naturalized during this period. Instead, most of the historical sources demonstrate that during this period essentialism came to dominate *scientific* discourse on race and indicate that commonsense views of race were increasingly guided by that scientific discourse. Neither of these things establishes that essentialist construals of race are in themselves a historical product. There has been a dramatic decline in essentialist reasoning in scientific discourse on race since the middle of the twentieth century (Barkan 1992), and most scientific writing on race is now openly anti-essentialist (see Gould 1981; Gill and Levidow 1987; Herrnstein and Murray 1994). Yet there is no evidence that commonsense essentialism about race has declined. In fact, I will present data in chapters 4–7 suggesting that it is alive and well, even in liberal Northern communities. There is no *a priori* reason to tie this directly to the prominence of modern biological thought or to the political projects which the theory clearly serves—the touchstones on which historians generally link essentialist notions about race. This should not surprise us. As Medin (1989) observes, essentialism may be good epistemology regardless of the nature of the essentialized category.

Accordingly, conceiving of essentialist reasoning as the product of a specific context fails to advance our understanding of folk reasoning about race because it fails to engage the most pertinent aspect of essentialism: its believability. Acknowledging this does not require us to conclude that the power essentialist reasoning has to enter into so many discourses—to become crucial to so many cultural expressions—is ahistorical. The role that essentialism played in organizing nineteenth-century biologistic thinking about race is related to the importance systematizing natural science had during the nineteenth century and to the prominence that eugenicist strategies for regulating human populations had during the first decades of the twentieth century. However, we need not conclude that the proliferation of discourse in natural sciences *caused* this. The fact remains that essentialist reasoning about race took on a scientific mantle just when the natural sciences were abandoning essentialism as a biological doctrine.

A fuller appreciation of these events (both psychological and historical) demands that we appreciate how our cognitive endowment enables and shapes specific cultural traditions by providing them with easily thinkable forms. This in no way suggests that historical and cultural variations are less essential to the construction of racial thinking than are mental processes. I simply start from the observation (convincingly documented in the vast literature on children and race) that race is an easy idea to think, and then ask why this is. As will be clear from the following chapters, we (and our children) mentally represent racial groups with remarkable facility, easily invest them with significance, and readily communicate our ideas about them. It could be that this facility is learned, that it derives from a dominant cultural ideology. I will have considerably more to say about that. But to anticipate that discussion, I will show that in no small measure children construct racial ideas on their own. This suggests that the ease with which members of modern secular societies hold racial notions is related to the ease with which members of other societies have held strikingly similar beliefs. Whether these beliefs represent antecedents to racial thinking or are instantiations of racial thought is in the end a fairly technical question of historiography. What is more crucial is that we find evidence of both continuity and difference in racial thinking. I am trying to provide a framework in which to understand both the continuity and the difference.

Race is about both concrete relations (corporeal and political) and vague, changing, fluid, and uncertain relations. I propose that this tension emerges from the distinct contributions psychology and context make to racial thinking. Without conceptual endowment we would not have race. Without historical context we would not have race. This is not the facile claim that nature and nurture cannot be separated. Our psychological endowment and the cultural environment do not contrive to produce race. Each contrives independently to produce an object of thought that has resonance across both historical events and mentation. It could be otherwise. Not all ideologies have the same conceptual fluency. Class, for example, is as potent an explanatory concept. Many would argue that it is more explanatorily potent. Yet class is not easy to *think*. One of the reasons that class often discursively transforms into race may well be that race is so much easier to think. As Hall (1980) remarks, race contains within itself something that other ideologies have to construct: the conviction that it captures an essential and universal aspect of nature. It is the child's discovery of this naturalness that I explore in the remainder of the book.

Chapter 3

Domain Specificity and the Study of Race[1]

Despite efforts by historians, anthropologists, and other comparative scholars to show that race is a singular socio-political notion, there has been no parallel proposal to explore how race might be a similarly unique *mental* phenomenon. Psychologists, with remarkably few exceptions, have avoided theorizing race as a construct distinct from other attributes of a person. Rather, it has been assumed that people learn about race the way they learn about other discriminable objects and their properties: through the operation of a general capacity to process category-relevant information.

According to the standard view, which is based on a small industry of psychological and ethnographic studies, children learn to discern patterns of racial variation by simply opening their eyes and looking. Although this view clearly accords with the realist assumption about race that is widely held in psychology, in view of the comparativist critique of this assumption we might expect constructivists to approach the acquisition of racial categories somewhat differently. Surprisingly, they did not. Their description of the acquisition process is much the same as the psychologists'. Little that is internal to the child or specific to race goes into the development of racial thinking. According to researchers in both traditions, children are "passive receptors of information" rather than active participants in its construction (Thornton et al. 1990, p. 408). The only major point of difference between comparativists and psychologists in this regard is that the former believe that it is the cultural rather than the biological environment that gives substance to racial categories. On this view, racial thinking so saturates the cultural environment that there is nothing to motivate researchers to explore the ways in which children's psychological endowment might contribute to its acquisition (Troyna and Hatcher 1992; Gill, Mayor, and Blair 1992; McCarthy and Crichlow 1993).

Both the constructivist approach and the psychological approach clearly situate racial concepts in a widely shared view of the mind

1. This chapter draws heavily on material presented in Hirschfeld and Gelman 1994a.

according to which human beings are endowed with a general set of reasoning abilities that they bring to bear on any cognitive task, whatever its specific content. A common set of processes applies to all thought, whether it involves solving math problems, learning natural languages, calculating the meanings of kinship terms, categorizing disease concepts, or constructing racial categories. It should be clear that I find this account problematic, at least for racial categories. My central claim is that the concept of race develops out of a psychological propensity to learn about a specific phenomenon: the world of human kinds. Most important, I suggest that this propensity is best viewed as a special-purpose cognitive faculty. Our notion of race is unlike our notions of other things. This claim about the specificity of race would be more convincing if it could be shown that special-purpose processing is a hallmark of a broad range of concepts. If my position is that only racial concepts are shaped by a specialized cognitive facility, then its plausibility is a good deal less than if it could be demonstrated that much of our conceptual repertoire involves specialized processing. In this chapter I will review recent work from several disciplines that supports the view that humans learn about and represent many aspects of the world (not only racial ones) in distinct and specialized ways. Taken together, this work suggests that the human mind is an assembly of domain-specific devices specialized to handle specific types of information, not a general-purpose problem solver.

The notion of domain specificity is not new. Indeed, intriguing (although brief) hints emerge in the epistemologies of Descartes and Kant and in the psychologies of Thorndike, Vygotsky, and de Groot. For example, in *Mind in Society*, Vygotsky (1978, p. 83) argues that "the mind is not a complex network of *general* capabilities such as observation, attention, memory, judgment, and so forth, but a set of specific capabilities, each of which is, to some extent, independent of others and is developed independently. Learning is more than the acquisition of the ability to think; it is the acquisition of many specialized abilities for thinking about a variety of things. Learning does not alter our overall ability to focus attention but rather develops various abilities to focus attention on a variety of things." Still, in recent years, increased and detailed attention has turned toward the question of domain specificity. Psychologists with concerns ranging from animal learning to emergent theories of mind and body, cognitivists exploring problem solving and expertise, anthropologists working with color terms and folk taxonomies, psycholinguists investigating auditory perception, and philosophers and others examining reasoning schemata have concluded—often independently—that humans simply could not come to know what they do know in a purely domain-neutral fashion. In this chapter I will review major themes that emerge out of this multi-disciplinary work, with an eye toward picking out the sorts of empirical questions that are relevant to determining whether racial thinking is in fact domain specific.

Language and the Domain-Specificity Hypothesis

To date, the most sustained and detailed account of special-purpose knowledge flows from Noam Chomsky's approach to language. Chomsky's work has played a crucial role in the development of the approach, and virtually all subsequent domain-specificity accounts bear the imprint of his arguments about cognitive architecture. Though previous researchers had recognized the need for conceiving thought as composed of discrete mental functions, Chomsky's speculations about the mind's design have reshaped the way we view human cognition. Given their influence on subsequent theories of domain specificity, I will review relevant claims in some detail, despite the fact that at first blush they seem far removed from questions of race and human kinds.

Central to Chomsky's view is the contention that language represents a body of knowledge that emerges from the operation of a specialized acquisition device. Both the kind of linguistic knowledge that we possess and the way we acquire that knowledge are distinct. Knowledge of language is simply not like the knowledge we have of other phenomena, and gaining it relies on a mode of acquisition that is not like the way we acquire knowledge of other phenomena: "We should, so it appears, think of knowledge of language as a certain state of the mind/brain, a relatively stable element in transitory mental states once it is attained; furthermore, as a state of some distinguishable faculty of the mind—the language faculty—with its specific properties, structure, and organization, one 'module' of the mind." (Chomsky 1986, pp. 12–13)

According to Chomskian theory, language-specific rules of grammar (e.g., those that govern word order in English) are derived from a universal set of language principles, and these principles take certain distinctive forms. Consider one of these principles: structure dependence. According to this principle, knowledge of language relies on structural relations between abstract linguistic categories (such as verb phrase or noun phrase) rather than on surface properties of the utterance (such as the sequence of words in the sentence). As an illustration, consider how a grammatically well-formed question is derived from a declarative sentence[2]:

(1) The man is here.

(1a) Is the man here?

2. The examples are from Chomsky 1980a.

(2) The man will leave.
(2a) Will the man leave?

Two hypotheses fit the data. In the first, the speaker processes the sentence from beginning to end, word by word. Upon reaching the first occurrence of a class of words (say, a verb such as "is" or "will"), the speaker transposes this word to the beginning of the sentence. This hypothesis makes no reference to an underlying linguistic phrase structure. The alternative hypothesis is the same as the first—i.e., look for the occurrence of a verb such as "is" or "will"; in this case, however, what is looked for is such a verb following the first *noun phrase* of the declarative. The first hypothesis is less complex and is independent of deeper linguistic structure. It relies on superficial features of linear word order, rather than require the speaker to interpret sentences with respect to components of their constituent phrase structure (such as "first noun phrase").

If language learning proceeded by using simple general problem-solving strategies, we would expect to find evidence of language learners' holding, even if only momentarily, the hypothesis of structure independence. That is, before discovering that language is in fact structure dependent, the language learner would consider the alternative, simpler hypothesis that it is independent of structure. Yet, as Chomsky notes, there is no evidence that children ever entertain this as a candidate hypothesis. Consider in this light the following declaratives and the derived interrogatives.

(3) The man who is here is tall.
(3a) Is the man who is here tall?
(3b) *Is the man who here is tall?

(4) The man who is tall will leave.
(4a) Will the man who is tall leave?
(4b) *Is the man who tall will leave?

Not only are 3b and 4b ungrammatical, Chomsky (1980a, p. 40) argues that sentences of this form are virtually never encountered in children's speech: "Children make many errors in language learning, but none such as [3b or 4b], prior to appropriate training or evidence. A person might go through much or all of his life without ever having been exposed to relevant evidence, but he will nevertheless unerringly employ [the structure-dependence hypothesis], never [the structure-independence one], on the first relevant occasions. . . . We cannot, it seems explain the preference for [the structure-dependence hypothesis] on grounds of communicative efficiency or the like."

Chomsky further contends that the principle of structure dependence is not a general feature of the mind but a property of a specific *module.* There are two ways to read this modular claim, one involving what might be called a *faculty interpretation* of modularity and the other involving a *task interpretation.* A *faculty interpretation* entails that the mind is made up of a number of distinct (though interacting) systems (e.g., the language faculty, the visual system, a module for facial recognition), each characterized by its own structural principles (Chomsky 1980b, 1988). This interpretation helps provide answers to questions about commonsense ontology and causality: What entities are in a particular domain, and what is the nature of their relations to one another? Sometimes, as with the classification of living kinds or the attribution of behavior to underlying and hidden mental states, a module under the faculty interpretation is associated with and gives rise to theory-like knowledge (widely shared and culturally specific discourses) about these domains. Faculties encompass big pieces of cognition.

The task interpretation of modularity captures a somewhat different set of phenomena, involving smaller chunks of cognitive architecture. On this interpretation, modules are identified not with cognitive faculties but with sets of operations that produce faculty-like processing. That is to say, task modularity involves proposals about cognitive structure that stress the organization and the contribution that each of the system's subcomponents makes to accomplishing distinct tasks. When Chomsky (1988, p. 135) refers to "modules of grammar" (the lexicon, syntax, binding theory, government theory, case theory, etc.), it is this sort of structure that he appears to have in mind. Here the notion of modularity is tied to specific operations *within* the language faculty rather than to the modular uniqueness of the language faculty itself. The grammar, or the language faculty in the traditional sense, is an emergent property of the interaction of these distinct modules. Descriptions of such systems adhere to what Marr (1982, p. 102) called the *principle of modular design,* "the idea that a large computation [such as vision or language] can be split up and implemented as a collection of parts that are as nearly independent of one another as the overall task allows." A task interpretation closely informs questions having do with implementation and with the evolutionary history of a module (Tooby and Cosmides 1992; Pinker and Bloom 1990).

Issues in Domain Specificity

Constraints

The acquisition of natural-language grammars is not the only developmental task that requires a learner to limit the range of hypotheses that he or she entertains. It has long been acknowledged that knowledge development generally could not occur if the child's candidate hypotheses were not constrained in some way. Of course, domain-specific constraints are not the only possible ones, and a variety of non-domain-specific solutions relying on general notions like similarity or contiguity have been suggested (Russell 1948; Quine 1960). Increasingly, however, developmentalists have acknowledged that "there are highly restrictive constraints specifically and uniquely tailored to various cognitive domains, and there are good reasons for this specificity" (Keil 1981, p. 198). The most important of these "good reasons" is the problem of induction. Experience is simply inadequate to explain how children come to share the concepts of their elders. On the one hand, tokens of many of the critical concepts children need to learn never appear in their environment. On the other hand, countless concepts are encountered that are never entertained (e.g., "all red things before Tuesday afternoon"). Take a restricted class of concepts that children acquire: those for which verbal labels exist. A child trying to learn word meanings without constraints is akin to an alien's trying to discover the laws of nature by examining the facts listed in a census report. Both would be doomed to positing thousands upon thousands of meaningless hypotheses. The child might wonder whether "rabbit" refers to a certain patch of color or to the positioning of a limb; the alien might wonder whether there is a meaningful causal relation between the number of babies born in Cancun and the heights of women in Brazil whose names start with Z. If left unconstrained, induction would yield meaningful knowledge only rarely if ever, and then only by chance.

Thus, all theorists acknowledge the need for constraints of some sort. Even traditional learning theorists propose constraints on learning (e.g., perceptual constraints; contiguity). Disagreement remains as to the importance of constraints, how much focus they deserve, and how best to characterize their nature (Behrend 1990; Nelson 1988). There may be a natural affinity between constraints and domain specificity. If constraints are appealing because they make the induction problem easier, then domain-specific constraints are all the more appealing because they make the induction problem all the more easy (Keil 1981). The argument is as follows:

> . . . it is necessary to grant infants and/or young children domain-specific organizing structures that direct attention to the data that bear on the concepts and facts relevant to a particular cognitive domain. The thesis is that the mind brings domain-specific organizing principles to bear on the assimilation and structuring of facts and concepts, that learners can narrow the range of possible

> interpretations of the environment because they have implicit assumptions that guide their search for relevant data. (Gelman 1990, p. 5)

Theories

Constraints are not the only domain-specific mechanisms that guide learners to a certain range of hypotheses. A number of researchers have argued that naive or folk theories are fundamental to the way knowledge is gained and organized (Karmiloff-Smith and Inhelder 1975; Carey 1985; Murphy and Medin 1985; Wellman and Gelman 1992). Theories, like constraints, seem to bear a natural affinity to the notion of domain specificity, in part because theories are by nature domain specific. A theory of biology cannot be applied to the phenomena of physics. They make different ontological commitments (biologists appeal to species and DNA, physicists to quarks and masses). They put forth domain-specific causal laws (e.g., that gravity does not affect mental states; biological processes such as growth or respiration cannot be applied to force dynamics). Thus, if human thought is in important ways analogous to scientific theories, it should be organized separately for distinct domains.

Of course, theories are not in principle required for getting around the world. It is possible to form relevant biological categories without the benefit of theories, as when pigeons classify birds and trees (Herrnstein 1979). By the same token, it is possible to respond to others' mental states by simply reflecting on one's own (Harris 1994). In fact, the claim that everyday knowledge is theory laden may at first blush seem implausible. If "theory" means "scientific theory," then it is certainly not the case that everyday knowledge is organized into theories. It is clear that few of us have the detailed, explicit, formal understanding that professional biologists or physicists have. Lay folk rarely, if ever, conduct scientific experiments to test everyday hypotheses.

Still, the need for positing naive theories is clearer if we consider the alternative view. According to a long tradition in psychology and philosophy, theories are not part of folk thinking. According to this tradition, word meanings, concepts, and categories are constructed on the basis of relatively simple algorithms, e.g., the similarity that members of a category have to one another. You don't need a theory of dogs to construct the concept DOG; you simply have to attend to the ways in which all dogs are similar. Obviously this puts considerable weight on our ability to attend to and recognize similarity, and considerable research has explored how these similarities might be computed (e.g., in terms of prototypes, feature lists, and similarity to exemplars; see Smith and Medin 1981).

The problem, as Goodman (1972) points out, is that similarity is not sufficiently constrained to solve the problem of classification or induction. Depending on what counts as a feature, any two objects could have indefinitely many features in common (e.g., a lawnmower and a hummingbird both weigh less than 200 pounds, less than 201 pounds, less than 202 pounds, . . .). Thus, we need a system of coherent limitations on what counts as a feature and how to weight features. Theories seem a plausible candidate. To appreciate this, consider a relatively simple problem involving similarity. Rips (1989) told subjects about hypothetical circular objects 3 inches in diameter. He then asked them to rate these objects on four dimensions: similarity to pizzas, similarity to quarters, likelihood of being a pizza, and likelihood of being a quarter. Rips discovered that similarity judgments and categorization judgments diverged. The object was judged more similar to a quarter than to a pizza, but more likely to be a pizza than to be a quarter. Theoretical beliefs about the possible features of pizzas and quarters yielded the classification; a general similarity metric did not (see also Medin and Shoben 1988).

It is not difficult to imagine that the development of rich categories of human kinds are also guided by constraints and theories. This guidance could take at least two forms. On one hand, a child's attention might be guided toward the discovery of the collectivities into which humans around the child have coalesced. On the other hand, a child might be led to discover only those collectivities predicated on certain properties, say the putative intrinsic nature of a groups' membership. In either event, the notion of constraint appears to be informative. As with other domains, similarity appears to be an insufficient explanation for racial categories. Similarity between individuals in itself does not determine whether two individuals are of the same intrinsic human kind. Like natural kinds, membership in human kinds is tied to appearances but is not defined by them. Membership is based on sharing a kind's essence.

The Acquisition of Domain-Specific Theories

Where do theories and constraints come from? According to a long tradition in psychology and philosophy, children's initial concepts are constrained by an innate sense of similarity, which is eventually supplanted by emergent theories (Quine 1960; Piaget 1951).

Recent work suggests that this account is not very plausible. Consider a study on living kinds in which Keil (1989) told children stories about a skunk that was surgically altered to resemble a raccoon but still had the parents and the internal structure of a skunk. By approximately second grade, children reported that the animal was still a skunk despite its changed outward appearance. However, when children of the same age were asked if a coffee pot altered to resemble a bird feeder was a bird feeder they reported that it was. What appears to be driving older children's answers is an emergent theory of living things—that is, of biology. Carey (1985) and Gelman (1988) have shown that the ability to overcome appearances in reasoning about living kinds develops even earlier than Keil's data suggest. There is controversy on how best to interpret these findings; developmentalists continue to debate how these theories emerge and about their scope and their nature. What is evident is that young children's common sense is both theory-like and domain specific. Knowledge accrues through the operation of special-purpose conceptual devices that guide children's attention to a specific range of information for each domain and a specific range of hypotheses about the relationship between items in each domain.

Evolution and Domain Specificity

Domain-specific competences are solutions to specific tasks. I have framed these tasks in terms of a general *class* of problems, namely those of induction. Human children are not the only animals that acquire knowledge. The induction problem is faced by other species and by humans during evolution. Not surprisingly, students of animal cognition and evolution have stressed the need to interpret a range of adaptations in domain-specific terms (Rozin and Schull 1988). Cosmides (1989) suggests that conditions of social exchange have selected in humans for certain very specific reasoning schemata. Symons (1979), Langlois and Roggman (1990), and Buss (1994) argue that notions of physical attractiveness may be governed by innate modular mechanisms. Gallistel (1990) contends that animal systems of navigation, dead reckoning, and temporality, are similarly domain specific. More generally, several researchers have argued that learning of any sort could hardly proceed without the aid of domain-specific devices (Cosmides and Tooby 1989, 1994; Gallistel et al. 1991; Symons 1979).

What about the emergence of human-kind and racial cognitions? Developing skills for discriminating between individuals and categories of conspecifics is a problem encountered by many social animals, not just humans. Ethological studies indicate that nonhuman primates are able to keep track of cooperative behaviors and other kinds of interactions. Moreover, they predicate future behaviors on this record. As Cheney and Seyfarth (1990) have shown with vervet monkeys, nonhuman primates do so not only by relying on memory for individual actors but also by making judgments about groups of conspecifics whose membership is based on status and kinship. As a consequence, nonhuman primates are able to "identify individuals that associated together" but also to "infer general properties of social relationships and compare relationships on the basis of these properties" (ibid., p. 61).

Clearly, then, the discrimination of social kinds has antecedents in our evolutionary history. I would not want to infer from this that the discrimination of a highly salient human kind, like race, is a solution to a problem encountered by prehumans. There is reason to believe that race is a historically recent phenomenon, at least in its modern guise of populations who are markedly different phenotypically. Moreover, though it seems worth asking what insights into racial thinking might be gained by exploring the sorts of group-discrimination problems our nonhuman ancestors encountered, there is considerable resistance to envisioning racial thinking (or any other thinking with unwanted political implications) as having any biological, let alone evolutionary component (Degler 1991). Understandably so. We recoil from the notion that one of the most pernicious aspects of human cognition is somehow rooted in the way our ancestral populations solved evolutionary problems—and plausibly part of the way we will resolve contemporary ones. It is therefore important to reiterate that I am *not* proposing the existence of a domain-specific competence for perceiving and reasoning about *race*. Instead, I am suggesting that racial thinking may be parasitic on a domain-specific competence for perceiving and reasoning about human kinds. One sort of human kind, the one based on the putative sharing of unforeseen and intrinsic properties, is especially important to conceptions of race. But that same sort of human kind likely is the basis for notions of kinship as well.

Domain Specificity and Problems of Cultural Variation

There is an important difference between the sorts of special-purpose cognitive devices described so far and the one I believe is linked to racial thinking. Racial thinking has a component that varies significantly across cultures and historical epochs and a component that is widely shared across cultures and historical epochs. In this regard it resembles the phenomena that have attracted the attention of psychology-oriented anthropologists (who, like their counterparts in psychology, have pointed out that human knowledge is task specific and domain specific) (Sperber 1974; Shweder 1982). The domains in which this has been most clearly articulated are color terms, folk biology, and symbolic representations.

Color terms Different languages appear to segment the color spectrum in dramatically different ways. Some languages have only two color terms that distinguish light from dark chroma. Others, including English, have rich and varied color vocabularies. Under the prevailing doctrine of linguistic relativity in anthropology and psychology, the prevalent interpretation of these data was that language differences reflect differences in how colors are experienced as well as in how they are named. Berlin and Kay (1969) directly confronted this view. They analyzed color terms in 98 languages and found that there are 11 basic color terms.[3] In principle, 2048 combinations of these 11 terms are possible (e.g., black/white, red/blue, white/green/yellow, . . .). Berlin and Kay discovered, however, that only 22 of these combinations actually occur. Moreover, they found a distinct pattern in the order in which basic color words enter a language. If a language has only two terms, they are invariably black and white; if three, they are for black, white, and red; if five, they are for black, white, red, green and yellow; and so on:

$$\begin{bmatrix}\text{white}\\ \text{black}\end{bmatrix} > [\text{red}] > \begin{bmatrix}\text{green}\\ \text{yellow}\end{bmatrix} > [\text{blue}] > [\text{brown}] > \begin{bmatrix}\text{purple}\\ \text{pink}\\ \text{orange}\\ \text{gray}\end{bmatrix}.$$

Another set of universal principles appear to govern color perception in a way that admits considerable cultural variation. The color space is fixed, but the number of named categories a particular language uses to describe it varies. Consequently, different languages draw boundaries within the color space in quite different ways. Berlin and Kay, however, found that the focal point of each basic color (i.e., the point in the array of reds that is judged to be the reddest of red) is largely the same across languages, regardless of the particular color boundaries. Subsequently, Heider and Oliver (1972), working with Dani tribesmen in New Guinea (whose language has only two basic color terms), provided cross-cultural evidence that memory for color as well as the naming of colors is largely independent of color vocabulary.[4] Again, the findings suggest that an invariant set of principles of nomenclature and conceptual organization underlies a set of distinct language-specific color-naming practices.

Folk biology As was the case for color terms, until recently the predominant view in anthropology has been that folk biological classification is

3. Berlin and Kay (1969, pp. 5–6) define as basic those color terms that (among other properties) are monolexemic (so that the meaning of the term is not predictable from the meaning of its parts), apply to a broad range of phenomena (thus excluding "blond," a term that applies only to hair), and are psychologically salient for all speakers (thus excluding the color of something with which only a few individuals are familiar).

4. The domain of color remains contested. Berlin and Kay's conclusions regarding linguistic relativity have been tempered by Kempton and Kay (1984) and challenged by Lucy and Shweder (1979, 1988) and by Lakoff (1987). Yet even if there is significant cross-linguistic relativity in basic color terms, the principles organizing the color lexicon are everywhere specific to the conceptual and perceptual domain of color.

culturally relative. This seems plausible in view of the enormous variation in the plants and animals that any local population encounters, and particularly in view of the great differences in saliency different parts of this local flora and fauna have for each culture. However, Berlin (1972, 1978) and his associates (Berlin et al. 1973) found that the basic principles of classification of biological kinds appear to be quite stable across cultures and over marked differences in learning environment and exposure. Although some cultural effects on the development of biological classification have been found (Stross 1973; Dougherty 1978), these differences are minor relative to the points of similarity across cultures in children's biological reasoning (Hatano and Inagaki, in press). These findings led Atran (1990), following Sperber (1974), to propose that folk biology represents a domain-specific device. Atran suggests that folk biology is uniquely organized insofar as a presumption of underlying essence applies to all living things and a strict taxonomic hierarchy spans all and only living kinds.

Symbolic representations Anthropologists have long remarked that the impetus to interpret the world symbolically is a hallmark of human cognition. A predominant view in anthropology has been that this sort of symbolism is a kind of language provided by the culture. Symbolic systems encompass networks of meaning that infuse speech, action, and other forms of representation with significance and coherence. Meaning, on this view, derives from public forms of expression, not psychological endowment.

Geertz's (1973, pp. 45–46) appraisal of the relative contributions psychology and culture make to symbolic forms is a typical one:

> . . . what are innately given are extremely general response capacities, which, although they make possible far greater plasticity, complexity, and on the scattered occasions when everything works as it should, effectiveness of behavior, leave it much less precisely regulated. . . . Undirected by culture patterns—organized systems of significant symbols—man's behavior would be virtually ungovernable, a mere chaos of pointless acts and exploding emotions, his experience virtually shapeless. Culture, the accumulated totality of such patterns, is not just an ornament of human existence but—the principal basis of its specificity—an essential condition for it.

In a major rethinking of the anthropology of symbolism, Sperber (1975a) argued that symbols are not signs, do not figure in code-like structures, and do not have paraphrasable meanings. The true cognitive role of symbolic beliefs, Sperber proposed, is to focus attention and to evoke representations from memory. He depicts symbolic representations as meta-representations of hard-to-process beliefs (such as the not-fully-interpretable notion of the Trinity, in which three is one). Sperber goes on to link symbolic representations with the relative availability of domain-specific competences. In an important extension of this proposal, Boyer (1990, 1994; see also Bloch 1993) demonstrates how religious representations may also be shaped by domain-specific principles even in the absence of a genuine domain of religious beliefs.

Domain-Specific Competence: A Characterization

Given this survey, is it possible to extract what researchers mean when they talk of domain specificity? In spite of the wealth of research, we lack an explicit and well-articulated account of what a domain-specific competence is. It is easier to think of examples than to give a definition. Naive conceptualizations of physical entities and processes, substances, living kinds, numbers, artifacts, mental states, social types, and supernatural phenomena are all candidate domain-specific competences. Are there features common to all domain-specific competences? This review, though brief, allows us to identify areas of accord, often implicit, in much domain-relevant research. I take the following to be a fairly uncontroversial characterization:

> A domain-specific competence is a body of knowledge that identifies and interprets a class of phenomena assumed to share certain properties and to be of a distinct and general type. A domain-specific competence functions as a stable response to a set of recurring and complex problems faced by the organism. This response involves difficult-to-consciously-access perceptual, encoding, retrieval, and inferential processes dedicated to that solution.

Let us consider each part of this characterization in turn.

Domain-Specific Competences as Guides to Partitioning the World

Most accounts converge on a view that domain-specific competences function conceptually to identify phenomena belonging to a single general kind, even when these phenomena fall under several concepts. For example, living kinds can be classified in a number of different ways, ranging from foodstuffs to zoo animals. The psychological correlates of competing classifications and their internal structures have significant effects on the way many common categories for living things are sorted, recalled, and recognized (Rosch et al. 1976). Yet, in spite of these competing ways of classifying living things, certain beliefs about living kinds typically emerge early, are acquired effortlessly, and vary little across cultures. This does not mean that domain-specific competences necessarily provide rigid constraints. They may serve rather as "guideposts" for organizing knowledge in coherent systems (Waxman 1991, p. 137). That is, domain-specific competences bias belief toward some interpretations or toward the relative weight an interpretation may assume, but domains do not always determine that a particular interpretation will prevail.

Domain-Specific Competences as Explanatory Frames

Most researchers would also accept that a domain competence systematically links recognized kinds to restricted classes of properties. Thus a cognitive domain is a class of phenomena that share among themselves, but not with other kinds, a number of relevant features. Though virtually all domain-specific competences seem to make reference to causal or otherwise model-derived connections, there is considerable variation across competences in how flexible these connections are.

It is not even necessary that all and only members of a given domain share a property. It is a recognized property of humans—recognized through the agency of a naive psychology—that human beings behave in association with their beliefs, whereas artifacts do not. Still, we have little trouble accepting that there are humans who do not have beliefs (e.g., people in deep comas), or humans who do not recognize that others have beliefs (e.g., autistic individuals), or artifacts that are most sensibly dealt with as if they had beliefs (e.g., a chess-playing computer). In other domain-specific competences (say, auditory processing of speech) there may be substantially less flexibility in the degree to which common characteristics of the input are mentally represented (e.g., all speech is perceived categorically).

Domain-Specific Competences as Functional and Widely Distributed Devices

Domain competences are a restricted set of the cognitive skills the organism may develop: they are the knowledge structures that target recurring problems faced by an organism.[5] Domain-specific competences are also generally seen as highly (though not universally) shared among members of a species, not as idiosyncratic solutions to individual problems. Even if a domain skill is unevenly distributed within a population, it must be a solution to a repeatedly encountered problem. To the extent that chess playing is governed by a domain-specific com-

5. Cases where the adaptive aspect of the competence has been challenged, as with the language faculty, have been much debated (Pinker and Bloom 1990; Greenfield 1991; Burling 1993).

petence, the development of perceptual strategies for analyzing chess positions arises *because* chess masters frequently encounter chess problems. Nonmasters do not have a less developed domain competence of chess; they lack the competence entirely. This relationship between frequency of encounter and domain skill, however, is complex. Some domain skills may appear to be closely tied to differences in the learning environment even if the underlying domain competence does not depend on environmental conditions. "The ability to develop and understand mathematics may be rooted in some fairly specific cognitive mechanisms, which human beings are innately endowed with. But if so, many cultures do not require that people use this ability. Nor is it occasioned by every environment. Mathematics does not spontaneously arise irrespective of social context, but seems to require a richer and more sustained sequence of experience and instruction in order to flourish than, say, basic grammatical knowledge, color perception or appreciation of living kinds." (Atran 1988, p. 8) Such mathematical skills, involving a formal language of mathematics, are distinct from other, universally emerging arithmetic competences, such as the principles underlying counting and cardinal enumeration (Gelman and Brenneman 1994; Gelman and Gallistel 1978).

Domain-Specific Competences as Dedicated Mechanisms
Domain-specific processing is involuntary and difficult to access consciously. This property is blatant in special-purpose knowledge structures such as color perception or phonetic interpretation, where some innate mechanism is difficult to doubt. But it is also apparent when an innate mechanism seems less likely, as in a more marginal domain competence like chess. Chess masters differ from chess novices in visual-perception processing of chess information, not in logical-deductive thinking or in general memory skills (Chase and Simon 1973). Accordingly, domain operations generally involve focused, constrained, and involuntary perceptual, conceptual, or inferential processes.

Do Domain-Specific Competences Correspond to Domains of the External World?

Some domains appear to carve the world at its joints. When we think of domains, we think of ranges of phenomena comparable to the ranges of facts that are the subject matters of the various sciences. Naive linguistics, biology, psychology, physics, mathematics, and cosmology have all been proposed as domains. It is tempting to go from this to a view that some causal link exists between the structure of empirical sciences and domain competences (Carey 1985). Domain-specific competences, on this view, would necessarily be comparable in size to the subject matters of the various sciences. Is there reason to believe that we are unduly influenced by the way scientific disciplines partition the universe?

Yes. For example, some domains less carve nature at its joints than create such joints. Colors appear to be perceived as discrete categories despite the fact that the distal stimulus on which they are based is a continuous natural phenomenon. In processing speech we automatically ignore within-category variation, engaging what is called categorical perception. Yet when we listen to a human voice singing, we attend to within-category variation in pitch just as automatically. Color and speech perception are less discoveries about nature than interpretations of it. A fairly extensive literature documents domain-like competences that span contrived phenomena not typically associated with a unique science or discipline (ranging from chess to chicken sexing (Biederman and Shiffrar 1987) to reading x-rays (Lesgold et al. 1988)), while others encompass phenomena that lack scientific validity or correspondence (for example, magic, the supernatural, and race—to the extent that racial thinking represents a domain-like competence).

The degree to which a domain is dependent on the world is complex and variable. Some domain-specific competences (for instance, naive biology and physics) may be less closely linked to our scientific understanding of the world than is sometimes appreciated. Some changes in scientific understanding are incorporated into common sense quite rapidly. Thus, whales are widely understood to be mammals and not fish, even by children. Examples of this sort prompted Putnam (1975) to speak of a linguistic division of labor in which science is seen as determining the meanings of natural-kind terms. But changes in the validity of a given scientific or formal description do not always alter our commitment to the commonsense conceptualization of that phenomenon (Resnick 1994; Strauss and Shilony 1994). Anthropologists, for example, have shown that the notion "tree" is central to our understanding of the plant world (Witowski et al. 1981). Nonetheless, tree does not represent an interesting evolutionary line and is therefore not a concept in modern systematics. Unlike instances where our commonsense knowledge is altered by scientific discovery (e.g., the reclassification of whales as mammals), the concept of tree maintains its conceptual salience in the face of scientific challenge. This appears to be true even for experts. Botanists in everyday contexts continue to hold the commonsense notion of tree (Atran 1990). The empirical and structural parallels between folk beliefs and science are indeed informative; however, from the perspective of understanding mental domains these parallels are more pertinent to the cognitive than other sciences.

Conclusion: Toward a Domain-Specific Account of Racial Thinking

A number of distinct intellectual traditions have converged on the view that human cognition can be fruitfully considered domain specific. Strikingly, with few exceptions (Turiel 1983; Jackendoff 1992; Bloom 1994; Premack 1994), researchers have not examined the possibility that social beliefs also derive from a domain-specific competence. Understanding persons and their social environments is a central task for all humans. Clearly, then, the notion that there are specialized capacities for classifying and reasoning about the social world is at first blush plausible. In the following chapters I will make the case that the conceptualization of human kinds (and, by extension, races) is a prime candidate for a domain-specific social competence. Evidence of this comes from various sources. Paradoxically, the strongest support comes from the interpretive literature's thick documentation of variation in systems of racial thought. As I argued in chapter 2, despite this marked variation, recurrent conceptual properties—in particular, abstract principles that constrain the construction of all racial theories—map onto otherwise quite distinct systems of racial reference.

Admittedly there is more than one way to interpret these shared features. For example, we might infer from these commonalities that there is a common external thing in the environment to which our perceptual and conceptual systems grab hold. As I suggested earlier, a parallel logic is implicit in most psychological work on the concept of race. Alternatively—and this is the position I am supporting—we might interpret recurrent conceptual properties mapped onto diverse cultural and historical contexts as supporting the notion that racial thinking represents a specific sort of thought more than a specific sort of shared experience. White (1994) makes much the same point by posing a quite different question: How is it that so many people tell such strikingly similar stories about being abducted by UFOs? White suggests two explanations are plausible. On the one hand, the stories may be true. Abductees may tell similar stories because they have had the same experience with similar aliens. On the other hand, the stories may reflect the mutual recruitment of a shared story *genre*. White opts for the latter, arguing that it is the commonsense notion of race that provides the underlying structure to these accounts. White's concern is with narrative genres or story structures in a cultural sense. My concern is with psychological genres—causal stories in a cognitive sense. It is not surprising that the idea of race should figure prominently in both our programs. As I remarked at the outset, race is just the sort of idea that lends itself to appropriation and extension. Race stories spread easily, are easily learned, and are readily recalled.

Other phenomena—e.g., explanations for endemic poverty or for inferior or superior performance on some set of tasks—recruit race in much the same way. It is not that race necessarily has anything directly to do these phenomena. Indeed, the naturalness of race has a lot to do with how expediently and convincingly racial explanations migrate to seemingly unrelated phenomena. Race stories spread easily in the sense that other stories are readily retold as racial ones. Class, many scholars have observed, is often re-presented in racial terms (Stoler 1995; Winant 1994; Roediger 1991; Anderson 1983; Fields 1982; Harris 1964; cf. Scarr 1988). The sociological mode here is one of false consciousness—the recasting of relations of power in terms of more palpable and palatable relations of blood. But such a move, like any invoking common belief, depends on a psychological mode as well. As Sperber (1985, 1990) has argued, the distribution of ideas is a jointly cognitive and cultural enterprise, and our understandings of that distribution must be similarly conjoined. The advantage of the domain-specificity approach is that it provides a framework in which differential susceptibility to belief is adequately explained in mental as well as sociological terms.

Much of what follows will explore what a domain-specific account of racial thinking might look like. There are several possibilities, all of which start from the same observation: whatever else racial thinking is, it is a theory (or a theory-like constellation of beliefs) about human variation, its meaning, its scope, and its social significance.

In the next chapter I will continue to explore what a theory of race entails and whence it emerges. For the moment I want to underscore that a domain perspective suggests at least two ways to approach such folk theories. On the one hand, folk theories might correspond to a specific domain. That is, a given folk theory might be the output of a special-purpose domain device. Race plausibly fits this model. To the extent that a propensity to identify group membership has evolutionary consequences, it has even been argued that a racialist (or ethnic) perspective has contributed to reproductive success (van den Berghe 1981). On the other hand, folk theories might derive from domain mechanisms that are independent of the particular folk theory in question. That is, although theories are necessarily domain specific, they are not necessarily special-purpose domain devices. Sperber (1975a,b, 1985, 1990) and Boyer (1990, 1994) have offered detailed accounts of folk theories of the symbolic and supernatural realms that depend on and are constrained by domain-specific mechanisms but are not in themselves special-purpose devices.

The symbolic and the supernatural are parasitic on the operation of such devices. These cultural forms involve entities that are at once constrained by deeply entrenched folk beliefs (as when otherwise unnatural creatures, such as ghosts, are thought to be motivated by belief/desire psychology, or when space aliens are seen as being compelled by human sexual interest) and freed from them (as when such entities can pass through solid objects or abduct humans from earth to spaceships). In the next chapters I will examine how cognitively unique commonsense beliefs about race are, how we should characterize their emergence, and whether we should attribute their form to more familiar belief systems, such as folk biology.

Chapter 4
Do Children Have a Theory of Race?[1]

How children acquire racial and ethnic concepts has long been of interest to both anthropologists (see, e.g., Goodman 1970; Holmes 1995) and psychologists (for reviews see Porter 1971; Katz 1982; Phinney and Rotheram 1987; Aboud 1988; Cross 1991). With this history of extensive study, it may seem curious that the question as to whether children have a theory of race remains open. Not only is there a vast literature on the acquisition of racial concepts by scholars interested in social development, but race is just the sort of commonsense concept that cognitive scientists concerned with folk theory have found compelling to explore. Like other naive theories, notions of race are culturally ubiquitous, developmentally salient, and entrenched in human behavior. Moreover, contrary to the widespread folk belief that it is a relatively late discovery, race is one of the earliest-emerging social dimensions to which children attend (Katz 1982; Davey 1983; Ramsey 1987), and this pattern of development appears to be stable across diverse cultures (see Hirschfeld 1988 for a review). Furthermore, racial thinking clearly develops into a theory-like knowledge structure, representing a coherent body of explanatory knowledge sustaining inferences about category members that go far beyond the range of direct experience (Allport 1954).

However, racial thinking appears to differ from other commonsense theories in at least two important regards. First, although the pattern of the development varies little, the content of the beliefs does. Systems of racial belief seem to display considerably more cultural and historical specificity than most other well-studied commonsense theories. Second, although systems of racial belief eventually become theory-like (as do other commonsense knowledge structures), they supposedly do so only relatively late in childhood (Aboud 1988; Katz 1982). In contrast, naive physics, folk biology, and theory of mind all cohere into theory-like conceptual systems early in childhood. And this pattern of

1. This chapter draws heavily on material presented in Hirschfeld 1995b.

development varies little from one cultural environment to the next.[2] Presumably both of these differences are tied to the fact that naive physics, folk biology, and theory of mind are all fairly directly tethered to stable referents in the real world—the events and objects picked out by the theories vary little across cultures or across historical epochs.[3]

In contrast, according to the standard view, racial content is distinct from one culture to the next because it is linked to locally varying, culturally constructed systems of social differentiation. The disjuncture between stability in the acquisition process and variation in the end result is a function of the generality of the former. Unlike other commonsense theories that emerge out of content-specific programs for the development, race is thought to derive from the operation of general learning mechanisms. Moreover, the learning that this involves is supposedly not only general but also unnuanced. It is widely argued that children rely predominantly on perceptual cues in modeling racial categories—or more specifically, in learning to match racial labels with some range of perceptual cues—so that the development of social categories generally (and racial categories in particular) is characterized by low level computational processes (e.g., judgments of similarity) involving attention to superficial differences. According to this argument, preschoolers group people into racial categories "on the basis of attributes perceived in common" (Vaughan 1987, p. 91), relying on "conspicuous" differences (Goodman 1970, p. 37), on the "concrete reality" of physical differences such as skin color (Clark and Clark

2. Major aspects of the lay understanding of physical phenomena appear to be fixed by birth (Spelke 1990) and to remain virtually impervious to cultural and other environmental influences (Kaiser et al. 1985; McCloskey et al. 1980). There is also striking regularity in the developmental course and in the structure of naive psychology, again despite considerable cultural variation in the way people talk about other people, their internal states, and what motivates their behavior (Avis and Harris 1991; Gardner et al. 1988; Wellman 1990). Systems of folk biological classification and reasoning also appear to be remarkably stable across cultures and historical epochs, despite the radically different cultural importance such systems often have (Berlin 1992; Atran 1990; Boster et al. 1986). Gelman and Wellman (1991), Springer (1992), and Keil (1989) argue that naive biology is among the most precocious of commonsense theories. To the extent that Carey (1985) argues that naive biology is not an autonomous domain before middle childhood, one could interpret her as suggesting that naive biology is not theory-like until then. I believe a more plausible reading of her argument is that naive biology is theory-like earlier in development—the theory is simply part of naive psychology.

3. This is not meant to suggest that common sense reflects an accurate reading of the external world. Many precocious beliefs that are commonsensically compelling are bizarre when viewed from the vantage point of science. Even in the case of folk biology, where systems of native classification closely correlate with scientific systematics (Berlin 1992; Atran 1990), it is not clear that it even makes sense to speak of a single system of scientific systematics against which folk belief might be compared (Hull 1992).

1940b, p. 168), on "overt or superficial characteristics" (Holmes 1995, p. 108), and on other "overwhelmingly" external properties, such as costume, cuisine, or language (Aboud 1988, p. 106). A corollary to this attention to superficial and concrete differences is a supposed inability to grasp that race is tied to abstract and intrinsic qualities. Initially, according to most researchers, race concepts are empirical summaries (based on superficial features) rather than explanatory constructs (involving causal principles), to borrow Yuill's (1992) distinction.

In chapter 2 I argued that the greater variability in surface content in racial thinking may be misleading since this diversity may well derive from a common set of abstract principles that are remarkably stable across history, culture, and individual experience. Herein lies a cognitive puzzle. It does not make sense to claim that a stable system of racial concepts emerges out of fundamentally dissimilar systems of local knowledge (for picking out, naming, and coordinating relations between supposedly distinct human types). Yet this is what is entailed in the standard account of the formation of racial categories. Virtually all previous work assumes that children derive their racial categories not from the relatively stable theory underlying adult systems of racial thinking but from the highly varying and local conditions of racial referencing.

Cognition, Race, and "Mature" Representations

Still, there is little doubt that adult reasoning about race is theory-like. Like other theory-like knowledge, racial thinking consists of a commitment to an ontology, a specific pattern of explanatory causal principles, and a specified set of concepts. The relevant ontology in the case of race is the expectation that humans can be partitioned into a number of distinct physical types. Adults the world over believe race to be a natural phenomenon and thus expect race to be governed by a range of folk principles about nature.

Three principles are primary: immutability, differentiation, and heritability. First, race supposedly derives from physical (specifically, anatomical) differences. Moreover, the physical properties characteristic of a given race are considered immutable—at least from the perspective of an individual's lifetime. Second, there is differentiation among the contributions that various physical properties supposedly make to race (i.e., not all physical properties contribute to racial identity in the same way that not all anatomical properties contribute to biological identity). Third, racial differences are seen as derived from family background, transmitted through and fixed by birth.

In the contemporary American system of racial thinking, the physical interpretation implicates the operation of two related biological processes: growth and inheritance. Both involve understanding of systematic and correlated patterns of resemblance, and both entail judgments about stability and invariance in the context of morphological change. The concept of growth explains why a person is the same person at two points in time despite dramatic changes in physique, mental aptitudes, and even personality. A further feature of growth is that not all points of continuity across the life span are predictable. The precise elements of a person's appearance that will be maintained cannot be known in advance. Similarly, offspring resemble their parents in a predictable class of ways, but the specific points of resemblance cannot be known in advance. Some children take after their parents in body build, others in the structure of their faces (or aspects of facial appearance), others in temperament, and so on.

Enmeshed in all three of these aspects of racial thinking (differentiation, immutability during growth, and inheritability) is a notion of a material and nonobvious *essence*. Note the peculiarity of racial essentialism relative to other characteristic and essentialized properties that are passed along family lines. Manifestations of underlying essence that emerge in personal identity (a characteristic physical or mental feature that simultaneously "runs through" a family) are thought to be graded. Some family members may share more of a property or propensity than others. In contrast, racial identity, and by extension racial essence, is fixed. In the folk view, a child does not simply resemble its parent in being black; the black child *is* black in virtue of having black parents. In this sense, the biological expectations associated with race more closely resemble naive conceptualization of interspecies difference than intraspecies (i.e., individual) variation. In other words, the notion of essence is a conceptual attempt to capture kinds rather than properties or attributes. Although kindhood may be defined in terms of large numbers of shared attributes (Dupré 1987), it is precisely the putative homogeneity of a kind that is crucial, not the number of attributes each member of the kind actually shares (Schwartz 1979).

As happens with commonsense essentialist understanding of nonhuman living organisms, racial essentialism recruits the complex relationship between attributes and kinds to serve another function: it provides the conceptual flexibility that permits psychological representations of race to match the social conditions of racial meaning. Race is thought to be an intrinsic feature of a person, attributable to his or her physical being. Despite this widely shared physical interpretation of race, it is also generally accepted that surface features alone do not predict membership in a racial category. On the basis of mere inspection one can be mistaken about a person's racial status, in part because there is not universal agreement about which traits identify a racial group (Molnar 1992). Adult common sense captures both a sense of physicality and the indeterminacy of that physicality by appeal to a notion of racial essence, which is part of each individual's underlying nature derived from *group* membership. Like the notion of species essence in folk biology, this conceptualization links group differences to a class of physical differences. But it also explains instances in which these physical differences are not evident: just as a three-legged albino tiger is a tiger in virtue of its nature, a light-skinned black who "passes" for white is a black (at least in the United States) because of his or her intrinsic nature.

Where does this naturalized and essentialist construal of race come from? Recall that according to standard view children first develop categories that capture little more than superficial regularities. Later these categories metamorphize into theory-laden and essentialized concepts. The consensus is that the mechanism underlying this transformation involves reasoning by analogy. There are striking parallels (both cognitive and historical) between the species model of living-kind difference and the racial model of human difference, and these parallels have repeatedly been explained as a *transfer* of biological principles of inference to the human domain (for a cognitive perspective see Rothbart and Taylor 1990, Atran 1990, and Boyer 1990; for a historical perspective see Guillaumin 1980 and Banton 1987). The idea is that knowledge-based adult processing of social categories is derivative: racial categories become essentialized when general categorization biases (Allport 1954; Hamilton 1981) combine with the transfer of specialized reasoning strategies from better-grounded domains (such as folk biology) to social objects (Rothbart and Taylor 1990; Boyer 1990; Atran 1990).

Nonetheless, as self-evident as the blatant similarities between the essentialism of living-kind categories and that of racial concepts seem, the evidence for reasoning by analogy is largely indirect. Virtually no work has actually examined this putative transfer process. We have no description of what underlying mechanisms might be involved (save a vague reference to analogical reasoning) and little more than speculation on how principles of causal reasoning transfer from the biological to the human realm.

Children's Racial Thinking

Perhaps the most striking feature of young children's racial knowledge is the remarkable ease with which it is acquired. As Katz (1982) observes, we can easily find school-age children who can neither read nor subtract, but it is impossible to find any that do not know about racial stereotypes. We now know that by the late preschool years children come to sort people into culturally appropriate racial categories and to evaluate them on the basis of racial-category membership (Clark and Clark 1940a,b; Horowitz 1939; Katz 1982).

However, while it is widely accepted that the extensions and stereotypes of adults' and children's categories match, their *meanings* are thought to be quite different. According to standard accounts, young children do not have a naturalized notion of race—they do not share adults' biologically grounded model of race. Young children classify people into racial categories (and social categories generally) on the basis of surface perceptual cues rather than abstract, nonobvious criteria such as essences (Aboud 1988; Katz 1982; Vaughan 1987; Clark and Clark 1940a,b). Preschoolers do so, it is argued, because before the age of 8 they do not view race as having the biological (i.e., natural) implications with which adults impute it (Aboud 1987; Semaj 1980). For example, Aboud (1988) reports research showing that young children do not grasp that a person's race is both immutable and derived from family background. Similarly, Ramsey (1987) contends that preschool children believe racial features to be temporary and changeable, caused by local environmental conditions (e.g., the tanning effects of the sun) or superficial factors (e.g., clothing).

In this chapter I will revisit these claims. I will show that even young children's beliefs about racial difference are essentialized and naturalized. Young children's racial thinking is embedded in a coherent system of knowledge, involving domain-specific causal attributions and sustaining inferences that go far beyond what either direct experience or similarity-based reasoning delivers. Specifically, I will show that young children's thinking about race encompasses the defining principles of theory-like conceptual systems, namely an ontology, domain-specific causality, and differentiation of concepts. This is not as surprising as previous work on racial cognition might lead one to believe. We know that even young children have an elaborately developed system of folk biology (ignoring for the moment whether young children's folk biological beliefs represent a distinct or a derived domain of knowledge). There are glaring parallels between the system of social categorization embodied by racial thinking and the system of nonhuman-living-kind categorization embodied by folk biological thinking. If children are aware of this, their gaining a theory-like representation of race may be a fairly modest move.

An extensive body of work now exists on biological reasoning among preschoolers (Carey 1985; Inagaki and Hatano 1988; Keil 1989; Gelman 1989). Although considerable controversy remains about how best to characterize this understanding, significant areas of agreement have emerged. First, it is widely accepted that commonsense biology recognizes the following:

> *a class of entities (living things) that fall under the theory* Young children's naive biology includes a unique ontology that discriminates biological phenomena at several levels, including animate from inanimate (Mandler 1992; Gelman et al. 1983; Spelke and Gelman 1981). A small number of cross-cultural studies suggest that this core set of taxonomic distinctions underlies children's biological classification everywhere (Stross 1972; Dougherty 1978).
>
> *domain-specific causal processes of growth and inheritance* Young children understand that the natural transformations that occur in biological entities differ from changes that occur in nonbiological things (Rosengren et al. 1991; Hatano and Inagaki, in press). Springer and Keil (1989, 1991) provide evidence that even preschool children differentiate between causal mechanisms appropriate to biological and nonbiological kinds, and that young children have a biological notion of inheritance.
>
> *conceptual differentiation among structural features (e.g., bones vs. internal organs) and among processes (e.g., intentional vs. involuntary processes)* Not all properties or features have the same biological implications or the same relevance for biological identity (Carey 1985), and young children appear to recognize this (Gelman and Wellman 1991; Springer 1992; Inagaki and Hatano 1988).

I will show that children's racial beliefs include all three of these features of folk biology.

There are several ways in which children could come to believe that race is biologically grounded. One possibility is that race *is* a biological phenomenon and that children's knowledge accurately captures this fact; however, as I have noted several times, racial thinking does not pick out biologically coherent populations. Another possibility is that children's racial thinking is naturalized (or biologically grounded) in the sense that it involves beliefs that accord with principles of biological causality. If the notion of race is naturalized or biologically grounded in this sense, then it is plausible that it receives this grounding through some sort of analogical relationship. That is, race would be biologically grounded to the extent that it borrowed (or imported) principles of naive biology and applied them to human variation. Alternatively, both folk biology and the notion of race might share principles of causality because knowledge in both domains is animated by some higher-order mode of understanding. In this sense, both naive biology and racial thinking might be naturalized though causally independent of each other. One goal of the present chapter is to determine which of these possibilities is most likely.

A Note on Methodology

The empirical studies I report are experimental. They involve presenting numbers of children with the same series of closely specified tasks. Performance is interpreted with respect to how the various groups of children—typically determined by their age—respond. Though this sort of design is familiar to psychologists, controlled investigations in a laboratory setting have often been viewed as contrived (or worse) by anthropologists. Skepticism about the generality of such findings is not unwarranted. Indeed, many in psychology now share this concern (Markus and Kitayama 1991; Moghaddam et al. 1993; Cole 1990; Rogoff 1990; Wertsch 1985; Rogoff and Lave 1984). My decision to employ an experimental strategy flows from unique methodological considerations facing researchers concerned with young children's racial beliefs. A number of important things about young children's thinking in this domain simply would not be discovered without recourse to experimental methods.[4] The issue is not whether young children have sufficient expressive skills to be objects of ethnographic study; ethologists working with nonhumans have shown that even language is not a prerequisite. More to the point, a number of researchers have conducted insightful ethnographic research among young children (Corsaro 1986; Dunn 1988), and several have profitably explored the racial beliefs and behaviors of older children (Troyna and Hatcher 1992; Troyna 1993; Schofield 1989; Goodman 1970). The primary reason that I, an anthropologist, turned to this experimental strategy is that the phenomenon I am interested in is related to the fundamental data of ethnographic study in a unique fashion: young children's racial cognitions have almost no impact on routine behavior and speech. That is, everyday behavior and speech provide little purchase on children's beliefs about race and ethnicity. If we relied simply on what children say and do in their normal interactions and in their typical settings, we would have little evidence that young children deeply cognize race at all.[5]

4. We would not know about the existence of many robust phenomena in the absence of experimental studies. For example, we now know that even young infants show surprise at demonstrations of action at a distance. This was a startling finding precisely because the infant's natural behavioral repertoire is too limited to provide evidence of this knowledge. Only by using experimental facilitation to extend the infant's ability to react (which relies on decidedly non-normative techniques for elicitation and measurement, such as habituation protocols that use electronically monitored pacifiers) did we become aware of these capabilities.

5. Holmes's (1995) recent ethnographic work among kindergartners is a case in point. Holmes looks at many of the same issues I explore here, but she comes to quite different conclusions, arguing that young children are overwhelmingly concerned with "superficial characteristics" and "observable differences" in classifying people (p. 107).

Consider young children's talk about race. Using the Child Language Data Exchange System, a computerized database of children's naturally occurring speech (MacWhinney and Snow 1985, 1990), I searched the spontaneous speech of two preschoolers (a total of over 80,000 utterances) for common ethnic and racial terms. The effort revealed no racial use of a number of common terms, including "black," "negro," and "colored" (cf. Holmes 1995, pp. 40–41). Virtually all mentions of other ethnic labels (e.g., Chinese) involved *national* labels (Japanese, Chinese, etc.), typically used as descriptions of costumes or cuisine rather than people. Or consider playmate choice, a behavioral arena in which racial beliefs might but do not appear to guide everyday action. Although experimental studies have shown that young children maintain strident racial prejudice (for reviews see Aboud 1988 and Katz 1982), race turns out to be a poor predictor of who a young child chooses to play with or actually plays with (Doyle 1983; Finkelstein and Haskins 1983; Singleton and Asher 1979; McCandless and Hoyt 1961; Lambert and Tachuchi 1956). Indeed, studies comparing levels of prejudice with aversive activity have, paradoxically, found little correlation between attitude and behavior in the same child (Katz 1982; Porter 1971; Stevenson and Stevenson 1960).[6]

Indeed, to call these controlled investigations laboratory experiments may well be misleading. More accurately we might say they took place in a "quasi-laboratory setting," since they were carried out in familiar, quiet rooms of the schools and preschools that the children attended during school hours. To the extent that schools are naturalistic settings, the studies were conducted in a natural environment. To the extent that schools are contrived settings, the studies were conducted in a contrived environment. To the extent that an adult posing familiar, answerable, and relevant questions to children in a school setting is naturalistic, these studies were naturalistic. To the extent that such cross-age interactions are contrived, the studies are contrived. As Cahan et al. (1993, p. 209) pointedly observe, the laboratories in which developmental research occurs are "*arranged environments* [that] are not totally unnatural to a child; they are one of a number of settings created by adults in which children are constrained to follow adult-stipulated rules."

6. Below I will say more about how this paradoxical situation may have come about. It is important to bear in mind that it is not a function of the modality in which the data were collected. The issue is not one of laboratory versus naturalistic studies. There is a well-established gap between the findings of naturalistic and laboratory studies. Naturalistic studies often reveal levels of competence not evident in controlled experiments. However, in this case the laboratory studies do not underestimate children's performance abilities; they overestimate them relative to observations made in everyday environments.

In any event, it is not obvious that the question of unequal power, authority, and contrivance is *in principle* more severe here than when it is faced by European and American ethnographers working in traditional societies (Marcus and Fisher 1986).

How Do We Know What the Young Child Thinks When Thinking Racially?

According to most researchers, when children think about race they are thinking about surface appearances rather than about underlying natures, biological principles, or nonobvious essences—things that adults think about when they are thinking about race. Recall that racial (and other) essences serve to preserve identity over significant changes in time, appearance, and behavior. As a result of this failure to grasp racial essence, young children supposedly do not realize that racial identity is impervious to environmental influences (Aboud 1988; Aboud and Skerry 1983; Ramsey 1987). Young children, in short, do not recognize that racial identity is constant.

This may be part of a more general inability to grasp identity constancy. According to several scholars, young children view as variable many of the identities that adults see as immutable. Guardo and Bohan (1971) found that many kindergartners believe that they will be a "different person" when they grow up and that they can take on the identity of another person. Keil (1989) presents evidence that preschoolers fail to understand that biological-category identity is determined by internal and nonobvious factors rather than surface features (5-year-olds believe that an animal that looks and acts like a horse is a horse even if scientists discover that it has cow "blood" and cow "insides," whereas they do not believe that a cow wearing a horse costume is a horse). Gelman et al. (1986), Carey (1985), Emmerichet al. (1977), Slaby and Frey (1975), and Kohlberg (1966) all report that young children do not understand that a person's gender remains constant in the face of changes to superficial outward appearances (as when a little boy is dressed up like a girl and given a long-haired wig).

These studies generally assess identity constancy by asking children whether a certain attribute is contingent or essential to a creature's gender, species, or racial identity. For adults change of dress is not a change in identity, and hence is contingent, whereas change of sex is a change in identity and hence is essential. Change of race, at least according to American folk wisdom, is not conceived as a genuine possibility at all. In short, an attribute is considered essential or contingent to the extent that an individual changes identity when gaining or losing that feature. The principal manipulation in identity studies typically involves comparing children's judgments about the possibility of changes in characteristic but nonessential cues (such as dress) with judgments about the possibility of changes in characteristic and essential features (such as skin color). Hence, children are asked: Is a creature that looks like a horse necessarily a horse? Is a boy dressed up like a girl really a girl? Is a Jewish child in Eskimo clothing Jewish, or Eskimo?

While such tasks use familiar properties, they do not necessarily involve familiar transformations: children may well know that skin color is relevant to racial identity, but they have had little or no experience with an individual who changes skin color before their eyes. Accordingly, asking children to determine whether a person's identity remains the same under several different meaningful but unfamiliar changes in appearance may confuse young subjects since it is not clear whether the pre-transformation and the post-transformation individual are supposed to be (as opposed to *could* be) the same individual (Bem 1989). Inasmuch as subjects have been asked to reason about personal identity in the face of unfamiliar or difficult-to-explain changes in a person's appearance, studies using such tasks may underestimate young children's understanding of identity constancy.

There are, however, contexts in which children encounter marked patterns of change (in the face of other continuity) in physical appearance and do not attribute the change to a change of identity. I have already discussed two such phenomena that are both familiar to children and biologically grounded: growth (which occurs over the life span) and inheritance (which occurs across generations). Understanding growth involves understanding that a person is the same despite dramatic changes in size, behavior, other obvious features. Understanding inheritance involves grasping, among other things, that physical resemblance transmits along family lines. Children give evidence of understanding both. Rosengren et al. (1991) showed that young children allow for dramatic (but only asymmetrical, e.g. from small to large) changes in living things over the life span. Preschool children also grasp that growth is an involuntary physical process rather than a voluntary and psychological one (Hatano and Inagaki, in press). Children also understand that kinship encompasses both variation and continuity in appearance, in that preschoolers infer that offspring resemble their parents (Springer and Keil 1989; Gelman and Wellman 1991).

Study 4.1: The Identity of Race

I exploited children's familiarity with growth and inheritance as a way of assessing their understanding of racial identity. Earlier studies suggested that young children believe that a person whose skin color suddenly changes also changes race. I wanted to know whether young children also believe that a person's race could change gradually, in the context of other physical changes that occur during a lifetime. If they truly are confused about racial constancy, they should also accept that racial change is possible in the "natural" context of growth. Similarly, I wanted to know whether young children believe that race is stable over generations. For adults, knowing that a person is black means that the person's offspring are also black. Do children draw a similar inference? If young children don't grasp racial identity constancy, then they should accept the possibility that race can change in the "natural" context of inheritance.

This method has other advantages. By questioning children about the possibility of change in both growth and inheritance, we not only assess whether children believe that change is possible; we also gain insight into what underlying principles children appeal to in explaining identity change and stability. That is, by exploiting children's knowledge of natural transformations, we will be in a position to compare patterns of causal reasoning about the resemblances inherent in growth and those inherent in inheritance. Adults typically ground the two resemblances in the same set of biological principles, so that they expect certain parallels in the two phenomena. Features that remain relatively constant over the life span are likely candidates for features that are inherited across generations: my nose is much the same in general shape as it was when I was young (although it is considerably bigger, even proportionally now), and it also bears a striking resemblance to my father's (adult) nose. Clearly adults believe that racial features display a similar constancy across the two modalities of change. It is an open question whether children recognize the same parallels. If the continuity manifest in each of the transformations has a distinct mode of presentation (the stabilities of growth are not always the same as those of kinship, even though the features involved may be), children who are innocent of the biological connection between growth and inheritance should not infer that the patterns of change and stability in the two cases are much the same. However, if children do provide evidence of similar reasoning about racial features under transformations of growth and inheritance, this suggests that both are attributable to the same "natural" or biologically grounded cause.

We presented 109 children in three age groups (3-, 4-, and 7-year-olds) living in Ann Arbor, Michigan, with two sets of color-wash line drawings. Each set consisted of a picture of an adult (in one set a male, in the other a female) and three pictures of children of the same gender. Children were presented with three triad combinations for each picture set. That is, they were shown the adult picture with two of the children

Figure 4.1
Examples of drawings used in study 4.1. Male items illustrate race-occupation contrast; female items illustrate occupation–body build contrast.

(say, child A and child B). Then they were shown the same adult with another child pair (say, child A and child C). Finally, they were shown the same adult with still another child pair (say, child B and child C). Each adult was depicted in terms of his or her race, body build, and occupation (e.g., the male items showed a stocky, black police officer). Each of the comparison pictures depicted a child who shared one of the three marked dimensions (say, a stocky white child dressed up as a policeman versus a stock black child without a uniform). (Black and white samples are presented in figure 4.1.) We assigned each child to one of three groups: a Growth group, a Family group, and a Similarity group. Children in the growth group were asked which of the comparison pictures was the target as a child, children in the Family group were asked which of the comparison pictures was the target's child, and children in the Similarity group were asked which of the comparison pictures looked most like the target.[7]

The logic of the task is straightforward. In each triad, each of the comparison pictures shares two features with the target adult, but they share only one feature between themselves. One triad set contrasts race to body build, one contrasts race to occupation, and one contrasts occupation to body build. When asked to choose which of the comparison pictures is the target as a child, the target's child, or most similar to the target, children must decide which of the contrasted properties is most relevant. If children simply rely on outward appearances in making identity judgments, then they should be as likely to rely on one form of outward appearance as on another. Accordingly, they should choose at random. If they believe that one dimension contributes more to identity than another, they should rely on that dimension in making their choices.

The decision to use race, occupation, and body build as the dimensions of contrast was based on four considerations:

All three are named categories.

All three are marked by conspicuous visual cues.

Knowledge of all three develops at approximately the same age. During the late preschool years young children develop an awareness of and vocabulary for variations in race (Katz 1982), occupation (Blaske 1984; Garrett et al. 1977), and body build (Lerner 1973).

All three are associated with preferences and stereotypes (for racial categories see Aboud 1988 and Katz 1982; for occupation categories see Cordua et al. 1979, Blaske 1984, and Gettys and Cann 1981; for body-build categories see Lerner 1969 and Lerner and Schroeder 1971). This last feature is particularly important because it suggests that category membership may be the basis for inferring nonobvious properties about persons (that doctors are helpful, that heavy people are friendly, and so on).[8]

7. Judgments about inheritability theoretically are indeterminate without specification of the mate's race. Anecdotal data indicate that preschoolers expect couples to be racially matched (Holmes 1995), so this lack of specification probably does not pose a problem in the present study. In chapter 7 I will discuss a study that explored children's beliefs about interracial children. To anticipate somewhat: it is not until preadolescence that children begin to show the adult pattern of biological reasoning about mixed-race children (namely, that children with one black parent are black).

8. The drawings were designed to avoid unnecessary distractions yet provide rich portrayal of all three category types. I was particularly concerned that the race pictures be racially and not merely chromatically identifiable. Earlier studies of children's racial understanding used pictures that varied only in skin color (see, e.g., Clark and Clark 1940a,b), and to the extent that folk discourse describes race in terms of skin color this

Results

Types of comparison Do children believe that some individuating properties are more important to the preservation of identity than others? The results indicate that they do: children's performance varied as a function of the type of comparison they were asked to make. Race was chosen over body build (i.e., was judged to be more identity-relevant) more often than race was chosen over occupation, which in turn was chosen more often than occupation over body build.[9] Children also chose race over body build more often than race over occupation, and they chose race over body build and race over occupation more often than occupation over body build. In sum, the children expected that race was more likely to be inherited and to remain unchanged over the life span than either occupation or body build.

Did children's performances vary as a function of age? In some respects they did; in others they did not. Although older subjects displayed more consistency in their judgments than younger subjects, the pattern of reasoning was largely the same for children in all three age groups. As figure 4.2 indicates, younger children were less likely than older children to believe that race was more relevant to a person's identity than his or her occupation, although all children believed that race was more pertinent to identity than body build. Equally significant, children's responses in all three age groups cannot be attributed to chance. Race over body build choices were significantly above chance for the youngest group. All three comparisons were above chance for the 4-year-olds. Race over body build choices were above chance for the oldest subjects. In short, although the effect was more powerful in the older children, children in all three age groups selected a comparison picture that racially matched the target more often than the picture

---

makes sense. However, race is a compound feature, thought to have a complex physical instantiation. In fact, young children's racial discriminations are based on a broad set of perceptual cues, not only on skin color (Lemaine et al. 1985; Aboud 1988; Sorce 1979). In preparing the drawings I followed the now-common practice of depicting racial differences with variations in skin color, facial features (lips, nose, overall shape), and hair color and texture. The body-build contrast was also designed to portray more than differences in body weight. Although body weight may vary considerably during an individual's lifetime, body build is much more stable—indeed, body build is both heritable and relevant to group identity (Bodmer and Cavalli-Sforza 1976). The drawings capture this by portraying body build with a complex of physical features (stature, body type, facial and neck shape, etc.). Finally, occupation was represented by uniforms and tools.

9. Unless otherwise noted, throughout differences cited are statistically significant. Methodological details, such as counterbalancing and randomization of questions and tasks, have also been omitted. Complete descriptions of the studies can be found in the original publications cited at the beginning of each empirical chapter.

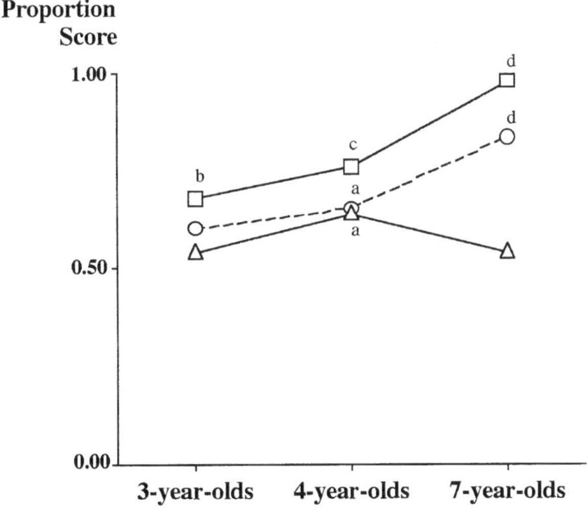

[a] significantly above chance, $p < .05$
[b] significantly above chance, $p < .01$
[c] significantly above chance, $p < .001$
[d] significantly above chance, $p < .0001$

—□— Race over body build
--○-- Race over occupation
—△— Occupation over body build

Figure 4.2
Mean proportion for each contrast in identity study.

that matched the target's physique. Thus, even 3-year-olds make a clear distinction between the contribution of race and body build to the preservation of identity.

The results also show that young children do not expect all conspicuous cues to be equally important to identity. If, as previous work argues, children focus only on changes in physical appearance when making identity judgments, modifications in body build should signal a change in identity as readily as variation in race does. To the contrary, even 3-year-olds believe that race predicts personal identity more than body build does (although they are less committed to this proposition than older children). Despite the fact that all three attributes are conspicuous, socially relevant, commonly labeled, and stereotyped dimensions, by the age of 4, children come to believe that race is a better predictor of identity than either body build or occupation. In summary: even preschoolers see race as immutable, corporeal, differentiated, derived from family background, and at least consistent with biological principles of causality.

Table 4.1
Proportion of times that each type of comparison was chosen in the first study for each question.

Comparison	Question	
	Inheritance	Growth
Race over body build	0.81	0.81
Race over occupation	0.62	0.78
Occupation over body build	0.55	0.60

Growth versus family Do children's responses to the growth and inheritance questions reliably differ from each other? The results suggest that they do not. As can be seen from table 4.1, young children see the social qualities that preserve identity in growth as essentially those that are inherited across generations. It is important to bear in mind that this would not be predicted on most accounts of children's understanding of identity. If children lack a biological understanding of identity, there is no reason to believe that they will infer that patterns of canonical resemblance displayed during growth will match those exhibited in transgenerational family resemblance.

Similarity versus identity Finally, are children's judgments about the natural transformations accompanying growth and inheritance based on judgments of outward similarity, or are they governed by other principles? We can answer this question by looking at whether children's inferences about similarity reliably differ from their inductions about identity (i.e., growth and inheritance). As can be seen from figure 4.3, they do. Of particular interest, as can also be seen from figure 4.3, is the fact that responses to the similarity question were more balanced (i.e., closer to what would be expected if children guessed at random) than responses to the other two questions.

Follow-up 1

Although these results lend considerable support to the claim that young children possess a theory-like understanding of human variation, other interpretations of the data cannot be ruled out. For example, while children's judgments about race may not be attributable to perceptions of global similarity, it is possible that a more specific or channeled similarity underlies their choices. What I interpret as judgments about race, for example, might actually be judgments about skin color—a real possibility in view of the salience color has for young children's sortings (Sugarman 1983). To rule out this possibility, we showed another

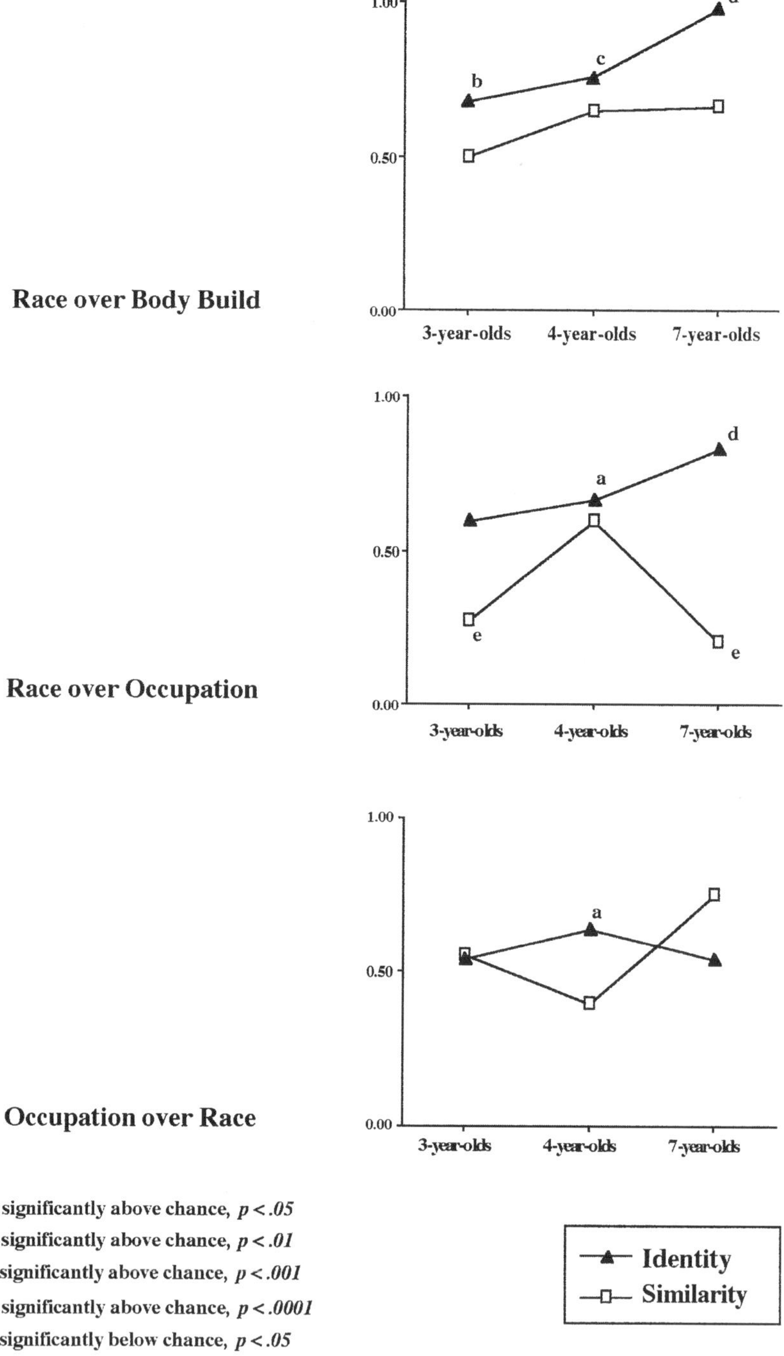

Figure 4.3
Mean proportions for each pattern of inference on similarity-versus-identity questions.

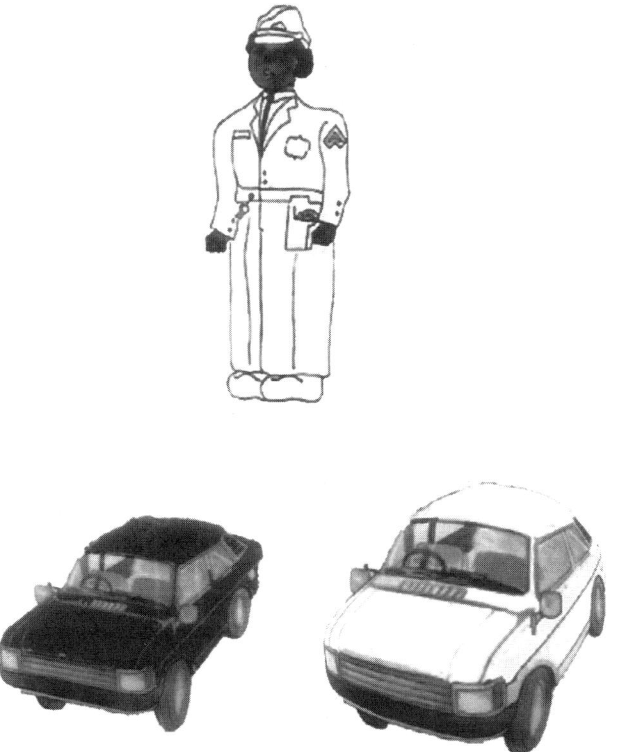

Figure 4.4
Example of drawings used in color-versus-shape study.

group of 3-, 4-, and 7-year-olds the black target picture used in study 4.1 with two new comparison pictures: a cream-colored car modified to appear bulbous or "fat" and an unmodified car recolored to match the skin color of the black target male.[10] Children were asked to choose which of the comparison pictures was the car of the target. Figure 4.4 is a black-and-white representation of the sample. If children chose on the basis of perceived similarity in body shape in the first task, their scores should tend toward the higher end of the scale. If they chose on the basis of perceived similarity between skin and surface colors, their scores should tend toward the lower end of the scale. If they found both dimensions equally relevant, their scores should tend toward the scale's midpoint. The results were unambiguous: children in none of the age groups showed a color bias in their responses.

10. For the female (Latina) picture set from study 4.1, the comparison depicted two dogs that had been similarly modified to match the shape of the target in the one and the skin color of the target in the other.

Follow-up 2

In the initial study, children's pattern of judgment about growth did not differ from their pattern of judgment about inheritance. I interpreted this as evidence that their beliefs about the two phenomena are governed by a single set of principles, much as adults' beliefs about the same phenomena are. An alternative explanation is that the children did not understand that they were being asked about two distinct phenomena. That is, children's responses to the growth and inheritance questions would not have differed if the children had difficulty in distinguishing the growth from the inheritance question. This is a plausible possibility, since the wording of the two questions was quite close:

> One of these two pictures is a picture of John's son. Show me which of these is a picture of John's son.
>
> One of these two pictures is a picture of John as a boy. Show me the picture of John as a little boy.

Perhaps subjects interpreted the second question as "Show me a picture of John's little boy." To rule this out, we showed another group of 3-, 4-, and 7-year-olds four new target pictures, one at a time. Two of the pictures showed adult males; two showed adult females. As in study 4.1, for each target the children were shown a pair of comparison pictures. All pictures were matched for racial category. One depicted a female child, the other a male child. For two of the targets, each subject was asked to choose which of the comparison pictures was the target picture as a child. For the other two targets, each subject was asked to choose which of the comparison pictures was the target's child. If children do not distinguish between the question "Show me X as a child" and the question "Show me X's child," their responses to the two questions should not differ. If children can readily distinguish between the two questions, they should choose the comparison picture of the same sex as the target when asked "Show me X as a child" (in virtue of an expectation of gender constancy) and should show no preference for either of the comparison pictures when asked "Show me X's child."

As figure 4.5 illustrates, children in all three age groups overwhelmingly chose the comparison picture of the same sex in response to "Show me X as a child." In contrast, in response to "Show me X's child" the 3- and 4-year-olds chose at random; the 7-year-olds were more likely to choose the child *not* of the same sex as the target.

Follow-up 3

One aspect of the results of study 4.1 is particularly puzzling: young children, especially the 3-year-olds, judged occupation to be almost as resilient over the life span and across generations as race. Why did the

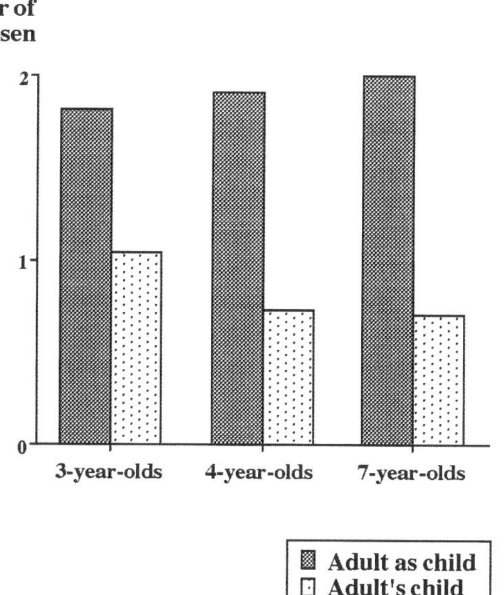

Figure 4.5
Mean number of times the same-sex child was chosen for "child of" and "as child" questions.

youngest children weight occupation almost as heavily as race in their identity judgments? The result is curious, because reasoning about occupation and race arguably involve distinct expectations about the sorts of people there are, and we would accordingly expect preschoolers' reasoning about the contributions race and occupation make to identity to be quite different. Reasoning about race presumably emphasizes intrinsic, corporeal attributes, whereas reasoning about occupation presumably emphasizes the activities a person engages in, the instrumentality of these activities, and the artifacts that accompany that instrumentality (tools, uniforms, etc.). That children's pattern of reasoning in study 4.1 did not reflect this is therefore a surprise.

It is possible, however, that the aggregate results from study 4.1 are misleading in this regard, since the aggregate pattern of results obtained is consistent with two patterns of individual response. The group means for the race-over-occupation question would be the same if children based identity judgments on race and occupation in equal measure (i.e., if children did not distinguish the contribution race makes to identity from the contribution that occupation makes) or if children based their identity judgments *either* on race *or* on occupation consistently, *and* about the same number of children used a race strategy as used an occupation strategy. Assessing which of these is the case

Table 4.2
Distribution of individual patterns of inference.

	Age (years)		
Type of Inference	3	4	7
Transitive, race first	22	29	40
Transitive, occupation first	14	10	6
Transitive, body build first	5	5	0
Nontransitive	9	14	2

is straightforward; all we need do is look at individual children's patterns of response to the task in study 4.1.

We need to know whether children believed that any of the three dimensions consistently determined identity. We also need to know how evenly the consistent patters of inference were distributed—that is, what percentage of children consistently inferred that race determined identity and what percentage consistently inferred that occupation determined identity?

A child was scored as consistent if his or her responses were transitive (on a particular triad set, if a child selected race over occupation and occupation over body build, the child was consistent only if race over body build was also selected); otherwise he or she was scored as mixed. As table 4.2 shows, most children used a consistent strategy. Eighty-three percent of the 3-year-olds' judgments, 75% of the 4-year-olds', and 95% of the 7-year-olds' were consistent. In contrast to older children, who seldom used an occupation-first reasoning strategy, a substantial proportion of preschoolers relied on occupation-first reasoning. Thus, the younger children used two reasoning strategies for thinking about social difference. In one strategy intrinsic, physical, and biologically relevant properties predominated; in the other strategy patterns of habitual behavior and possibly functional (goal-directed) considerations predominated.

Follow-up 4

I interpreted children's responses in study 4.1 to be about the category of occupation, not occupational apparel. This may seem too expansive an interpretation. After all, the pictures about which children were making judgments depicted occupation in terms of distinctive apparel (uniforms) and tools of the trade. It is possible that the children's identity reasoning was really about dress, not the more abstract categories of occupation. If so, their judgments are even more curious than they seemed at first blush. Previous work suggests that children consider dress the least important factor (relative to race, age, and gender) in sorting people. When asked to make undirected sortings, Ramsey (1987) found that preschoolers, and Davey (1983) found that slightly older children, considered dress the least important factor relative to race, age, and gender. One explanation for the curious results of study 4.1 is that the children in my study invested apparel with more meaning than the children studied by Davey and Ramsey. The goal of this fourth follow-up is to assess whether the pattern of inductions revealed in study 4.1 is attributable to "deep" reasoning about occupation rather than superficial reasoning about clothing.

Another group of 38 children of ages 3, 4, and 7 were recruited and presented with a task much like the one used in study 4.1. They were shown two sets of color drawings, each consisting of a target and two comparison pictures. Each target depicted a child wearing an occupationally relevant costume of a certain color. In the first set the target child was dressed as a fireman, in the other set as a waitress. Each comparison pair portrayed an adult version of the child depicted in the target picture. In one comparison picture the adult wore clothes of the same color as in the target picture but without occupational emblems; in the other he or she wore clothes of a different color but having the same occupational emblems. Subjects were asked to identify which of the comparison pictures showed the child portrayed in the target picture after he or she had grown up.

The logic of the task is as follows. If children reason that a person's occupation is more identity relevant than the color of that person's clothing, they should choose the comparison picture with the same occupational emblems more often than the comparison picture with the same clothing color. If they reason that color of clothing is more identity relevant than occupation, they should choose the comparison picture with the same clothing color more often than the one with the same occupational emblem. Alternatively, if children reason that the two dimensions are equally relevant (or irrelevant) to identity, they should choose at chance.

The responses across all four items provide little evidence that children's beliefs about occupation are produced by a theory-like knowledge structure. Collapsed across items, no preference for shared occupation over shared clothing color emerged. However, as figure 4.6 shows, when the male and female items are examined separately a different pattern of reasoning emerges. Overall, children in all three age groups believe that occupation is more relevant to identity when the contrast involves a male than when it involves a female. The effect is most powerful for 3-year-olds, whose inferences about occupation in study 4.1 had some of the characteristics of their inferences about race. Individual

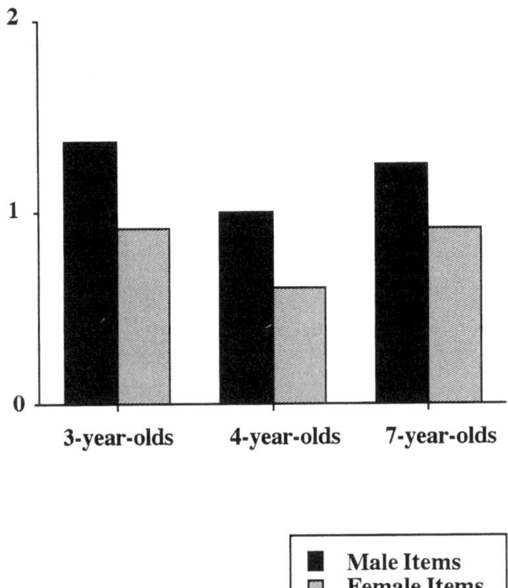

Figure 4.6
Mean number of times occupation was chosen over shared clothing color for male and female items.

children's responses in study 4.1 also provide evidence that children believe a male's occupation is more important to identity than a female's. In study 4.1, 45% of 3-year-olds who made transitive judgments inferred that race was the most important predictor of the male's identity, whereas 40% of the 3-year-olds inferred that occupation was the most important predictor. In contrast, for the female item, 62% of the 3-year-olds inferred that race was the most important predictor; only 29% judged that occupation was the most important predictor of identity. This is not unexpected in view of American gender ideology: a man's occupation is seen as more relevant to his identity than a woman's occupation is to hers.

These data indicate that young children believe that occupation is more than a feature of a person's appearance. Rather, it represents for them an important aspect of identity, especially of male identity—an aspect that is maintained over time. Occupation, like race, is tied to the kinds of people there are in the world. This is not a small matter, since kindhood, in virtue of expectations about a range of phenomena, is often inferentially very powerful. Kindhood captures deep commonalities. The notion that an occupation may encompass an expectation of kindhood may seem odd to those of us living in modern secular societies in which profession or trade is more closely associated with place of employment, functional goals, uniforms, and special purpose tools than it is with intrinsic nature. It is important to bear in mind, however, that kindhood and occupation, on the one hand, and functional apparel and naturalized identities, on the other, have been linked in many historical and cultural contexts. For example, in South Asia occupation, kindhood, and essential nature are tightly bound in a single cultural discourse of caste (Daniel 1984).

A similar identification of occupation with natural social kindhood is found in both American and French culture. In the United States, many ethnic costumes (such as those of organ grinders, pirates, and fortune tellers) are identified with specific occupations, as if being one meant being the other. In fact, the embodiment of natural coalitions may have its roots deep in our evolutionary past: costume, clothing, and ornaments were surely the most marked physical differences that our ancestral populations encountered. (Recall that frequent encounters between individuals of greatly different external anatomy is a fairly recent development, largely a function of overseas colonialism). In Parisian French several names for subcultural regions in France came to be terms for specific occupations, again as if being the one meant being the other. For example, "savoyard" (literally "person from the Savoie") was a term for chimney sweeps. Similarly, "auvergnat" (literally "person from the Auvergne") referred to the proprietors of cafés in which coal was sold. One possibility, of course, is that this reflects lexical economy derived from empirical summary: most X do Y for a living, so why not use a single term to refer to both? Alternatively, this may reflect the fact that occupations are good kinds to think in terms of. The results from our 3-year-olds suggest that there may be a conceptual reason to opt for this latter interpretation.

Study 4.2: Switched at Birth: Race, Inheritability, and Essence

The results of study 4.1 and its follow-ups paint a picture of children's reasoning that is quite different from that portrayed in most standard treatments. Even young preschoolers believe a person's racial identity to be immutable, related to family background, and derived from some physical properties but not others. In short, young children go beyond superficial attributes when reasoning about social difference. Moreover, inferences about racial differences appear to be naturalized, i.e., consistent with a biological grounding. First, beliefs about the continuities in growth and inheritance seem to derive from the same principles, something that cannot obviously be adduced from the limited experience that young children have with such continuity and variation. Second, children's beliefs about racial inheritance are consistent with (though they give only indirect evidence for) two crucial components of biological understanding: a belief in family resemblance and an understanding that the mechanism underlying this resemblance involves birth (see Carey and Spelke 1994).

These data, however, fall short of establishing whether a truly biological understanding is achieved before middle childhood. The issue is not limited to discussions of whether race is inherited. Considerable debate surrounds the developmental nature, the scope, and the chronology of biological thinking. Springer and Keil (1989) found that preschoolers expected offspring to resemble their parents physically. Similarly, Gelman and Wellman (1991) found that young children expected an animal's kind to be impervious to environmental influences (e.g., that tiger cubs would grow to be adult tigers even if reared by lions). They argue that preschoolers believe this happens because living kinds possess an intrinsic and inviolable potential that provides an underlying continuity over other changes that occur during growth. Carey and Spelke (1994), however, caution that these results do not fully support the conclusion that young children have a strictly biological understanding of inheritance. Children, they suggest, may believe that family resemblance derives from social rather than biological causes. Solomon et al. (1995) present data indicating that children's expectations about inheritance are far less adult-like than Springer and Keil, Gelman and Wellman, or the results of study 4.1 suggest. The contention of Solomon et al. has two parts: that children younger than 7 years do not understand that a child's resemblance to its parents is mediated by mechanisms of biological reproduction, and that young children fail to differentiate between the inheritability of psychological properties and that of biological properties.

In light of these contradictory findings, it is worth exploring whether children's beliefs about race include a biological notion of inheritance. Toward this end, I told eighteen 5-year-olds the following story about two families, one black and one white:

> I'm going to tell you a story about two girls and their families. It's important for you to understand that we made this story up. It really didn't happen. Look at this picture of the Smith family and the Jones family. Mrs. Smith just had a new baby. So did Mrs. Jones. At night in the hospital all the babies sleep in the same room, called the nursery. It looks like this. Can you find the Smith baby? The Jones baby? When they went home from the hospital,

> Mrs. Smith and Mrs. Jones were given the wrong babies from the nursery. So Mrs. Smith took home Mrs. Jones' s baby, and Mrs. Jones took Mrs. Smith's baby back home. But nobody noticed. So, the baby girl that the Smiths took home from the hospital grew up and started school. Look at these little girls. Can you tell me which is a picture of that girl? So, the baby girl that the Jones took home from the hospital grew up and started school. Look at these little girls. Can you tell me which is a picture of that girl?

With pictures of the couples and their (switched) infants still in view, children were shown pictures of two school-age children, one black and one white, and asked to choose which was each couple's baby several years later. If children use a "nurture" strategy, believing that racial identity derives from social contact and parenting, they should choose the child that racially matches the adoptive parents. In contrast, if they rely on a "nature" strategy, believing that racial identity is fixed at birth, they should choose the child that racially matches the birth parents.

The results were striking. Children showed a clear preference for the nature strategy: 13 of the 18 selected the school-age picture that racially matched the infant picture on both trials, and 5 selected the school-age picture that racially matched the infant picture on only one item. No child selected according to the nurture pattern (that is, no child chose a child of the adoptive parents' race on both items). Justifications were also informative. Only four children used explanations that could be termed psychological or experiential (for example, that the target child liked being this way). Thirty-nine percent justified their choice in terms of skin color, 22% in terms of hair color, and 16% in terms of the child's generally "looking like" the biological parents. These results are consistent with those of study 4.1, and lend further support to the claim that children have a naturalized model of race. Preschoolers do not attribute family (racial) resemblance to life experiences but to birth. The results also lend support to Gelman and Wellman's (1991) and Springer and Keil's (1989) contention that an adult-like understanding of the role of birth in inheritance is part of young children's naive biology.

Follow-up 1

There are at least three potential difficulties with this interpretation.[11] First, whereas adults associate hospital maternity wards with the events surrounding birth, for children the connection may be less evident. Second, the story I used mentioned the length of time the switched child lived with the adoptive family but did not emphasize

11. I thank Susan Carey for pointing these out to me.

aspects of family life (e.g., continuously provided care and affection) that might be necessary to trigger a nurture perspective. Third, since the picture of the target infant was in view when the subjects were asked to select which picture portrayed the adopted child at school age, subjects could have recruited their expectation that race is immutable in making nature-consistent judgments. The results, then, may not assess whether children believe that the reproduction of race is biologically mediated. To rule out these possible explanations, and to explore the possibility that younger children understand that family resemblance is biologically mediated, I conducted a second switched-at-birth study with 47 children of ages 3, 4, and 5. In this study, however, the relationship between the mechanism of pregnancy and birth and the infant was underscored, nurturing familial relations were stressed, and children were not shown a picture of the baby before being asked to judge what the switched-at-birth child would look like upon reaching school age (and therefore could not use a constancy strategy to reason about the child's race).

Each child heard two stories, one the inverse of the other. First, while hearing the following story, the child was shown color-wash line drawings of each couple:

> These two people, Mr. and Mrs. Smith, had a baby girl. [The child is shown a picture of a black couple.] That means that the baby came out of Mrs. Smith's tummy. Right after it came out of her tummy, the baby went to live with these people, Mr. and Mrs. Jones. [The child is shown a picture of a white couple.] The baby lived with them and Mr. and Mrs. Jones took care of her. They fed her, bought her clothes, and hugged her and kissed her when she was sad.

For each item, the child was then shown a two pictures—one of a white school-age girl and the other of a black school-age girl—and asked which of these girls was the infant grown to school age. The child then heard the inverse story, in which the white couple's child was taken home by the black couple. (The two stories were counterbalanced so that half the children heard the first story first and half heard the second story first.)

Again, the results are unambiguous. As figure 4.7 shows, both 4-year-olds and 5-year-olds clearly favored the "nature" hypothesis, choosing the child whose race matched the birth parents on both items. And again, children's justifications were informative: 34% of the 5-year-olds explained their responses in terms of the birth parents' skin or hair color, 21% of their justifications cited experiential, emotional, or apparel

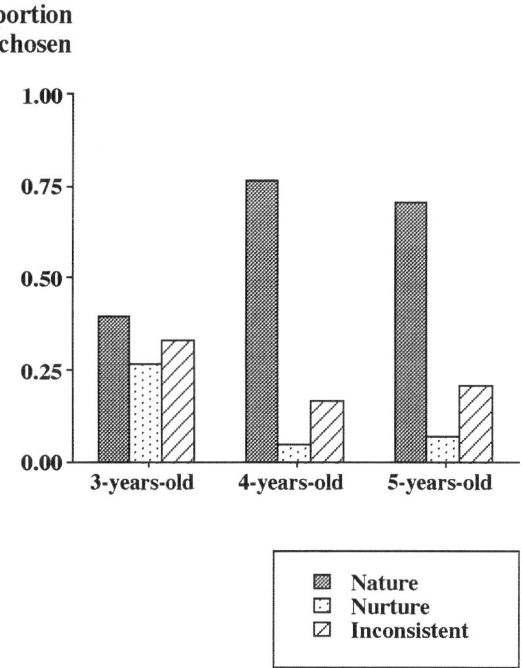

Figure 4.7
Distribution of "nature," "nurture," and inconsistent choices: race contrast.

associations ("I like her better," "She's wearing the same outfit," etc.), 9% made reference to the adoptive parents' skin color, and 24% offered no justification. Four-year-olds' justifications were similar: 37% justified their responses in terms of the birth parents' skin or hair color, 30% in terms of experiential, emotional, or other associations, and 33% gave no justification. Two points stand out from these justifications: that the difference in the formats of the two switched-at-birth tasks had little effect on children's reasoning (although the greater number of "don't knows" suggests that children in the second task were somewhat less able to reflect on their choices), and that, unlike the children in the first task, in the second switched-at-birth task a small proportion (2 of 16 children) used a nurture strategy. It is apparent from the justifications that these were not random choices, since these children explained their answers by referring specifically to the adoptive parents' race.

These results provide strong support for the claim that children believe race to be both biologically grounded (i.e., reproduced through a natural mechanism) and heritable. However, the results do not tell us whether children believe race to be more or less biologically grounded than other physical properties. Results of studies recently conducted by Ken Springer (1995) indicate that children do naturalize other physical properties. One of Springer's experiments used the same switched-at-birth task as the studies reported here, but instead of being shown pictures depicting physical differences the children were told about the properties. Springer found that preschoolers (a group including 4- and 5-year-olds) expected a baby to resemble its biological parents in visible nonracial physical properties (e.g., stature) as well as in invisible nonracial physical properties (e.g., having the liver on the right). In contrast, children expected a child to share psychological properties (e.g., beliefs and preferences) with its adoptive parents rather than its birth parents.

One question that remains unresolved by these results is whether children believe all heritable properties to be equally biologically grounded. That is, do they expect some properties to be more intrinsic than others? For instance, is children's understanding of the biological nature of race more precocious than their understanding of other physical properties? (If it is the case that young children naturalize race before they naturalize other properties, this might account for the difference between my results and those reported in Solomon et al. 1995. The question is of interest since, as we will see in chapter 7, adults believe race to be a particularly powerful and deeply rooted property and suppose race to control or regulate the distribution of many presumably nonracial properties, such as mental acuity.)

To explore the possibility that young children expect other properties to be similarly heritable as but less deeply rooted than race, I conducted two follow-ups using the same switched-at-birth task. In both follow-ups children were asked to make judgments about the role birth and rearing play in the development of specific body builds. Although body build is as much a physical property as race, recall that in study 4.1 children did not find body build a particularly identity-relevant attribute. That finding, however, is relevant to a specific set of judgments. Study 4.1 pitted body build against race (and occupation) in terms of contribution to identity. Thus, the results of that study do not tell us whether children believe that body build is controlled by a natural mechanism. All we can conclude is that young children expect race to be more identity-relevant than body build. Children may believe that both properties are heritable, equally mediated by pregnancy, and equally fixed at birth. Alternatively, the priority children attribute to race may extend beyond identity so that children believe it is more heritable, more directly mediated by pregnancy, and more likely to be fixed at birth than body build. A second follow-up tests this

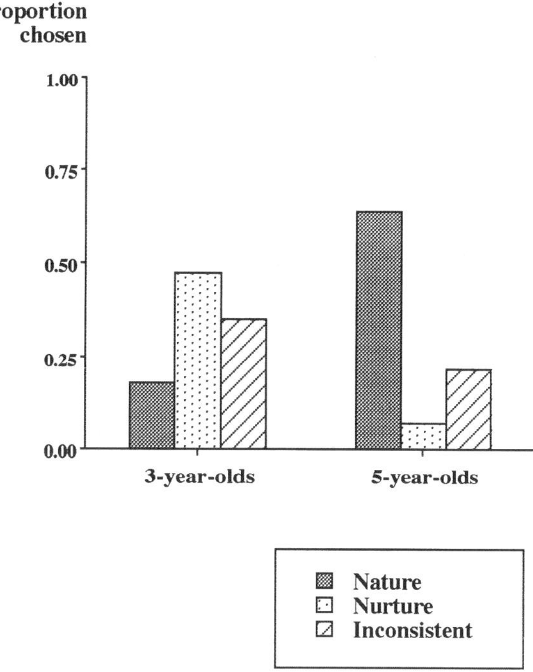

Figure 4.8
Distribution of "nature," "nurture," and inconsistent choices: body-build contrast.

possibility. Like study 4.1 it pits race against body build, but in this task the two attributes were crossed in a switched-at-birth paradigm.

Follow-up 2

Thirty 3- and 5-year-olds received a switched-at-birth task just as described above expect that birth and adoptive parents contrasted in body build rather than race. In each of two trials children were shown a picture of two couples, one stocky and the other slight, and told that a baby girl had come out of the stocky woman's tummy but that the thin couple had taken her home and cared for her, etc. They were then shown pictures of two school-age girls, one thin and the other stocky, and asked which was the picture of the little girl in the story. As can be seen in figure 4.8, although the effect was less pronounced than on the race task, the pattern of judgments was much the same: 5-year-olds but not 3-year-olds reasoned in accord with a nature hypothesis. As I remarked earlier, this is not implausible; body build is a heritable characteristic, and presumably children have as much opportunity to observe this as they do to observe that race is heritable.

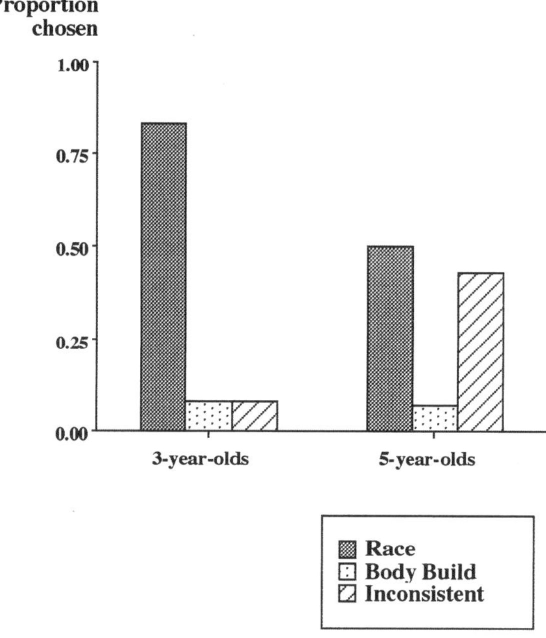

Figure 4.9
Distribution of race, body build, and inconsistent choices: race and body-build contrast.

Follow-up 3

Twenty-six 3- and 5-year-olds were told the same story about two couples whose infants are inadvertently switched. This time, however, the adoptive and birth parents differed in both race and body build, which were crossed: in one trial the birth parents were stocky and white, the adoptive parents slight and black. Children were then shown pictures of two school-age children, one black and stocky the other white and slight, and asked to identify the child in the story. Accordingly, the task asks children to identify which dimension (race or body build) is more heritable. As figure 4.9 shows, although most 5-year-olds favored race over body build, a substantial proportion displayed an inconsistent pattern (i.e., they chose race on one item and body build on the other). Most strikingly, even 3-year-olds displayed a strong expectation that race is more heritable (i.e., more likely to be fixed at birth) than body build. Recall that in the first switched-at-birth study 3-year-olds were more also likely to use a nature than a nurture strategy, although the trend was not significant there. It may be that having to choose between one of the two attributes as fixed at birth gave the 3-year-olds a sufficient purchase on the problem to reliably infer the nature pattern for race.

Together these data cast doubt on the claim that it is beliefs about shared life experiences that cause preschoolers to expect family members to resemble one another physically. Both 4-year-olds and 5-year-olds consistently, and 3-year-olds occasionally, expect identity-relevant physical properties such as skin color to be fixed at birth. Springer (1994) attributes this pattern of judgments to an expectation that there is a material but nonobvious link between biological parents and their offspring. Following Gelman and Wellman (1991), I further interpret this nondemonstrative link as a belief in an intrinsic essence shared by category members. In this case the relevant category membership involves the notion of family under a biological interpretation. Recall that in study 4.1 we found that young children believed that the same principles govern the canonical resemblance accompanying growth as govern canonical family resemblance. This finding is consistent with a view that children conceptualize the essence underlying the emergence of physical properties during growth as the same essence underlying family resemblance, a view that adults take to be part of a biological construal of life.

Conclusions: The Conceptual Origins of Folk Sociology

Children, even quite young children, clearly have an understanding of race that is both naturalized and theory-like. In this respect their beliefs are much like those of the adults among whom they live. Where do these expectations come from, and what meaning do they have? For example, does a naturalized and theory-like understanding of race mean that children acquire the race concept as part of their acquisition of folk biology? I will close this chapter by arguing that this is unlikely. I will suggest that, to the contrary, children's essentialist construal of race is not derived by analogy from folk biology. Instead, essentialist reasoning arises independently in racial and biological thinking.

Although there has been little speculation about how racial *theories* developmentally emerge, in the last few years several researchers have independently proposed a model of social categories that has important developmental implications. According to Atran (1990), Boyer (1990), and Rothbart and Taylor (1990), the notion of a racial essence is derived analogically from the commonsense notion of a species essence. In other words, adults model their theory of racial essence after their notion of biological essence. The developmental implication is that if children have an essentialized theory or race it must have been derived by analogy from their theory of folk biology. Analogy can involve either knowledge extension or knowledge transfer. For example, when adults and older children stop treating humankind as a taxonomic and ontological isolate and come to see humans as "one animal among many" (Johnson et al. 1992; Jackendoff 1992; Carey 1985; Keil 1979) they are extending rather than transferring knowledge, since learning that humans are biological creatures involves a shift in conceptual organization from the belief that humans are not part of the biological realm to an expectation that they are part of it. In contrast, according to the standard view, "true" transfer occurs when biological principles come to be applied to social groups, inasmuch as this involves the application of biologically specific principles of causality to categories that initially (in ontogenesis) did not encompass biological expectations.[12]

The idea that naive biology is imported to racial thinking seems plausible in view of the marked parallels between interspecies differences among nonhuman kinds and intraspecies differences among humans. Thus, physical variation among humans putatively comes to be conceptualized as an analogue to the interspecies phenotypic variation: ". . . apparent morphological distinctions between human groups are readily (but not necessarily) conceived as apparent morphological distinctions between animal species" (Atran 1990, p. 78). As a result, racial thinking comes to embrace the causal principles and ontological commitments that laypersons use to reason about biological creatures (see also Allport 1954).

Identifying the apperception of racial differences with the recognition of species differences is not without its difficulties. There are significant differences between the visual affordances of folk-biological concepts and those of race. For example, in contrast to the cross-cultural uniformity in folk-biological classifications (see Berlin 1992; Atran 1990), there is much variation in the ways different cultures choose to segment human beings into physically relevant categories. There are also psychological reasons for skepticism about the identification of racial thinking with folk biology. According to the analogical transfer model, children first perceive phenomenal variation in humans, then infer that this variation predicts discontinuous and discrete human types. Eventually children come to believe that these discrete human types are conceptually similar to nonhuman living kinds. Clearly this is

12. It might be argued that analogical transfer is more a description of a phenomenon than an explanation of it. Empirical studies of knowledge transfer disclose something of a paradox: although the intuition that problems are solved through analogical reasoning is robust, attempts to demonstrate such abilities experimentally have not been altogether successful (Novick 1988; Resnick 1994). Convincing instances of analogically or metaphorically driven episodes of conceptual change have of course been detailed, especially in the history of science (Wiser and Carey 1983). Still, replicating natural transfers across domains (as opposed to within a domain) with children under controlled conditions has proved to be a remarkably intractable research problem (Brown 1990). Thus, knowing *that* cognitive faculties interrelate in predictable ways is central to understanding thought, yet knowing *how* this comes to happen continues to be an unresolved question.

plausible only if the perception of racial differences *precedes* the formation of racial categories and racial theories. It is also plausible only to the extent that racial categories from the start are constructed so as to incorporate and make sense of the observed differences. In other words: according to this interpretation, racial categories are perceptually segregated before they are biologically understood. Despite the intuitive appeal of these claims, I argue that neither of these conditions is met.

Adults (and most 3-year-olds, as study 4.1 established) believe race is more important to a person's identity than body build. If visual input drives the child's theorizing about race, then one of two things must be true: either racial tokens are more visually prominent than other physical forms, or the environment delivers information that leads the child to infer that race is more relevant to identity than other physical forms. The pattern of response to the similarity question is not consistent with this first claim: clearly children's judgments cannot be attributable to purely perceptual processing mechanisms. The facts of biology, in turn, are not consistent with the second possibility: the environment provides information that differences in body build are relevant to identity, even racial identity. The correlation among climate, geographic region (and hence breeding population), and body build is marked (Bodmer and Cavalli-Sforza 1976). Body build, stature, and the like *are* inherited aspects of outward appearance. Indeed, the results of follow-up 4 indicate that children believe body build to be biologically grounded (see also Inagaki and Hatano 1988). Still, because admixture based on body build may be less carefully monitored socially than admixture involving skin color, the equally continuous variation in the latter due to history is less widely appreciated in both folk and legal wisdom.

The developmental and biological evidence together suggest that the biologically grounded understanding of race emerges neither gradually nor precipitously out of children's understanding of nonhuman biological kinds. The critical developmental difference between race and biology is that biological discontinuities are readily available from direct inspection of the environment. Folk genera, the basic level of biological taxonomies, are marked by highly correlated clusters of features (Rosch and Mervis 1975; Berlin 1992). For racial categories, in contrast, there is little correlation among features, either at the level of nonobvious traits (e.g., blood-group genes) or at the level of salient physical characteristics (e.g., skin color and facial structure). In short, the structure of the environment does not deliver racial categories as readily as our cultural intuitions imagine, nor does the environment deliver them as readily as it does biological species.

Still, we cannot deny the striking similarities between naive biological and racial thinking, particularly in folk expectations of underlying essence. Where do these parallels come from if not from transfer? Children and adults conceptualize biological difference in terms of a presumption of nonobvious essence (Atran 1990; Gelman and Wellman 1991). In much the same way, both adults and children conceive of racial types in terms of underlying essence (Allport 1954; Rothbart and Taylor 1990; see the findings of this chapter). Yet I propose that these parallels are not the outcome of a process of analogical transfer. This is paradoxical only if we imagine that essentialist reasoning somehow "belongs" to folk biology, a notion that some adherents of the domain-specificity approach appear to embrace (see, e.g., Atran 1990; Gelman et al. 1994; cf. Medin 1989). I suggest that it does not.

Keil (1994), Sperber (1994), and Leslie (1994) provide insight into why this may be the case. They propose that many faculty differences may lie neither at the level of perceptual structure nor at the level of conceptual organization but at the level of more abstract mechanisms or modes of understanding. For the present discussion the most relevant speculation is that causal principles (or the principles from which theory-specific causal principles are derived) may not evolve in tandem with ontological commitment. Rather, specific causal principles may be the precipitate of more abstract mechanisms for organizing conceptual knowledge. This view allows essentialism to be uncoupled from folk biology. Consider in this regard Keil's (1994, pp. 250–251) description of modes of construal:

> We may therefore want to distinguish between broad modes of construal and detailed sets of beliefs in our accounts of how knowledge becomes organized into domains and changes over time. We may be endowed with relatively few modes of construal (or stances, if you prefer), such as the mechanical, the intentional and the teleological, (and perhaps a half dozen more); but we may be able to use these as footholds into acquiring much more elaborated belief systems in an extraordinary number of specialized domains.

Modes of construal then are not directly linked to a set of phenomena (say, living kinds for an essentialist mode of construal); instead they should be "viewed as opportunistic, exploratory entities that are constantly trying to find resonances with aspects of real world structure" (ibid., p. 252).

These speculations also give some indication of the consequences of a naturalized and essentialized racial thinking for studies of cognitive architecture. Cognitivists tend to omit what Keil calls the "real world structure" from their considerations. As a result, they often pay scant attention to something that most anthropologists find self-evidently salient: that humans organize themselves into collectivities and define themselves into social kinds as a function of group membership (Hirschfeld 1995a). While considerable research in cognitive development has explored the perceptual and conceptual faculties that are sensitive to variations in human behavior and physique,[13] much less work has examined how cognitive endowment articulates with societal factors. We do know that young children have something like a theory of society, inasmuch as they closely adapt their speech to varying social situations (Chomsky 1988), social statuses (Andersen 1990; Becker 1982; Corsaro 1979), and social types (Hirschfeld 1989).

Still, there has been a powerful tendency to interpret children's theory of society (i.e., their expectations about the entities of society and their nature) as ultimately derived from theory of mind. Psychologists focus much effort on showing that children view social environments as constituted of people sorted in terms of mental traits or dispositions for a specific kind of personality (Hirschfeld 1995a). In so doing, they risk losing sight of the fact that the ontological commitments of naive theories of mind and society are not the same. At least one major task of a theory of society is to provide expectations about the intrinsic kinds of people there are—that is, to provide a set of expectations about the skeletal structure of society. I have tried to show here that race is a central component of the child's naive theory of society. Moreover, I suggest that the racial ontology stipulated by this theory of society provides the framework for specifying a class of phenomena that resonates with an essential mode of construal.

Rather than borrow principles for causal reasoning from naive biology, I propose that young children's racial thinking is organized around the same biases to prefer certain kinds of explanations over others (organized around the same mode of construal) that are embodied in naive biology. Thus, what naive biology and racial thinking share is not a commitment to a morphologically derived ontology but a common instantiation of an essentialist pattern of causal reasoning. In the case of racial thinking, this pattern of reasoning seems to *enable* (rather than derive from) an expectation that humans are biologically clustered. Although further work is needed before we can adequately evaluate this claim, the data I have presented here force us to consider this possibility seriously. Racial thinking is important to cognitivists not simply because a cognitive approach to race is worth pursuing (as many in social psychology have long acknowledged) but also because racial thinking, in its specificity and richness, is informative to cognitive theory.

13. And mental state: infants and young children attend closely to subtle variations in emotional expression (Campos and Sternberg 1981) and are clearly adept at construing behavior in mentalistic terms (Astington et al. 1988).

Chapter 5

Race, Language, and Collective Inference[1]

A hallmark of adult racial thinking is its comprehensiveness. Knowing a person's race is supposedly crucial to understanding other, nonracial things about that person. Does the young child also believe that race predicts other properties? If so, what sorts of properties? We know from previous work on racial attitudes that young children believe that a person's race is a predictor of at least some properties—whether that person is smart or dull, polite or rude, friendly or not, etc. The relationship between attitudes and beliefs is not easy to determine in all cases. Many accounts of children's racial attitudes attribute them to failures of cognition (e.g., overly egocentric reasoning) rather than to coherent expectations about property distribution (Aboud 1988). Whether children use race to predict other kinds of properties is important precisely because my proposition is that race is especially salient to young children's elaboration of social ontology (Hirschfeld 1988, 1995a, 1995b). To the extent that this is the case, it is plausible to anticipate that knowledge of race is closely linked to knowledge of other ontologically relevant aspects of the world. In this chapter I explore whether children believe that there is a special relationship between a person's race and the language that he or she speaks. I do this because other work has shown that children expect variations in the way one speaks to be associated with membership in a range of collectivities. This opens the possibility that children believe that language variation sheds light on the collectivities to which a person belongs.

Categories and Inference

How might this work? One possibility is that categories of language and categories of race have similar and overlapping inferential potential. Categories are generally important because they partition the world in a comprehensible fashion. But some kinds of categories (particularly natural-kind categories) are important because of the inferences they

1. This chapter draws heavily on material presented in Hirschfeld and Gelman 1991.

permit us to draw. In particular, they help us go beyond the knowledge afforded by everyday experience. Recent work on folk biological knowledge illustrates this well. Even quite young children are able to recruit living-kind labels to enrich and extend conceptual knowledge (Carey 1985; Gelman and Markman 1986, 1987; Keil 1989). These categories allow children to make educated guesses about nonobvious aspects of living kinds (e.g., that each living kind has an underlying essence that causes it to develop into a certain sort of creature (Gelman and Wellman 1991)) and to make predictions about novel events (e.g., that all living things undergo asymmetrical growth, becoming bigger but not smaller over time (Rosengren et al. 1991)).

I have argued that race has similar inferential potential. Of special interest is the likelihood that race is informative of the collectivities into which humans coalesce and around which everyday social interactions are defined, regulated, and organized. This raises the prospect that racial categories might have a special facility in promoting inferences about the properties, attributes, and competences relevant to the *collectivities* to which persons belong. In fact, if my claim is correct—i.e., if race is particularly important to the elaboration of a social ontology and if its salience in early childhood is tied to the role it plays in that elaboration—then race would *have to* capture knowledge of collectivity-relevant properties, attributes, and competences. We would further expect the notion of race to capture more of this knowledge than other social categories.

Language, Society, and Inductive Inference

A series of studies Susan Gelman and I conducted are relevant to this question. These studies probe young children's beliefs about the relationship between language variation and social-category membership. Arguably, no other acquired competence is more relevant to collectivities than language. A major school of anthropology held that each language embodies a unique worldview that sets the cognitions of its speakers apart from speakers of other languages. Though few continue to hold the strong version of this claim, it is standard wisdom in anthropology that language is a major medium through which cultural difference is enacted, expressed, and maintained. More important, the view that language is relevant to the collectivities to which people belong is not limited to professionals. Firmly rooted in folk belief is the idea that the language someone speaks, is allowed to speak, or is even capable of speaking is crucial to that person's membership in a collectivity. Consider the controversies over maintaining French in Canada and "pure" French in France; consider English-only rules in schools and workplaces in the United States.

Indeed, language *is* a good predictor of social-category membership. Members of different social categories speak in distinct ways, and children provide evidence that they understand this. It is less clear whether children grasp that different sorts of speech have different implications. Intuitively, intrinsic and deep language differences can be distinguished from more superficial and variable ones. Interlanguage differences (e.g., between French and German) are deeper than intralanguage ones (e.g., regional and individual accents). Categories associated with interlanguage differences (e.g., two different nationalities) tend to entail greater social distance than categories associated with intralanguage differences (e.g., two different occupations). Moreover, most nonlinguists conceive of language as a learned skill; in this respect, language and race are conceptually distinct types of phenomena.

When and how children come to understand these things is important because achieving both cultural and linguistic competence requires that language and other forms of social understanding be calibrated. As Chomsky (1988, p. 188) observes, "somehow, young children have a theory of society and a theory of language, and they are able to link them up in some fashion to indicate that you speak this language in this social situation."

Children's Understanding of Language Variation

Children encounter tremendous variation in the language spoken around them, including individual variation in speech quality (e.g., each person has a distinct, recognizable voice), a rich array of differences associated with social groups (e.g., gender, geographic locale, status, and social role), and differences in language itself (e.g., English versus Spanish). An important task for children is to determine which features of language are relevant to which kinds of inter-individual distinctions. This is no small feat: the mapping between language differences and variations among individuals and groups of people is complex. Variations in speech and language map onto variations between individuals in distinct, independent, and potentially conflicting ways.[2] Moreover, the kinds of inferences that children make about other people will be guided by their beliefs about these correspondences. Specifically, how children match up language and social variation has implications for how they think about the diversity in language and speech that they encounter daily. If children adopted a

2. In contrasting "language" and "speech" I mean the commonsense distinction between supposedly mutually unintelligible systems (e.g., English vs. Italian) and differences within a language (e.g., dialect or register).

strategy that ignored speech variation between individuals, there would be nontrivial consequences. Disregarding variation that adults find meaningful would lead children to miss out on important information regarding the social world: language differences (such as dialect, regional accent, and gender aspects of speech) are important (though fallible) cues to a range of nonlinguistic behaviors.

From the available research, we know that in their own production and on-line comprehension children pay selective and unequal attention to various aspects of speech variation. For instance, children (and adults) ignore nonmeaningful variations in sounds (e.g., collapsing together aspirated and unaspirated t in English) (Werker 1989) as well as variations in individual pronunciation (Kuhl 1985). On the other hand, we also know that children attend closely to a variety of speech differences, both in their own talk and in how they interpret what others say. For example, a 2-day-old infant can distinguish its mother's voice from the voices of other women (DeCasper and Fifer 1980). An infant can also discriminate its mother's native language from other languages (Mehler et al. 1988). On a larger scale, young bilinguals, even at early stages of language acquisition, have little trouble keeping their two languages distinct (Lindholm and Padilla 1977; Redlinger and Park 1980; Grosjean 1982) or selecting the appropriate language to use in different contexts and with different speakers (Volterra and Taeschner 1978; Grosjean 1982).

Several studies have found that young children also grasp that variations in speech are related to variations in the groups to which people belong (e.g., collections or classes based on gender, kinship, occupation, or age grade) (see Becker 1982 for a review). Andersen (1990) found that when young children were asked to take on different social roles (e.g., to talk like a doctor, a teacher, or a mother) they varied their speech along a number of dimensions (e.g., register, word choice, syntactic devices). This suggests that children understand the link between these properties of speech and social-category membership. In a study examining children's spontaneous role playing with peers at nursery school, Corsaro (1979) found that even younger children ($2\frac{1}{2}$–$5\frac{1}{2}$ years) produced appropriately modified language according to the familial or occupational role they were enacting (e.g., using more baby talk and requests for permission when taking on a subordinate role than when assuming a superordinate role). Kuczaj and Harbaugh (1980) found that by age 4 children believed that adult members of their own culture could learn to talk like them (and even 3-year-olds believed that they could learn to talk like members of another culture).

An understanding of the social differences that occur between languages appears to emerge somewhat later. For example, in clinical interviews Piaget and Weil (1951) asked children of ages 4–15 about national differences. They found that children of ages 6 and above cited language differences as evidence of national differences, and that they appealed to shared language as evidence for the absence of national differences (see also Jahoda 1963). Piaget and Weil were more concerned with children's comprehension of the notion of country and nationality than their metalinguistic understanding, and they concluded on the basis of their data that before age 7 or 8 children had little grasp of the notion of country. Intriguingly, however, they cite as evidence one 6-year-old Genevan who thought Paris was in Switzerland (because Parisians speak French) and that Bern was not (because residents of Bern do not speak French). Although this child's understanding of national boundaries may have been confused, he evidently was able to coordinate knowledge of social and linguistic entities rather impressively, recruiting the idea of homeland to infer shared language and the idea of shared language to infer homeland.

Jahoda (1963) provides further evidence of similar expectations. In a study of children's knowledge of foreign countries, he asked children of ages 6–11 what they could say about America and Russia. Overall responses varied considerably, particularly among the younger subjects. Jahoda did find, however, that children tended to link foreign countries with unfamiliar language behavior and with unfamiliar physique. Interestingly, these children did not link skin color *and* language differences to unfamiliar countries. Rather, they tended to associate *either* linguistic difference *or* skin- color difference with the foreign country, but not both. This pattern suggests that they saw language and race as relevant to collectivities but independent of each other, at least to some extent.

The most extensive study on these issues was conducted by Kuczaj and Harbaugh (1980; see Kuczaj 1989 for additional details). They found that preschool children understood that not all people speak the same way; that animals, plants, and vehicles neither talk like nor speak the same language as the child; and that even people who speak the same language may talk differently from one another. However, it was not until the age of 6 years that children consistently inferred that people from a different culture would speak a different language, and it was not until the age of 7 or 8 years that children reliably believed that people from a different culture could learn to talk like them (although even 3-year-olds expected that they could learn to speak like or speak the same language as members of another culture). In sum, available research indicates that children map language onto certain social-group differences.

Several questions remain unresolved, however. Studies that have looked at preschoolers' sensitivity to intralanguage differences show that younger children map such variation onto social-group differences. In contrast, studies that have looked at interlanguage differences indicate that these differences are not reliably mapped onto social-group differences until children are somewhat older. The realization that speech varies with social category thus may develop before the understanding that languages vary with social category. Methodological differences between studies exploring intralanguage versus interlanguage differences make it difficult to decide this question on the basis of available data. It is also not clear whether the link between social-group differences and language variation is learned on an *ad hoc* basis or as a general understanding. Piaget and Weil (1951) and Jahoda (1963) found that children's knowledge in this area was extremely varied and was shaped by specific local events (e.g., television reports). Ramsey (1987, p. 61) draws a similar conclusion about preschoolers, whose ideas about cultural differences, she argues, "are vague and undifferentiated associations rather than coherent concepts." Kuczaj and Harbaugh (1980, p. 225), in contrast, conclude that children do not learn to map language and social-group differences instance by instance; "Instead, they appear to learn the importance of cultural variation *per se* in a relatively broad sense." (Kuczaj and Harbaugh note, however, that this does not occur before middle childhood.) Finally, anecdotal data suggest that even younger children may associate interlanguage and social-group differences (Slobin 1978; Kuczaj and Harbaugh 1980).

Reviewing this and other evidence, I speculated that the awareness of multiple languages may derive not from children's knowledge of language *per se* but from their knowledge of intrinsic social differences (Hirschfeld 1989a). In addition to whatever metalinguistic knowledge may emerge during early childhood, the young child clearly develops a good deal of knowledge about social-category differences, both intrinsic and variable. It is possible that children recruit this knowledge to make inferences about types of language difference. This possibility is made more plausible by the fact that linguistic input alone does not appear sufficient to trigger inductions about multiple languages (Hirschfeld 1989a). For one thing, young bilinguals appear to become aware of multiple languages only *after* their ability to speak multiple languages is quite well formed (Chomsky 1988; Vihman 1985).

Clearly, then, a number of questions remain to be answered. When do children begin to associate language variation (as opposed to speech variation) reliably with social-group differences? What is the scope of children's understanding? Which social categories do children associate with language differences? Do children appropriately limit the range of these associations, or do they associate all social-category differences with language differences? If the latter, which categories are considered relevant? What language properties do children base their judgments on when linking linguistic and social variations? Susan Gelman and I conducted several studies designed to address these questions. Unlike earlier workers, we focused on younger (pre-school-age) children. To ensure that performance reflected children's beliefs about language (as opposed to speech) differences, we used actual speech samples in an unfamiliar foreign language. In the first study we asked preschoolers to infer the language spoken by people varying in race, clothing, and dwelling. The second study examined whether there are limits on which social differences are mapped onto language. The third study demonstrates that the effects observed in the first two studies are functions of children's beliefs about language and cannot be attributed to a superficial quality of the foreign speech samples we used.

Study 5.1: Mapping Languages onto Social Categories

Thirty-six 3-, 4,- and 6-year-old children were presented with a series of picture pairs while they heard a number of speech samples. Each picture pair consisted of color drawings depicting two individuals who contrasted either on race (black vs. white), clothing (Western vs. non-Western ethnic apparel), dwelling (Western vs. non-Western architecture), or orientation (forward facing vs. backward facing). Each speech sample consisted either of an adult male or an adult female uttering a short sentence in English or Portuguese. Just before hearing each of the speech samples, the children were given the following instructions:

> Here are two (men/women/houses). Listen carefully to the voice, and tell me which (man/woman) is talking. [Or, in the case of houses where no person was depicted, "and tell me which house the voice is coming from."]

We calculated two variables: one for the dwelling, clothing, and race items and one for the orientation items. The first variable represents how often children in each age group identified the Western items on the clothing and dwelling picture pairs and the white person on the race picture pair with the English speaker versus how often they identified them with the Portuguese speaker. The question is whether the children's attributions differed as a function of the language spoken. The logic of the design is straightforward. If children expect social-category differences to predict language differences, they should attribute Portuguese to the unfamiliar and non-Western individuals and English to the familiar and Western ones. If children do not expect social-category differences to be systematically related to language differences, their attributions would be random. The second variable represents

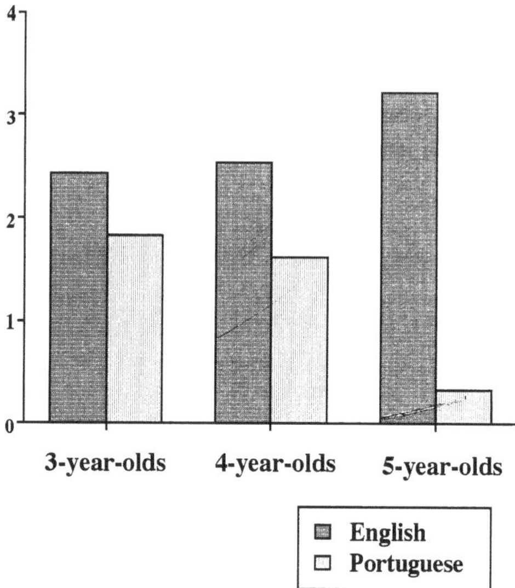

Figure 5.1
Mean number of times white or Western items were chosen for each language.

how often children in each of the age groups attributed English to the forward-facing person, and how often they attributed Portuguese to the forward-facing person.

As can be seen from figure 5.1, responses were not random. Children in all groups selected the white and Western items more when hearing English than when hearing the Portuguese. That is, children in all age groups reliably mapped language differences onto the social dimension (race, clothing, and dwelling). Although the pattern was most pronounced with the oldest children, it was clearly evident in the younger children's responses too. We found marked age differences on the forward-facing-vs.-backward-facing items, with 4- and 5-year-olds assigning language to orientation at random. This pattern of response to the control items allows us to rule out a simple matching strategy of familiar to familiar and unfamiliar to unfamiliar as an explanation for their choices on the dwelling, clothing, and race items. That is, they did not assign Portuguese to the teepee dweller simply because both were unfamiliar items, since they were as likely to attribute English as Portuguese to the backward-facing pictures (which are anomalous poses for a portrait). In contrast, 3-year-olds tended to attribute the

English utterances to people facing forward and Portuguese to the people facing backward. Accordingly, a simple matching strategy cannot be ruled out for these subjects.

Study 5.2: Are All Social Contrasts Informative of Language Differences?

This control study had two parts. In the first, we examined whether children mapped language differences onto any social contrast, particularly one that is not racial. In the second, we looked to see whether children mapped race onto all social contrasts, particularly ones that are not collectivity relevant.

Language Differences and Social Contrast

We can better understand the youngest children's performance on the control items if we know whether 3-year-olds attribute language differences to *any* social contrast or whether they limit such attributions. For this study we selected a social contrast that 3-year-olds were expected to know does *not* map onto language: age. Children are sensitive to age-group differences (Pope Edwards 1984; Taylor and Gelman 1993) and recognize that age differences are predictive of intralanguage differences (specifically, differences in speech register; see Becker 1982 and Corsaro 1979). But age is not an appropriate dimension on which to map interlanguage differences. If children attribute language variation to *any* recognized contrast, then they should be as likely to attribute language differences to differences in age as to differences in race, clothing, or dwelling. However, if children realize that only some social contrasts are relevant to language differences, then they should not map language differences onto age differences.

Eleven 3-year-olds were presented with pictures of two people and then heard a sound sample in either English or Portuguese. Each child was then asked to identify which of the people made the sound. Unlike the picture pairs used in study 5.1, these picture pairs contrasted on only one dimension: age. Each pair of drawings depicted one youthful adult and one considerably older person.[3] In contrast to their performances on the previous task, children on this task chose at random. They were as likely to attribute Portuguese to the old person as they were to attribute English to the old person. Clearly, then, even 3-year-olds do not match all language differences onto all social contrasts.

3. We pretested the age items by asking children to choose which one looked most like a grandmother or a grandfather. We selected only those which children were reliably able to distinguish on the basis of age.

Race and Social Contrast

I took the results of study 5.1 to be evidence that children coordinate knowledge of society and knowledge of language. Since social differences have varying levels of importance, this interpretation would be more compelling if it could be established that children do not map race onto all social differences. The results of the language-to-social-contrast study demonstrate that children are not biased to map language onto any social contrast. An alternative interpretation of these results, however, is that children are biased to map race onto any social contrast. On this alternative account, it is not the case that children specifically believe that race is predictive of language differences. Rather, the child's attention is drawn to the racial contrast depicted in the pictures, and she uses this contrast in sorting whatever further contrast the experimenter presents. If this is the case, then children should map race onto any contrast the experimenter provides. If children have a specific belief that race is predictive of language differences, we should not find such a general pattern.

To examine this possibility, we looked at children's expectations about the relation among race, language, and music preferences. If children have a bias to map race onto any behavioral contrast, then they should expect race to predict music preferences as readily as it predicts language differences. However, if they have a specific belief that race and language are linked (perhaps because they are both informative of intrinsic nature; see Hirschfeld 1989a), then children should not expect race and music preferences to be related. Forty-two 4- and 5-year-old children were shown a series of picture sets, one at a time. Each picture set consisted of a pair of color drawings depicting two groups of four individuals. Some groups consisted of two children and two adults all of the same race (either all black or all white). Other groups consisted of two whites and two blacks all of the same age (either all adults or all children). Each picture set accordingly contrasted a mixed race group with a mixed age group (e.g., one set consisted of a picture of four girls, two black and two white, and a picture of four white females, two girls and two women). Children were shown the picture sets twice. In one block children were asked to identify which group of people all speak the same language, in the other they were asked which group of people like the same kind of music.

The results are informative. The 5-year-olds were more likely to map language onto race than music onto race. The 4-year-olds, in contrast, responded at chance, mapping race onto music as often as race onto language. We interpret this as evidence that older preschoolers map race onto language contrasts but do not map race onto contrasts involving nonintrinsic preferences (specifically, music). One potential difficulty is that children may know more about language variation than about variation in music preference and hence may be more reasoned in their judgments involving race than in those involving music. To rule this out, before beginning the main task we asked children a series of questions meant to tap their knowledge of variations in language and of differences in music preferences. We found that 88% of the children could name the language they spoke, and 98% could identify a type of music they liked. Similarly, whereas 53% of the children reported knowing someone who spoke another language, 57% reported knowing someone who liked another kind of music. In short: children seem to be as knowledgeable about variations in music as they are about language, at least on the basis of this pretest measure.

Study 5.3: Intelligibility, Language Structure, and Race

Studies 5.1 and 5.2 support the claim that even preschoolers are able to coordinate knowledge of race with knowledge of interlanguage variation. This pattern of reasoning has important implications for understanding the scope of racial concepts because we have assumed that interlanguage variation is a collectivity-relevant property. One problem with this argument is that the *basis* of children's judgments may not really be collectivity relevant, even if those judgments involve interlanguage variation. For example, rather than judging the native-language and foreign-language speech samples as tokens of two different types of language, children might have based their judgments on the fact that one set of speech samples was intelligible and the other unintelligible. If this were the case, then children's willingness to map racial differences onto linguistic ones might be interesting but irrelevant to whether racial concepts entail a special ontological commitment on the child's part. The reason for this is that judgments of intelligibility need not involve reflection on language *per se*. They could instead involve the child's awareness of his or her own mental state (comprehension vs. incomprehension). If children base their judgments on intelligibility, they may be making inferences about their own mental states rather than about the speech signal. However, if they base their judgments on a property of language (say, prosodic information), their judgments are about language *per se*.

One way to test between these possibilities is to render unintelligible *all* the speech samples that children are asked make judgments about—not just those in the foreign language. If children's judgments are based on their understanding of differences in language structure, then their pattern of inference should be no different from that uncovered in study 5.1. If children's judgments are based on intelligibility, then they should randomly associate (distorted) language with race.

Twenty-five 5-year-olds participated in the experiment.[4] As other children had in studies 5.1 and 5.2, these children looked at pictures of people contrasting in race, heard a sound sample, and were then asked to identify which of the people made the sound. In contrast with the earlier tasks, however, the speech samples were electronically distorted (using a low-pass filter) so that only prosodic information was maintained.[5] In pretests we found that children had difficulty attending to the highly distorted speech as speech, and we tried several stories to explain why the sounds were so unusual. Eventually we found an explanation that children found convincing. As children were shown each picture pair, they were given the following instructions:

> See, here's a stuffed bunny [a puppet in whose hand cavity a small speaker was placed]. It's a funny bunny because there's a hole inside where someone can sit and hide. I have different friends who took turns sitting inside the bunny and talking. You can't hear them too well when they're inside; it sounds kind of like this. [The experimenter demonstrates a very muffled voice.] I'm trying to figure out who was sitting inside the bunny when they talked. Okay here's my first friend. [The first picture pair is placed in front of the child, and the first speech sample is played.] Who do you think is inside the bunny?

Six picture sets were selected from those used in studies 5.1 and 5.2: two forward-facing vs.-backward-facing control items and the four race items. Six speech samples, three in Portuguese and three in English, were produced by two bilingual speakers. As in studies 5.1 and 5.2, the male Portuguese and male English samples were produced by the same person, and the female Portuguese and female English items were produced by the same person.

As they had in studies 5.1 and 5.2, children reasoned differently about the race of the English speakers and the Portuguese speakers.

4. Although it would be ideal to test 3-, 4-, and 5-year-olds as a comparison to the earlier studies, pilot testing made it clear that the task was too difficult for children below age 5. This could well be due to the difficulty of the speech samples. In any case, we included only 5-year-olds in the main experiment.

5. The filtered speech samples, though readily recognizable as speech, were markedly distorted, and both the English and the Portuguese were fully unintelligible. Mehler et al. (1988) showed that infants could discriminate between native and non-native speech on the basis of prosodic cues alone. If infants can discriminate on that basis alone, it is plausible that older children can do so. Still, since we know that some sound-discrimination skills degrade with age (Trehub 1976; Werker 1989), we pretested the stimuli in order to be sure that adults could also distinguish between native and non-native speech on the basis of prosodic information alone. Overall, adults easily distinguished the English from the Portuguese samples, although they were more accurate in judging that the Portuguese items were not English than in judging that the English items were English.

Although the size of the effect was modest, it is significant. Children chose the black person 72% of the time (reliably above chance) when hearing the Portuguese utterance and 48% of the time (at chance) when hearing the English. As predicted, children were at chance in their language attributions to the control items of forward-facing and backward-facing people, choosing the forward-facing person 68% of the time when hearing Portuguese and 53% of the time when hearing English. In contrast to the finding of studies 5.1 and 5.2 (in which 5-year-olds also linked variations of language with differences in race), these results cannot be attributed to a simple strategy of mapping race onto intelligible versus unintelligible speech. Children mapped race and language even when all utterances were equally unintelligible. Crucially, the children's judgments about who produced a given type of speech were based on properties of language, not on meaning alone.

Conclusions

Preschool children reliably coordinate knowledge across the social and language domains. They recruit knowledge about language differences to make inferences about social difference, and they recruit knowledge about social differences to draw inferences about language variation. Previous research suggests that children do not consistently infer that people from a different culture speak a different language until age 6. We found, in contrast, that even 3-year-olds make this association. Strikingly, children's beliefs do not appear to be made on an *ad hoc* basis; they reflect a coherent set of beliefs about the way categories of language and society are linked. Furthermore, we have been able to demonstrate that these judgments are specific to language and to meaningful social variation.

To what extent does the range of everyday experience provide a basis for these inferences? Study 5.1 showed that language differences are reliably mapped onto several social dimensions associated with human groupings. Children believe that people who live in unfamiliar homes or wear unfamiliar costumes speak an unfamiliar language. In view of the ubiquity of the multicultural curriculum, even at the preschool level, it is not implausible that children encounter materials that generally would support this inference (although it is unlikely that children have had direct experience with the stimulus language we used, Portuguese). Crucially, however, preschoolers also believe that people who have darker skin are more likely to speak Portuguese than English—indeed, children were actually more consistent in making this inference than in their attributions to clothing or dwelling (although the difference was not statistically significant). This association presumably is *not* an accurate reflection of reality, and presumably is *not* knowledge delivered through routine social interaction. The vast majority of blacks encountered by midwestern preschoolers in the United States are native English speakers—and, conversely, there is no reason to expect that the percentage of non-native English speakers is higher among U.S. blacks than among U.S. whites. This observation suggests that children construct these beliefs to some extent on their own, despite the lack of any empirical evidence to support them. I argue that children do so because they spontaneously combine and integrate knowledge across content domains.

We do not know what meaning children attribute to these various kinds of social differences, but there is some basis to speculate. Young children understand that both age and race are inherent to an individual. As was argued in chapter 4, even preschoolers believe that race is an intrinsic aspect of a person, fixed at birth, and immutable over the life span. They also understand that growth is biologically grounded and asymmetrical (Rosengren et al. 1991), that age is an important dimension on which to group people (Pope Edwards 1984), and that speech predictably differs with the age of the speaker (Andersen 1990). Whereas both race and age involve intrinsic qualities, race (unlike age) is a marker of stable cultural-group differences (as are clothing and architecture, dimensions which we found children also use to predict language differences). In short, race is collectivity relevant. Children also believe that languages are collectivity relevant, the properties of peoples. It is this common presumption that seems to underlie children's judgments about language and social variation.

One question that is not addressed here is how children interpret collectivity relevance. Race is clearly biologized (i.e., seen as part of a person's natural character). Adults see race as identity relevant for social reasons. We do not know yet whether children also hold both social and biological interpretations of race, although these data suggest that they may well. Clearly they associate language and race. I suggest that they do so because both are identity relevant. But they may be identity relevant under quite different interpretations. Language is identity relevant under a social interpretation. By late preschool age, as Kuczaj and Harbaugh's (1982) study shows, children see language as a learned capacity. The question is whether language and race are associated because they are both identity relevant or because they are both identity relevant and socially interpreted. In chapter 7 I will again take up the issue of race's multiple interpretations and how children come to coordinate them. To anticipate: It appears that younger children are more likely to see the biological interpretation of race as paramount. But before exploring this issue, I would like to turn to the question of what sorts of data are crucial in forming racial categories.

Chapter 6

The Appearance of Race: Perception in the Construction of Racial Categories[1]

By reference to what kinds of experience do children formulate racial concepts? Virtually all previous work assumes that visual experience plays a fundamental role. This presumption is paradoxical for at least two reasons. First, surface physical features provide at best confusing cues about racial-category membership.[2] Second, as I argued in chapter 4, the hallmark of racial categories—the notion that they are natural and

1. This chapter draws heavily on material presented in Hirschfeld 1993.
2. Consider the biology of skin pigmentation—the principle criterion of racial categorization in the United States. As we saw in chapter 4, even quite young children believe skin color to be both heritable and immutable. This accords well with adult belief. There is some question, however, as to whether it accords with our unmediated experience. Skin pigmentation is controlled by several genes, and different populations' skin colors appear to be governed by distinct combinations of genes (Molnar 1992). The degree to which skin color is inherited also varies across populations, and contrary to common sense (and the legal system of racial classification in the United States) dark skin color is not dominant over lighter tones (Robins 1991). The lack of dominance of one skin pigment over another, combined with the polygenetic (and varying) control of skin color, means that (again in contrast to conventional wisdom) parents often produce offspring with a broad range of skin-color blends (Byard 1981), and parents whose skin colors are not close tend to have offspring whose skin color does not closely match either parent's. In short, there is significant and fairly continuous variation in the skin color both within "homogenous" racial categories and among members of the same immediate family. Nor does the environment provide unequivocal support for the expectation that skin pigment is immutable over the life span. In fact, nongenetic factors play a significant role (Robins 1991). Even though skin color is highly (though varyingly) heritable, a substantial portion of variance is not accounted for by genetic factors (estimates range between 20% and 40%). Furthermore, nontrivial changes in an individual's skin color do take place. Tanning, for example, is a familiar process even to young children. There is also considerable darkening of skin color (and hair color) with age (Byard 1981), so that infants of dark-skinned parents are often relatively light-skinned (Molnar 1992). Accordingly, though populations may maintain characteristic central tendencies which serve as racial prototypes, population differences in skin color imperceptibly blend over time and over space. In the absence of geographic isolation or social intervention against mixed-race unions, racial differences tend to disappear (van den Berghe 1981). But race is generally not conceptualized as this variable: in societies where skin color is socially relevant (e.g. the United States), children (and presumably adults) appear to perceive skin color categorically, whereas in those few societies in which skin color lacks such social implications (e.g. Sweden in the 1970s) children perceive skin color accurately, as a continuously varying attribute (Hughes 1975).

naturalized groupings of like beings—is largely independent of appearances. Nonetheless, children naturalize race as readily as adults do.

Why then should we imagine that appearances play a crucial role in the development of children's racial categories? In significant measure, the presumption has nothing to do with race. Instead it reflects a foundational belief about the way children learn about most things in the world. That is, most accounts of the acquisition of racial and ethnic awareness have much in common with major theories of cognitive development. In all cases, children are seen as having to use obvious surface cues to sort exemplars into different categories. Only later are they granted the ability to use "abstract" criteria.

I have suggested that this strategy misses racial thinking's relation to a domain-specific competence for constructing and reasoning about human kinds. From this perspective there is no reason to trace the peculiar qualities of racial thinking (in particular its heightened salience in the human conceptual repertoire) to special aspects of its appearance (in particular, the attention-demanding nature of its physical correlates). In fact, I will show in this chapter that, rather than being overly dependent on appearances, young children's racial concepts involve encoding and retrieval processes that are in many ways independent of perceptual factors. I do not mean by this that young children do not use perceptual (i.e., observable) cues in constructing racial categories. Instead, on the view I propose, such cues are not *defining* of racial categories, as previous researchers have suggested. Children may have quite rich perceptual knowledge of race, but this knowledge may be less integrated with conceptual knowledge than is usually imagined.

For example, it might be that preschool children develop overlapping but distinct kinds of knowledge about racial targets: perception-oriented knowledge structures on one hand and domain-oriented (or ontology-oriented) ones on the other. If this were the case, children might build categories that discriminate individuals on the basis of perceptual criteria and might also build categories that discriminate individuals on the basis of ontological criteria. Previous research has proceeded on the assumption that these two kinds of knowledge are aspects of the same structure, and that racial terms name discriminable kinds of persons as well as the putative physical correlates of these kinds. Against this view, I will argue that the two sorts of knowledge are distinct. Both types contain information about physical appearance, but the importance that such information has in domain-oriented knowledge structures is limited.

An Alternative Model

In chapter 4 I suggested that young children's racial thinking can be best viewed as part of an endogenous curiosity about the social world.

Children understand at least two things as a result of this curiosity: that people come in "racially" different kinds and that these "racial" kinds encompass some sort of pertinent perceptual differences. It is not until later that children come to know which specific surface cues are relevant to specific kinds because it is not until later that they integrate their perceptual knowledge with their ontological knowledge. Previous researchers suggest that there is considerable conceptual development in racial thinking during the preschool and early school years (Aboud 1988; Katz 1982). I suggest, in contrast, that what develops during this period is the ability to calibrate and eventually combine the perception-oriented and domain-oriented knowledge structures. The conclusion that perceptual information is central to early racial categories may reflect previous researchers' focus on the process by which perception-oriented and domain-oriented knowledge converge, not the processes by which racial concepts are actually formed. This further suggests that what happens during the late preschool years may be less a restructuring of the conceptual system than an accumulation of factual knowledge about the culturally relevant perceptual correlates of the concept in question.

This pattern of conceptual development, in which young children initially focus on the elaboration of a conceptual domain and only later come to know specifically how individual exemplars might be perceptually differentiated, is found in other domains. For example, though even very young children can readily categorize objects on the basis of color (Sugarman 1983), according to Carey (1978) the conceptual domain of color emerges somewhat later. Carey found initial mappings of novel color terms to indicate that young children are better at picking out a domain of color than they are at pairing specific terms and specific colors. Recently other researchers have argued generally that much of early conceptual development involves top-down processes in which superordinate levels of the conceptual hierarchy emerge before lower levels (Mandler et al. 1991; Wellman and Gelman 1992). As a result, conceptual development often involves closer attention to verbal or discursive environmental cues than to visual ones.

The model I propose for the development of the race concept is consistent with what we know from other areas of conceptual development. Whether or not it is plausible is something else. Is there another reason to believe that this pattern of development actually applies to the domain of racial cognitions? In this chapter I will present evidence that children develop an ontological commitment to race (i.e., an early appreciation of the conceptual domain of race) before they begin to attend in earnest to the physical correlates that adults believe are important in racial classification. Although this model of development turns conventional wisdom on its head, there is nonetheless evidence from previous research to support it.

For example, anecdotal data indicate that, although young children clearly attend to perceptual cues in discriminating racial kinds, they seem to be strikingly unable to decide which perceptual cues (or even which range of perceptual cues) are relevant. Ramsey (1987, p. 60) reports that a white 3-year-old looked at a photograph of a black child and declared "His teeth are different!" Then the subject "looked again, seemed puzzled and hesitantly said, 'No, his skin is different.'" At the age of 4 my daughter made a similar observation. She and I were stopped at a traffic light in France. She looked at an ethnically Asian family in the car next to us, seemed startled, and then exclaimed that they looked like her friend Alexandre, a Eurasian child. I asked her in what ways she thought they looked like Alexandre. She mulled over the question for a moment, staring intently at the family as we waited for the light to change. Finally she said "They all have the same color hair." Of course she was right. Alexandre and the members of his family all had black hair—but so did I, at the time. More critically, the majority of the inhabitants of France have black hair, whether they are ethnically French, Southeast Asian, or North African. The point to be taken from both stories is that preschoolers are aware of perceptual differences between members of racial groups and are aware that perceptual cues play a role in defining racial groups, but they do not appear to reflect on precisely which perceptual factors are important.

Less anecdotal work lends further, though indirect, support to the model. There is a body of literature on the queston of why young minority children tend to identify themselves with ethnic groups other than their own. The finding is fairly straightforward: when asked to choose which person they look most like, many black preschoolers choose representations of white rather than black children. There is considerable controversy on how to interpret this. What is of importance for the present discussion is the conditions under which such misidentifications almost never occur. Misidentification is extremely rare when verbal racial labels are used (Aboud 1987), and almost all misidentification occurs in studies in which children are asked to choose among pictorial (or doll) representations of racial status. In short, children appear to know quite well which *named* group they belong to. What they are unsure of is which physical correlate is most relevant to identity.[3]

3. In misidentifications, this ambiguity may be recruited in an attempt to reconcile identity judgments and identity politics in an unproblematic way. Nonwhite children know that being white in a physical sense is socially favored and that they belong a named category that is not "white." The question for them is whether their own skin color is the physical quality diagnostic of the named category to which they belong. Their (so-called) misidentifications reflect the fact that children's verbal identification of their own race may run well ahead of their perceptual self-categorization, and particularly ahead of their ability to match the physical correlates adults associate with race with racial labels.

Ironically, evidence that there are overlapping perception-oriented and domain-oriented knowledge structures also comes from studies meant to establish that race and gender are especially salient precisely because of their perceptual correlates. As was noted in chapter 4, when presented with an array of people who can be classified along several dimensions, young children prefer to sort by race and gender rather than by other social dimensions (Aboud 1988; Davey 1983; Davey and Norburn 1980; Katz et al. 1975). These findings have generally been interpreted as demonstrating that race and gender demand a lot of attention *because* of the richness of their physical correlates. If this were the case, we would expect race and gender to drive sortings regardless of the task involved. In fact, this is not what has been found. Young children favor race on free-sorting tasks, but they rely little on race in choosing playmates. An apparent exception to this is informative: ethnic differences predict children's interactions if those ethnic differences are accompanied by language differences (Finkelstein and Haskins 1983; Doyle et al. 1988). Not all observable correlates of ethnicity, therefore, guide playmate choice. Some are treated as relevant and some are not. Certain perceptual contrasts (such as language) but not others (such as skin color) influence playmate choice.

The crucial manipulation in these directed-sorting versus free-sorting tasks is that children are asked to focus on a specific social context (Milner 1984). In directed-sorting tasks children are encouraged to make judgments about the individual's social status rather than the individual's physical appearance. Precisely because everyday contexts contain many competing dimensions of interest, experimentalists design tasks that seek to obscure or efface this range of contextual cues. In order to make the study of social judgments tractable, experimenters provide children with tasks that guide their attention to a limited number of contextual features. In a typical racial awareness study, skin color is pitted against age and against style of dress. This move may have unforeseen consequences. In particular it may keep us from appreciating the subtlety of young children's social understanding (Dunn 1988). Although results from free-sorting tasks that incorporate very limited contextual information indicate that young children recognize that individuals can be sorted in terms of their skin color, these performances do not establish that children attach the same meaning to the resulting sortings that older children and adults do.[4] Natural sortings, such as playmate choice, by

4. In fact, studies with adults show the same thing. Stimulus situations in which richer social information is presented produce quite different processing than stimulus situations in which a small and focused amount of social information is presented. Richer levels of social information, which are more likely to approximate the levels of information encountered in routine social contexts, tend to trigger category-based top-down processing; more constrained levels of social information tend to enhance person-based bottom-up processing (see Brewer 1988 for a review).

definition involve contrasts that are meaningful for the child. Perceptual cues lacking in intrinsic meaning may demand less attention in these situations and thus may be less conditioning of children's choices.[5]

Implications of the Alternative Model

A number of empirical predictions follow from the claim that children first understand race in terms of discrete ontological rather than visual kinds. Clearly these predictions differ from those coming from the standard view that young children's racial categories are derived from observed differences.

> *Prediction 1* To the extent that race is important to young children for ontological rather than perceptual reasons, there is no reason to believe that all social categories with equally rich perceptual correlates will be equally salient to young children. In contrast, the standard model predicts that all social categories with similarly attention-demanding physical correlates will be equally salient.
>
> *Prediction 2* The salience of race will be higher on verbal than on visual tasks, because social ontologies are initially derived principally from discursive information. The standard view predicts that racial cognitions should be better evoked by visual than by verbal stimuli.
>
> *Prediction 3* Given prediction 2, I predict that verbal cues will not readily elicit visual information about racial categories. The standard view predicts that racial concepts will be closely linked to visual information.

Testing the Model

I designed two studies to assess these predictions. In both, children were presented with racial and other social information incorporated in complex narratives. There are three rationales for this design. First, narratives hold the interest of even quite young children (Dunn 1988). Second, preschool children are adept at encoding and retrieving complex texts (Denhière 1988; Mandler 1985; Stein and Glenn 1979; Poulsen et al. 1979), and these skills have been found to develop over a broad range of learning environments (Heath 1982). Therefore, memory for narratives should provide good evidence of those aspects of social behavior that young children find significant. Third, a more nuanced understanding of

5. The modality in which information about context is conveyed may also affect the nature of children's judgments, as it does adults' memory for social information (Lynn et al. 1985). Responses to visually represented contexts may reflect children's ability to bring together and articulate both racial and perceptual categories. In contrast, verbal descriptions of contexts may reflect the child's higher capacity to reason about domain-oriented categories than to reason about perception.

the conceptual content of social categories may be achieved by examining category saliency in contexts that approach the complexity of everyday life. Complex narratives make it possible to present children with representations that approximate the complexity of routine social interaction. Keep in mind, however, that the issue is not whether the narrative is a more complex stimulus, but whether the narrative allows us to represent a more complex social environment and thus to see how the child deals with social complexity.

The principal question is whether patterned variation in children's memories for social information emerges. Both of my studies focus primarily on encoding and retrieval processes (although recognition and identification processes are also probed in supplementary tasks). The first study explores the social information preschool children extract from a detailed verbal narrative. The goal is to see if various social categories are remembered differently. Since the task is entirely verbal, and immediate perceptual input plays no role, responses should reflect information about appearances already in memory. The second study examines the social information preschoolers recall from a parallel but nonverbal (pictorial) narrative. The central question is whether memory for racial and other social information is affected by modality of narrative presentation—in particular, whether the pattern of recall for a visual story differs from that for a verbal text.

The second study also examines an allied issue: the relationship between verbal labels and visual information. Even if racial categories are less perceptually rich than previously thought, it seems implausible that they should contain *no* perceptual information. Visual information and perceptual cues can be related in a number of ways, ranging from a direct association (in which seeing something brings to mind its label), to a mediated one (in which seeing something brings its label to mind only after verbal priming), to a tenuous one (in which, even with priming, seeing something does not bring the label to mind). The narrative tasks are conducted under two conditions to test the relationship between racial labels and perceptual cues. In the primed condition, the tasks are carried out before the visual narrative task. Immediately before collection of narrative identifications and recall, children participate in several tasks in which they match verbal labels to pictures of what they represent. In the unprimed condition, these tasks are performed after the narrative task.

A note on methodology The social dimensions used were race, gender, occupation, nonracial physical features (including body type and age), and behavior. The rationale for contrasting children's judgments about race, occupation, and body type were reviewed in chapter 4. Age and behavioral cues were also assessed, because during the same age period children are also beginning to discern, label, and draw inferences about individuals on the bases of age (Pope Edwards 1984), nonobvious psychological states (Wellman 1990; Miller and Aloise 1989), and dispositions and traits (Eder 1989, 1990). Unlike the other studies reported here, this one was done in France, a country with an especially rich ethnic and racial environment. With few exceptions (Alejandro-Wright 1985; Corenblum and Wilson 1982; Durrett and Davy 1979; Hunsberger 1978; Morland 1969; Vaughan 1963), research on racial awareness involves Euro-American and African-American children's performances on tasks using only two racial categories: white and black. Almost by definition these categories turn on marked differences in appearance. However, many systems of racial thinking involve much more subtle and graded differences in appearance. By working in France, where blacks, North Africans, and Asians are numerous, I was able to explore the processes underlying racial awareness in a considerably more complex environment.

Study 6.1: Appearances and Memory for Narrative

Sixty-four 3- and 4-year-old French preschoolers were read a simple four-episode story in which a young protagonist (male or female, corresponding to the sex of the child being tested) is faced with a problem he or she is trying to resolve. Each of the story's four episodes begins with a solicitation in which the child asks for help from an adult. Each adult reacts differently. The first and third encounters are neutral. The second episode is disagreeable: the adult yells at the child. The final episode is agreeable: the adult warmly provides the needed assistance. Each adult character is described twice in terms of race, occupation, and a nonracial physical feature (body type or age).[6] (The complete story, in French and in English, is reproduced in the appendix.) Importantly, the characters' social descriptions are irrelevant to the story's plot and structure. Thus, any variation in rate of recall is attributable to the relative importance of the social descriptions themselves, not to their role in the story. Children were read the test story and immediately afterward were asked to freely recall it. Immediately after this recall, the experimenter reread the story to the subject and again asked for free recall.[7] The assignment of characters to the four episodes was counterbalanced.

6. The race of one adult (the young saleswoman at the newsstand) was not mentioned. In view of the pragmatics of talk about race, this implies that she is a member of the majority racial or ethnic group (in this case, white). Explicitly mentioning her race by describing her, for example, as "the young, white saleswoman at the newsstand" would have violated conventions of everyday speech, possibly biasing recall (Bigler and Liben 1985).

In order to assess memory for social information, I computed how often children in their retellings of the story mentioned each character's race, occupation, nonracial physical feature, gender, and behavior. The gender measure was not meant to capture merely whether the character's gender was mentioned; that information is implicit in virtually any use of a pronoun to refer to the character. Rather, I was interested in knowing how frequently children recalled the character *only* in terms of gender. Therefore, gender was scored when the child referred to a character as either "le monsieur" or "la madame" without further detail. Clearly this underestimates how often the child recalled a character's gender. Behavior in the scoring system I used encompassed only behavioral evidence of a character's state of mind, such as smiling, raising one's voice, or offering assistance.

Two recall scores were computed. The first was based on the number of times the social description appeared in the story. It was computed by dividing the number of times the descriptive label was recalled by the number of times the label was mentioned in the original story. For example, a child who mentioned occupation three times received an occupation score of 0.375, because occupation was mentioned eight times in the story. In contrast, the second scoring method was based on how many of the characters the child recalled. It was thus sensitive to how well the child recalled the story as a whole. Here recall was calculated by dividing the number of times each child mentioned each social description by the total number of characters that child actually remembered. Thus, a child who mentioned occupation three times but recalled only three characters received an occupation score of 0.5, because the occupation of those characters was mentioned six times.

We calculated this second recall measure because two children, each using quite different strategies to store and recall social information, might have the same score on the first measure. For example, one child

7. The use of two readings and two recalls was unusual but not unprecedented. Earlier work on narrative comprehension (Denhière 1984, 1988; Denhière and Le Ny 1980) suggests that a second test and a second recall significantly enhances performance. Denhière (1984) found that younger children's performance on a second reading and recall test was comparable to older children's performances on a first reading and recall test. This led him to argue that differences between younger and older children's performances are attributable to differential access to information stored in memory rather than to distinct, age-related strategies for encoding story information. Although my concern is with differential rates of recall of social information that are not relevant to categories of story grammar, this methodology is useful. From previous studies I expected to find developmental differences in the first recalls of older and younger subjects. To provide a more sensitive measure of younger children's competence, and to ensure that differences between younger and older children's performances could be attributed to differential salience of each social description rather than differences in retrieval acuity, a second test and a second recall were used.

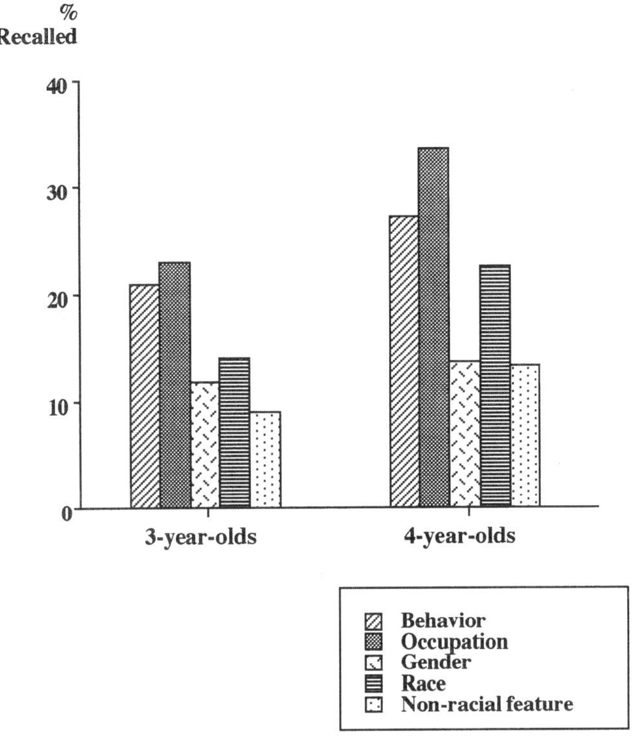

Figure 6.1
Percentage of times each social dimension was recalled after verbal narrative, computed by first method. Scores are averaged across first and second recalls.

might remember only two of the story's characters but recall the race of each of those two. Another child might recall all four characters but mention the race of only half of them. As computed on the first method, both children would receive the same score. The analysis would accordingly be insensitive to the *prima facie* greater salience race has for the hypothetical first child. The second method provides a measure sensitive to the overall performance of each child.

Results

The main findings obtained by the first method are summarized in figure 6.1. Each of the social descriptions was distinctly memorable: children were more likely to recall descriptions of an individual's behavior and occupation than the individual's gender, nonracial physical feature, or race. Older subjects recalled more descriptive labels than younger subjects. Younger subjects were more likely to recall a charac-

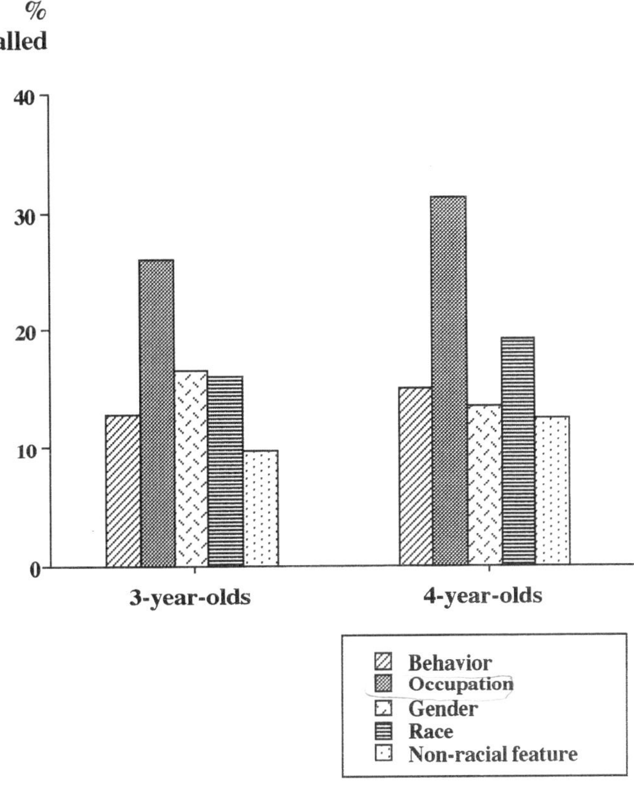

Figure 6.2
Percentage of times each social dimension was recalled after verbal narrative, computed by second method. (Scores take into account number of story characters recalled and are averaged across first and second recalls.)

ter's occupation and behavior (which were not significantly different from each other) than they were to recall their race, gender, or nonracial physical feature (which were also not significantly different). Older subjects were more likely to recall occupation than race, and they were more likely to recall race than gender or nonracial physical feature. The results obtained by the second method are summarized in figure 6.2. In the main they were very close to those obtained by the first method. Children recalled occupation more often than race, gender, behavior, or nonracial physical feature. In contrast to the results of the first analysis, there were no age-related differences in recall; this suggests that the developmental trend revealed in the initial analysis may be attributable to increases in the number of story elements recalled by older children rather than to changes in the salience of the various social dimensions.

Clearly, as my alternative model predicts, not all types of social description are equally memorable. There are unresolved issues, however. The study tells us little as to whether information about surface cues is integral to all social categories, since it relies on a verbal task to assess the salience of visual information. Perhaps there is a mode effect underlying distinct memorability of the various social descriptions. To rule this out, study 6.2 used visual stimuli and verbal labels. If the conceptual saliency of racial categories is influenced by the sheer availability of physical exemplars, then performance levels in this second study should exceed those in study 6.1. Another methodological issue might explain the differences in performance of children in this study and previous studies. Earlier studies indicating that race is a particularly salient social dimension did not rely on recall in assessing children's knowledge. Perhaps my results do not accord with previous findings simply because of memory factors. To rule out this possibility, in study 6.2 children's social descriptions are collected under two conditions, one which is memory-based (children describe from memory the characters they had just seen, as in study 6.1) and one that involves direct identification (children describe the story's characters with the pictures still in front of them). Finally, it could be argued that some of the findings of study 6.1 are attributable to factors of linguistic form. In the story used in the study, each character's occupation is the head noun of a descriptive phrase (e.g., "le grand facteur noir" and "la grosse épicière chinoise"). Occupation might be more readily recalled than either race or nonracial physical feature because the word used to describe it is a noun, not an adjective. This interpretation is can be rejected if the pattern of recall in study 6.2 is similar to that found in study 6.1, since the narrative in study 6.2 is visual rather than verbal.

Study 6.2: Verbal Descriptions from Visual Narratives

Thirty-two 3- and 4-year-olds from the same French public preschool participated in the second study. In addition to the main narrative task, the children were given an additional set of labeling and sorting tasks. I will describe these and report the results before turning to the main study.

The labeling and sorting tasks had two goals. The labeling task functioned as a priming condition for the narrative recall and identification task (described in greater detail below). In this task children were shown six color-wash line drawings depicting several common blue-collar and service occupations and several races. Children were asked two sets of questions. First they were asked if they could find any blacks, North Africans, Chinese, or whites among the people portrayed in the first six drawings. Next they were asked if they could identify which drawing depicted each of the occupations. The sorting tasks (actually match-to-sample tasks) were included in order to resolve whether occupation's greater salience in study 6.1 is ultimately attributable to conceptual or to perceptual factors. If occupation generally demands more perceptual attention than race, then children might preferentially sort by occupation even on a verbal task because the physical correlates of the category are brought to mind when the label is used. If race demands more perceptual attention than occupation, then the use of the verbal labels for race should prompt the children to sort preferentially by race. If both are equally perceptually salient, then children should show no preference.

In order to test whether one category demands more perceptual attention than the other, each child was presented with three triads made up from four drawings depicting a black male physician, a female physician, a black female nurse, and a male in a business suit. Each triad consisted of a target picture and two comparison pictures. The first triad, pitting race against occupation, consisted of the black male physician as target matched with the black female nurse and a white female physician. The second triad, pitting gender against race, consisted of the black female nurse as target matched with the black male physician and the white female physician. The third triad consisted of the white female physician as target matched with the black male physician and the black female nurse; here gender was pitted against occupation. As each child was presented with each triad, he or she was asked to put the target drawing with the comparison picture to which it was most similar.

Labeling and Sorting Results

As expected from previous studies, in the labeling task children in both age groups correctly paired occupational and racial labels with the appropriate drawings. The results of the match-to-sample sorting task were striking. In contrast to the pattern of results found in studies 4.1 and 6.1, children on the match-to-sample (or sorting) task were as likely to sort by race as by occupation or gender.

Narrative Tasks

In the main task, children were presented with a complex narrative and asked about the social information they extracted from it. As in the first narrative study, conceptual salience is construed in terms of the relative availability of social dimensions such as occupation, gender, and behavior in children's descriptions of and memory for a short narrative. In this case the narrative is visual, not verbal. The narrative study comprised a visual narrative identification task and a visual narrative recall

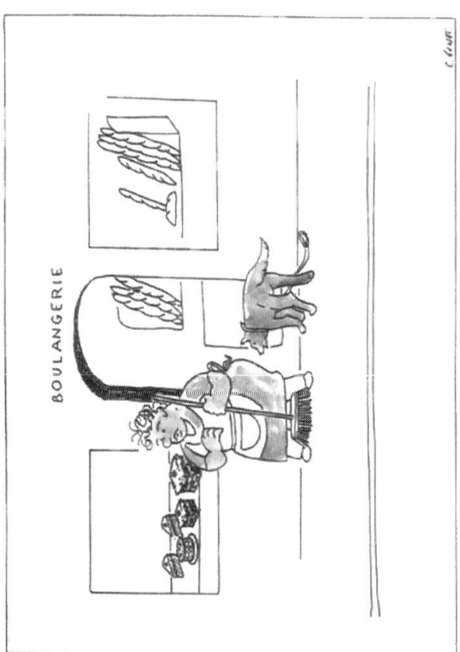

Figure 6.3
Example of drawings used in visual narrative study.

task. Children were presented with a visual narrative similar to the verbal narrative used in study 6.1. Following Poulsen et al. (1979), two sets of responses were recorded. In the first, subjects were asked to describe the events portrayed in a storybook while viewing it. In the second set, the same children were probed about their memories of the story.

Each child was shown a storybook with 14 full-page color-wash line drawings. Unlike the format of a traditional comic or other picture book, in our storybook each of the drawings was doubled so that a new story frame was always introduced on a recto page and each verso page reproduced the frame that had been on the preceding recto page. This design ensured that subjects were always presented with a sequence of two scenes at a time, thus underscoring the narrative momentum of the text. (Black-and-white examples of one sequence are reproduced in figure 6.3.) The plot line parallels that of the verbal narrative used in study 6.1. In the picture narrative the protagonist is a dog separated from his master, a little boy. In trying to rejoin the little boy, the dog encounters four adults in succession: a tall black policeman (male), a plump white baker (female), a bald Chinese waiter (male), and an old North African fruit seller (female). As in the verbal narrative in study 6.1, the first and third encounters are neutral, the second disagreeable, and the fourth agreeable. The story ends with the boy and the dog reunited. Each adult character figures in two action sequences, so that each adult is depicted in four frames.

Children were presented with the narrative task and the labeling/sorting tasks in one of two orders. Half the subjects were in a primed condition and participated in the labeling and match-to-sample tasks before being presented with the narrative task. The other half were unprimed and given the narrative task first. The narrative task itself had two parts, one involving identification and the other recall. In the identification task the experimenter guided the child to "read" through the storybook, at each page soliciting descriptions of what was taking place and regularly prompting for more detail. In the recall task, the experimenter put the book away and asked the child to remember the first person encountered by the lost dog. The experimenter then asked the subject to describe that person. After the child answered, the experimenter asked "What else was the person like?" If the subject offered a description, the experimenter solicited further detail. This procedure was repeated for all four characters. As with the verbal task, the picture task was conducted twice.

Narrative identification task The number of times each child described each adult character's gender, occupation, race, and nonracial physical feature was recorded. As in the first method used in study 6.1, a percentage score was then computed by dividing the number of times

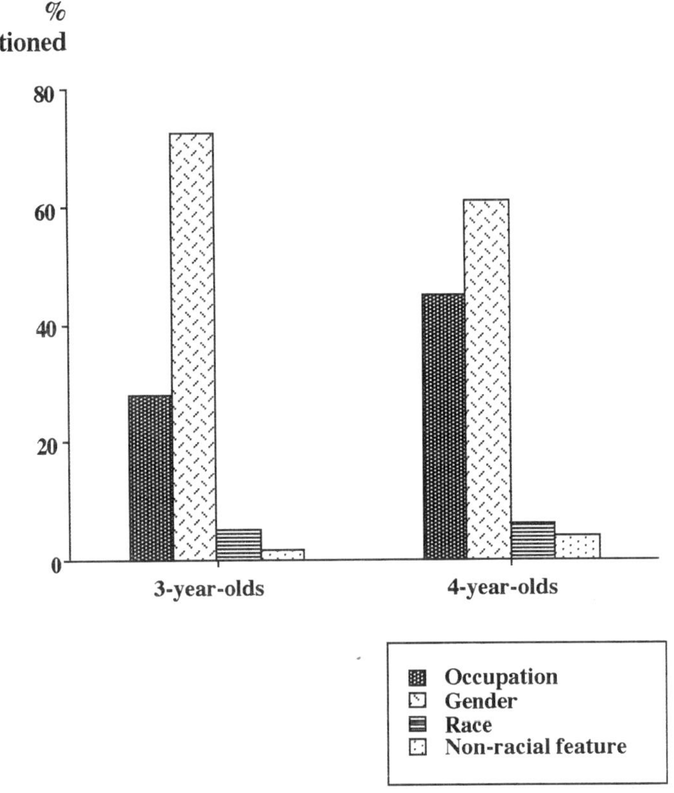

Figure 6.4
Percentage of times each social dimension was mentioned with visual narrative in view. (Scores are averaged across first and second readings.)

the description was mentioned by the child by the number of frames containing that description in the storybook. For example, all the characters had their occupations depicted in the storybook, so there were eight possible descriptions of occupation. Thus, a child who mentioned occupation twice received an occupation index of 0.25. In contrast, race was depicted in only six frames since we did not expect children to consider the white character's race salient in their descriptions. Thus, a child who mentioned race twice received a race index of 0.33.

As can be seen from figure 6.4, the main findings closely follow those from study 6.1. Each type of social category was distinctly salient, with gender mentioned significantly more often than occupation, which in turn was mentioned significantly more often than race and nonracial physical feature. As in the second analysis in study 6.1, children in both age groups performed in much the same manner. However, one striking difference from study 6.1 did emerge: looking at the picture book provoked almost no mention of race and a great many mentions of gender. One interpretation is that perceptual information is so closely tied to category representation of gender, but not race, that a visual mode of presentation prompts many more mentions of that dimension than a verbal one.[8]

Perhaps the most striking result of the narrative task is that no effect of priming was evident. Participation in a task that required children to put racial labels together with pictures of their referents had virtually no effect on visual identification. Pairing verbal labels with depictions of their referents (pairing tasks) did not facilitate retrieval of the labels when the child encountered similar representations of the same referent in an identification task. For example, pairing the picture of a North African man with the label "North African" did not increase the likelihood that subjects would subsequently refer to a picture of a North African man with the term "North African." This finding deserves comment.

Several studies indicate that preschool children can readily match social category labels with pictorial exemplars (Aboud 1988; Pope Edwards 1984; Blaske 1984; Lerner 1973). Clearly these studies provide evidence that some perceptual information is associated with the verbal category. However, contrary to the way these results are usually interpreted, these studies do not specify the scope of that association. The amount of perceptual information associated with verbal categories can vary considerably. The perceptual information associated with a verbal

8. There is a second possible interpretation of these results. I have proposed that racial categories are not (at first) perceptually rich and that, hence, visual depictions of race would not elicit descriptions in terms of racial labels. The results are consistent with this view. The findings are also consistent with the claim that race is so obvious that children would not think to describe the pictured individuals in terms of it. I am skeptical of this interpretation for two reasons. First, gender is a conspicuous feature of a person's identity and an obvious way to describe people, yet this did not lead to a dispreference for gender descriptions on the task. In fact, just the contrary: as figure 6.4 shows, gender is the most common social description used. More important, if race is too obvious to mention, we would expect race to be an especially memorable aspect of an individual's identity. Yet subsequent questioning revealed that children were not particularly accurate at recalling whether the various ethnic groups had been depicted in the picture story. After the probed recall task, children were asked whether there had been any whites in the story, then any Chinese, then any North Africans, then any blacks. Their recall was generally poor: 53% of the children correctly recalled a white, 37.5% a Chinese, 16.6% a North African, and 46.9% a black. If race is such an obvious feature that children do not find it worth mentioning, it is not clear why recall for the mere presence of racial information in the story was so poor.

category might be relatively fragmentary. You might, for example, recognize a representation of the label's referent only if your attention is directed toward a relevant domain of variation. Additionally, familiarity with the word might matter. If I say "armadillo" you might not be able to build a detailed mental image of the creature, although you might nonetheless easily recognize a specimen from a photograph.

These possibilities can be rephrased in terms of the relationship between exposure to a perceptual cue and retrieval of a verbal label. In the case of racial categories, recognizing that the verbal label and the perceptual cue go together could imply either (i) that the perceptual information is directly represented in the racial concept (such that observing the perceptual cue brings to mind a specific verbal label), (ii) that the perceptual information is contained in the racial concept, although in a less direct way, such that the perceptual cue brings to mind the specific verbal label only under certain conditions, or (iii) that only the fact that perceptual information is important (rather than any specific perceptual information *per se*) is represented in the racial concept. Hence, observing the perceptual cues brings to mind the verbal label only when attention is drawn to a relevant and present perceptual contrast *and* the verbal label is provided.

If the verbal label is directly brought to mind by the perceptual cue, we would expect the results of study 6.2 to parallel or exceed those of study 6.1. That is, race should be at least moderately salient in social description on both tasks. Clearly this was not the case. Race was considerably less salient on the visual task. If the label is brought to mind by the perceptual cues only when the child's attention is specifically directed toward the relationship of the label and its referent, then we would expect that the results of study 6.2 would parallel those of study 6.1 in the priming condition. They did not. Finally, if the verbal label and the perceptual cues are associated only if the two are immediately conjoined *and* attention is drawn to the contrast, then priming should have no necessary effect and performance on the two tasks should not be related. This is the pattern obtained, providing strong support for the claim that the relationship between the verbal category and a specific range of visual cues is not as close as previous researchers imagined.

Recall task The proportion of times that children recalled each character's gender, occupation, race, nonracial physical feature, activity, and clothing was computed. As in study 6.1, the recall measure was calculated by dividing the number of times each child mentioned a particular type of description by the total number of times he or she offered a description. As figure 6.5 shows, children's memories for the various

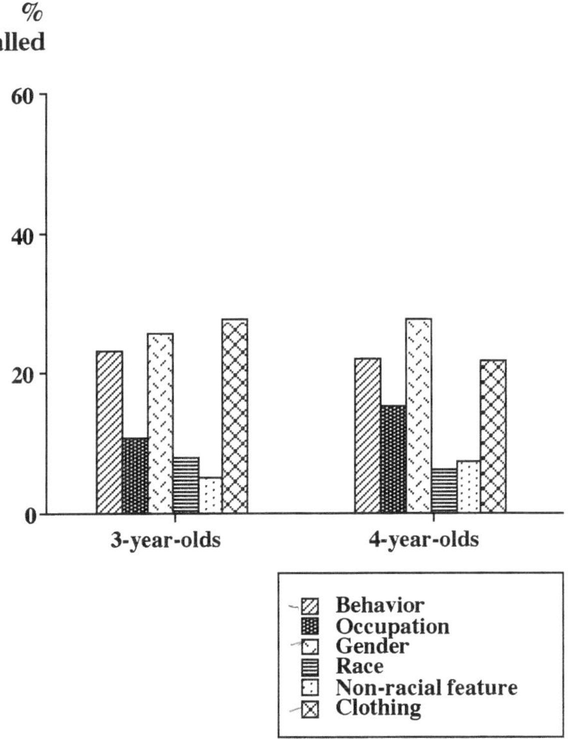

Figure 6.5
Percentage of times each social dimension was recalled after visual narrative. (Scores are averaged across first and second recalls.)

social descriptions varied. Recall of gender, clothing, and behavior were not different from one another but were significantly higher than the rates of recall of occupation, race, and nonracial physical feature, which were also not different from each other. As in the identification task, priming was found to have no effect. Several aspects of these findings are of interest. First, patterns of visual narrative identification and recall correspond closely; both tasks revealed an absence of developmental differences, very low levels of mention of race and nonracial physical features, and no effect of priming. Finally, these results suggest that discrepancies between my findings and those of previous research cannot be attributed to memory factors (since results of memory-based and non-memory-based tasks closely converge). Rather, they appear to be due to the embedding of social-judgment tasks in the sorts of complex contexts children encounter in daily life.

Conclusion

I began this chapter by wondering whether children learn racial categories by discerning patterns of discontinuity in human morphology, as others have argued, or whether they acquire racial categories by speculating over the kinds of people there are in the world. The studies I discussed in this chapter cast strong doubt on the widespread view that simple surface cues are a fundamental component of young children's racial categories. By extension these data cast doubt on the claim that such surface cues are the building blocks on which children rely when constructing racial categories. Children recalled considerably more about a character's race after listening to a complex verbal narrative than after viewing a complex visual one. In contrast, the visual narrative led to identification and recall of other kinds of social information, particularly gender, in greater detail than did the verbal text, suggesting that variations in memory derive from the distinct conceptual formats in which information about various social categories is stored. Strikingly, even when the link between the racial label and its visual referent was pointed out immediately before viewing of the picture-book narrative, children's use of racial labels was almost nonexistent. Finally, I found that embedding judgments in a social context significantly decreased the salience of race as a factor in classifying people. Children recalled considerably less information about race than about occupation or behavior. Perhaps as remarkable, these results contrast with the widely documented finding that racial awareness undergoes marked development during the late preschool years. Once memory factors were controlled for, I found no evidence of fundamental conceptual change.

Rather, as I suggested at the beginning of this chapter, much of the developmental change previous researchers have described is better explained as an alignment of initially relatively distinct verbal and visual categories. Young children readily differentiate people on the basis of racially relevant perceptual cues. Preschoolers also have racial categories: they recognize the existence of named, enduring groups of humans. Virtually all previous work on racial concepts has assumed that these two phenomena constitute a single system. I argue that they represent two distinct but overlapping conceptualizations. The systems cohere in two ways. First, racial concepts contain some perceptual information, but it is extremely fragmentary, specifying only that certain kinds of perceptual differences are pertinent to group membership (young children probably realize that skin tone is a pertinent dimension whereas finger length is not).[9] Young children are adept at

9. It is important not to overstate consistency among *adults* in knowledge of how perceptual cues and ethnic categories go together. Even if there are high levels of agreement

matching racial labels to individuals differing on relevant dimensions, but only when label and referent are made available simultaneously.

This position may at first blush seem paradoxical in view of the studies described in chapter 5. Recall that in those studies I relied on children's sortings of *pictures* to make inferences about their reasoning. If perceptual information is largely irrelevant to young children's racial categories, how appropriate is it to assess their conceptual knowledge through judgments about visual representations? Keep in mind, however, that my argument is not that perceptual input is irrelevant to emerging racial categories. Rather, I propose that, in building racial categories, obvious surface cues like skin color are not *defining* for young children. Perceptual cues are not extraneous to racial concepts; they simply (and grossly) underdetermine them. Young children's racial categories initially derive *less* from visual than from verbal (i.e., discursive) information. Though this means that such categories contain little perceptual but a great deal of conceptual (i.e., ontological and causal) knowledge, it does not imply that visual information is not represented. We see this in the differing features that children attend to relative to adults. For adults, skin color is a crucial diagnostic of race. The same does not appear to be the case for children. For example, although preschoolers find skin color to be one of the easiest racially relevant perceptual features on which to discriminate people, it is not the most salient perceptual cue in racial recognition (Sorce 1979; cf. Holmes 1995). Like the anecdotes that I related earlier in this chapter, the justifications children provided in the switched-at-birth studies discussed in chapter 4 lend support to the same conclusion. In explaining their "nature" choices, a substantial proportion of subjects (22%) cited the fact that parents and child have the same hair color. Thus, even though children at this age may be more concerned with elaborating a racial ontology than with specifying the physical features diagnostic of that system, they understand that some physical dimensions are racially relevant and others are not. This is the knowledge on which the tasks reported here are based.

If the learning of ethnic and racial labels is not directly conditioned on surface cues for color and the like, another empirical paradox in the literature on racial attitudes dissolves. As I mentioned in chapter 4, there is a marked lack of relationship between children's racial attitudes and the behaviors that we might expect these attitudes to warrant. Young children display strident racial prejudice, as measured on

---

among adults about what identifies an individual as black (which there is not), there is great disagreement as to what makes someone white. Waters (1990) found that most whites are not very clear about how ethnicity is linked to appearance. Many of her respondents, for instance, gave quite different physical descriptions of the same ethnic group.

a variety of experimental tasks. Yet generally race is a poor predictor of preschoolers' interactions, specifically playmate choice. It might be that young children's preferences simply do not influence their behavior. This is not unreasonable—we know that for adults attitudes are often poor predictors of behavior (Fiske and Taylor 1991). Nonetheless, if we consider *classes* of attitudes and their relationship to behavior, we can expect consistent patterns of enactment. Indeed, young children's attitudes about gender and body type appear to directly condition their everyday behavior (Lerner 1973; Fagot et al. 1986). Similarly, whereas race is a weak predictor of playmate choice, gender is a strong predictor (McCandless and Hoyt 1961). If attitude does not predict behavior, it is not obvious why two such similar concepts should have such different patterns of enactment.

I propose that the lack of correspondence between racial attitude and behavior can be traced to a quite simple cause: young children's racial beliefs are *unable* to influence their behavior in a systematic way. Young children's representations of racial categories are not rich with perceptual information (and therefore directly associated with specific differences in appearance). As a result, preschoolers are unable to translate their dispreferences for members of minority groups into behavior for the simple reason that they do not know exactly which individuals are members of the minority groups they don't like. In short, young children have little difficulty expressing racial prejudice once given the opportunity to do so in the experimental context, but they have considerable difficulty instantiating racial categories.

The results of the present studies also allow us to speculate on why race and occupation have distinct patterns of saliency for young children. Social descriptions are instrumental in that they permit the child to pick out relevant aspects of actors and actions. That is, they help render events meaningful. Presumably this accounts for the heightened saliency of behaviors in children's descriptions. As we saw in study 6.1, this is true even for behaviors that are (on the experimenter's account) not relevant to the unfolding stream of events. Occupation may be particularly salient in recall because occupations represent recurring and purposeful behaviors (policemen protect people, doctors cure them when they are ill, postmen deliver the mail, etc.) and are thus meaningful to the interpretation of events. In contrast, the race concept performs a quite different job—one whose contribution to understanding may be less directly evident, and thus one whose salience may be attenuated relative to other social constructs. Race is part of the child's expanding social ontology; it is an early step in cataloguing and discovering the relevance of human groups. Moreover, the fact that young children appear more concerned with developing a conceptual vocabulary for racial variation than with developing a catalogue of physical differences suggests that this impulse to find racial types involves the construction of global concepts rather than the differentiation of specific ones (Mandler et al. 1991; Hirschfeld 1988). As I have repeatedly stressed, on the folk model races are not simply groups of individuals, they are *kinds* of people. Also, being a member of a particular race means sharing certain intrinsic, physical properties with other members of one's race. And it means that one shares a common language with other members of one's race, lives in the same kind of dwelling, and wears the same kind of distinct clothes. Shared membership in any number of other social categories captures none of these commonalities.

Together these findings suggest that a single learning strategy, dominated by attention to appearances, does not operate over the development of all social categories, even those that have marked physical correlates. Rather, young children's early representations of racial and other social categories seem to be guided by expectations about the relations between category members and the kinds of data relevant to these relations. Occupational and other behavioral categories are integral to finding meaning in everyday experience; racial and gender categories are integral to finding the sorts of things there are in everyday social experience. Social categories, like natural ones, have this inductive richness because social categories are products of domain-specific devices, not because they are inferences from superficial differences. Children do not find races because they are there to be found; they find races because they are following an impulse to categorize the sorts of things there are in the social world. As I observed in chapter 2, social theorists have increasingly concluded that racial categories are historically constructed and relatively independent of the regularities in physiognomy adults often associate with them. It is intriguing that most 3-year-olds seem to recognize this too.

Chapter 7

The Cultural Biology of Race[1]

What roles do the cultural and political environments play in the formation of racial categories? Most people, I suspect, presume that the environment makes a crucial contribution. However, as in the case of the question I began chapter 4 with ("Do children have a theory of race?"), there is surprisingly little direct research on the topic. In my empirical studies I have focused almost all the attention on what the child brings to racial-category formation and left the issue of cultural and political influences largely to the side. In my theoretical formulation, however, I have made it clear that the environment is crucial.

In this chapter I explore how, when, and in what ways cultural systems of belief make contact with an endogenous strategy for making knowledge of human kinds. In doing so, I hope to show how, when, and in what ways a specific system of racial thinking emerges from racial theory. Racial thinking, of course, provides a rich set of comparative possibilities in which to undertake this sort of exploration. Even if there is a core set of underlying principles, systems of racial thinking vary considerably across cultures and across the individual's life span. One way to assess how these principles engage and are elaborated within specific cultural traditions is to see how and when culturally novel strategies for reasoning about things racial emerge in the child's mind. Although bearers of most systems of thought imagine them to be natural and uncontrived, it is evident that culturally unique aspects of virtually any system can readily be isolated. One such aspect of the North American system turns on the strategy most Americans use to reason about the inheritance of racial features and identity. The goal of this chapter is to sketch how that peculiar reasoning strategy emerges.

Race, Biology, and Society

Race, as we have seen, is a complex concept. Race is a folk category of biology, supposedly discriminating humans in terms of their biological

1. This chapter draws heavily on material presented in Hirschfeld 1995c.

heritage. It is also a folk category of power, discriminating groups in terms of their social status. The relationship between these two dimensions may well be contingent. As I noted in chapter 2, it has been argued that the concept of race historically derived from a concern about social rather than biological differences (Fredrickson 1988; Jordan 1968). Alternatively, it has been suggested that race became biologized as part of an effort to rationalize and legitimize those social differences (Fields 1982; Guillaumin 1980). As we have also seen, the biological interpretation additionally encompasses two more or less independent aspects. Racial thinking includes beliefs about patterned variation in inborn visible traits as well as expectations about an underlying and nonobvious essence shared by members of each race.

The notion of essence, of course, does not conflict with a physical or a material interpretation so much as shift the focus from perceptible and external qualities to nonobvious and internal ones. In North America, the essentialist construal of race is given a vague physical interpretation through the symbolic medium of "blood."[2] This notion serves to quantify and give concrete content to category status in terms of the amount a person possesses of each race's "blood" (i.e., its nonobvious but material racial substance). This notion is important for several reasons. First, it literally gives (i.e., attributes) substance to a vague perception of commonality. Second, and perhaps more important, it allows for the systematic classification of individuals whose racial history is complex. Not everyone conforms to his or her race's physical, behavioral, mental, and temperamental "prototype." One explanation for this is hybridity: although some (perhaps most) individuals have "pure blood," a significant portion of the population, in virtue of ancestral mixing between socially defined races, has "mixed blood."

We can gain a sense of how pertinent this issue is by examining, if only briefly, the anxiety that has historically accompanied various ways of resolving the question of "mixed-race" individuals in North America.[3]

2. For a detailed account of the American folk notion of "blood," see Schneider 1968. The notion of blood embedded in American commonsense beliefs about kinship and race—the idea that members of the same race or close relatives share a natural commonality described in the idiom of blood—is symbolic in the sense that it does *not* entail the belief that shared racial (or kin) essence is literally embodied in the circulatory system generally or in blood specifically.

3. I have used scare quotes around the phrases "mixed race" and "pure blood" to emphasize that these are biologically incoherent notions. Since various markers of race do not correlate, whether these markers involve physical features such as skin color and skull shape or less obvious ones such as ABO blood types, there is little possibility of determining what the standards of mixed and pure might be. Furthermore, as already noted, interbreeding across socially defined racial categories is more the norm than an exception. What is at issue with the notions of pure and mixed blood are folk (including legal) algorithms for resolving questions of hybridity.

As was noted in chapter 2, Jordan (1968) and Morgan (1975) point out that during the early colonial period racial hybrids were conceptually recognized as mulattoes but were not categorically recognized as belonging to an intermediate class. This is essentially the same system of classification used in North America today; racial mixing is not thought to produce a new category of racial hybrids.[4] Under this system of classification children of mixed racial origin are treated as belonging to one or another, but not both, of their parents' races.

Still, it would be a mistake to believe that this represents a continuation of a single policy from colonial to present times. For a considerable time, at least in parts of the lower South, an intermediate mulatto category was recognized, both socially (in terms of its nonslave status) and biologically (in terms of its supposedly intermediate physical status) (Starr 1987). However, as the Abolitionist movement gained force, anxieties emerged about the danger posed by an intermediate category bridging slave and freeperson. In the 1850s a new system of racial classification began to take hold: "The lower South gave up its peculiar sympathy with mulattoes and joined an upper South already in place. Miscegenation was wrong and mulattoes must be made black, both within slavery and without. There was no middle ground in the organic society, no place for one who was neither white nor black." (Williams 1980, p. 74)

The "the one drop of blood rule" was the strategy used to efface this intermediate status. According to that rule, a person is black if he or she has a traceable amount of black ancestry (Williams 1980; Davis 1991; Wright 1994). Exactly what is meant by "a traceable amount of black ancestry" varies with the culture, with the historical epoch, and—as we will see—with the age of the person doing the classifying. In some parts of the United States, including Louisiana (under a law that was upheld as recently as 1986), a person is classified as black no matter how he looks if one of his great-grandparents was classified as black (Domínguez 1986). In other states, a person has to have a much closer black relative in order to be classified as black.

Historically, the one-drop rule was part of a racist ideology that "explained" (in quasi-biological terms) how putative inbred proclivities, temperaments, and capacities mapped onto racial categories. It clearly also allowed race to serve as a way of fixing and biologically

4. For example, there is no formal or commonsense category "mulatto" in the American system (Davis 1991). The Census Bureau, at the behest of the Office of Management and Budget, is conducting research toward deciding whether to include a multiracial category for the 2000 census. The question is fraught with difficulties, in large part because there is no reason to believe that "multiracial" represents an even remotely coherent category. (What does the child of a black-white union have in common with the child of an Asian-Hispanic one?)

justifying social and economic boundaries (Morgan 1975; Fredrickson 1988). Despite this racist heritage, the one-drop rule is no longer limited to marginal or extreme views of race. Many blacks, for example, now defend the one-drop rule as a means of maintaining the black heritage (Russell et al. 1992; Davis 1991). According to one report, the U.S. government has adopted a version of the one-drop strategy in allocating mixed-race individuals to racial categories. Molnar (1992) reports that if a child has one white and one black parent, the Census Bureau assumes that the child is black. A child who has two nonwhite parents (e.g., one black and one Asian) is assigned to the race of the father.[5]

For our purposes the one-drop rule is interesting precisely because it is culturally specific. Kessen (1993) reports that Haiti's former leader "Papa Doc" Duvalier once told an American reporter that 96% of the island's population was white. In response to the reporter's surprise, Duvalier explained that in Haiti they used the same procedure for counting whites that Americans use for counting blacks.[6] There are also more empirically grounded examples of one-drop rules that do not accord with the North American system—for example, according to Popenoe (1994) the Nigerian Moors consider the children of a white Arab father and a black slave mother to be white. More important, many systems of racial classification do not rely on a one-drop rule at all, assigning interracial individuals to a third, hybrid racial status rather than to either parent's category. Davis (1991) reviews a number of these systems, including the South African category "Coloured," the Mexican category "Mestizo," and the French Canadian category "Metis." (See also Williams 1980 on mulattoes in the lower South and Domínguez 1986 on creoles in Louisiana.)

Hybrid racial categories represent more than an increase in the number of recognized racial identities; they often signal a different conceptualization of race. Consider the phenomenon of "passing"—adopting a racial status different from the one that would be assigned on genealogical grounds. Passing, and anxieties about it, are a recurrent theme in North American racial lore. One's race cannot change over one's life span, and any activity that suggests that it has changed involves subterfuge. Yet in many systems of racial thought passing is not an issue precisely because one's race is not necessarily fixed at birth. In South Africa, Cuba, and Brazil, for example, a person's racial status can change. But in contrast with the American system, in which such changes are generally made in secret and predicated on ambiguous

5. However, a child with one Hawaiian and one non-Hawaiian parent is assigned to the race of the mother.

6. The story may be apocryphal (Fields 1982).

physical appearance, the criteria for racial change in these systems are not principally physical (Davis 1991). According to American common sense (and a good deal of scientific speculation), physical form supposedly drives racial categorization. But in other systems common sense also recognizes that racial categorization may drive (at least the perception of) physical form, as the Brazilian saying "money whitens" implies (Harris 1964). Similarly, in some racial systems members of the same family may be designated as belonging to different races, depending on their socio-economic status. Such a situation, under the American one-drop system, would essentially be inconceivable.

It is important to bear in mind that these varied strategies for classification entail not only that there are both social and biological interpretations of race, but that there are both social and biological interpretations of the one-drop rule. As a biological claim the one-drop rule disengages the formal identification of race from physically observable criteria by focusing attention on essences supposedly discoverable only through genealogical inspection. Thus, racist and other ideological interpretations, in virtue of presumptions about shared racial essence, involve expectations about the inheritance of physical or biological qualities and potentials. For example, one widely reported folk belief is that a family that has a small amount of black heritage but whose members are visibly white can subsequently have children with markedly black features (Frankenberg 1993; Davis 1991).

On the other hand, the one-drop rule involves expectations about category membership that are independent of any obvious appeal to biological grounding. Race is often less a biological (or even a visual) category than a socio-cultural one (Smedley 1993; Stoler 1992; Martinez-Alier 1989). There is no reason to assume, for example, that the U.S. Census Bureau's distinct strategies for classifying the offspring of black-white, black–other minority, and Hawaiian-white unions reflect the government's endorsement of diverse beliefs about the extent to which black, white, or Hawaiian "blood" is inherited. Instead, these strategies have to do with racial identity as a subordinate category identity (Wright 1994). The one-drop rule, in this regard, is an instance of a more general classificatory strategy (called *hypo-descent*) that assigns children to the status of the subordinate parental category (Harris 1964). Again, these remarks are related to the earlier observation that historically racial categories may have had more to do with questions of power and social status than perceptions of biological difference (Fredrickson 1988).

Children's Understanding of the Inheritability of Race

The wide range of variation in systems of racial thinking and the principles underlying them have developmental consequences. For one thing, we cannot say that the American adult endpoint is necessarily accurate. Systems of racial thinking are cultural constructions, not inductions from experience with biological variation. For another, coming to hold a causal view of race based on the one-drop rule (or on any other referencing algorithm) involves acquiring a set of cultural representations encompassing at least two issues. First, the child must come to understand that a single categorical domain has two interpretations—i.e., that some social categories refer to both social and biological relations. Second, the child must come to hold a specific form of essentialist reasoning in order to have the appropriate expectations about the inheritance of racial status. Thus, the essentialist construal of race by a child in Rio de Janeiro is plausibly quite different from the essentialist construal of race by a child in Detroit.

Social versus Biological Interpretation

When do children begin to appreciate that a category can have both social and biological interpretations? One way to pose this question is to ask how and when children's interpretations of identity relations and identity-relevant resemblances develop. The belief that identities are inherited entails beliefs about resemblance across generations, and in the past few years several studies have established that even preschoolers expect offspring to resemble their parents in a number of ways (Springer and Keil 1989, 1991; Springer 1992; Gelman and Wellman 1991; Hirschfeld 1995b; Carey and Spelke 1994; Solomon et al. 1995). There is considerable controversy about how best to interpret this finding. Springer (1992) and Gelman and Wellman (1991) argue that the child's appreciation of family likeness, like the adult's, is part of an understanding of biological processes. Carey and Spelke (1994) and Solomon et al. (1995) suggest that children's understanding of family likeness is governed by a naive psychology, not by folk biology. Judgments of family likeness, according to this account, arc based on the child's beliefs about the constitutive nature of the social rather than the biological environment. Resemblance between offspring and parent does not necessarily indicate a biological understanding; it may simply indicate knowledge about parents and children, which are as much social roles as biological relationships.

This debate presumes that children interpret resemblance *either* biologically *or* psychologically (i.e., socially). There is some question as to whether it always makes sense to distinguish distinct kinds of causation (i.e., biological versus social causality) as applying to a specific domain, since the category resemblances embedded in identity relations are at times both social and biological. To take a familiar example, self-identification and other-identification often involve appeal to kinship categories that implicate both genealogical and social relationships: a mother is both one who gave birth and one who is consistently nurturing and supportive. A reference to someone's "real mother" could mean either the woman who gave birth or the woman who did the raising. Accordingly, learning the meanings of kinship terms involves acquiring knowledge of both social and biological properties and the causal principles underlying their distribution (Hirschfeld 1986, 1989b). One possibility is that young children see the biological and social interpretations as applying under distinct conditions (Hirschfeld 1994, 1995a). A second is that they conceive of the two kinds of causation as indistinguishable. A third possibility is that children have specific strategies for integrating biological and social causation. For example, they may integrate social and biological understanding when they conceive of biological causes as being *mediated* by social relationships. I will argue that such an integration occurs in pre-adolescent children's understanding of racial identity.

Essentialism in Children's Reasoning about Race

In chapter 4 I presented evidence that children's beliefs about race not only cohere into a theory-like knowledge structure but also involve essentialist reasoning. Children use essentialist reasoning in that they expect racial identity to emerge out of a nonobvious and material substance. This sort of inferencing is found in other domains of preschoolers' cognition, especially in the representation of nonhuman living kinds. Gelman and Wellman (1991; cf. Solomon et al. 1995) propose that children believe that biological development is governed by an *innate potential* or an intrinsic essence that causes living things to mature in a specific way whatever their initial appearances or environmental influences. We can recast the finding of the switched-at-birth studies in chapter 4 as showing that preschoolers believe race to have innate potential in that children believe race to be part of an individual's biological makeup, to be fixed at birth, and to be impervious to social experience. Of course, both my findings in chapter 4 and Gelman and Wellman's findings involve inductions about unambiguous cases in which both parents are of the same race or animal species. More relevant to the present discussion is the question of how and when children acquire knowledge of the cultural algorithm for resolving a person's race or an animal's species identity in ambiguous cases. Unfortunately, there has been virtually no work on children's reasoning under these more complex circumstances.

A major goal of this chapter is to explore how children resolve cases of ambiguous racial identity, and in particular when North American children begin to resolve such cases in accord with the one-drop rule. A second goal is to examine the meaning they give to this resolution. For example, knowing that children sort in accord with the one-drop rule does not tell us whether they learn the rule as a biological principle or a categorical one. Similarly, knowing that some children eventually acquire a one-drop-like rule does not tell us whether all children in the same cultural environment will acquire it. One possibility is that the interpretation of the rule may not be evenly distributed in the population—in part because we do not know *a priori* what the boundaries of any cultural environment are. For instance, is adherence to the one-drop rule distributed with prejudice, or as a *response* to prejudice? Even though the one-drop rule is no longer limited to racist ideology, it is clearly associated with certain strains of prejudice—particularly under its biological interpretation.

To examine when children acquire the one-drop rule and to assess the meaning they give it, I conducted four studies of adults' and children's beliefs about the inheritance of racial identity. Study 7.1 looks at adults' and children's beliefs about racial-category membership and family resemblance by probing reasoning about the category identity of offspring of same-race and mixed-race couples and the degree to which a child resembles each parent. That study's principal goal is to assess the extent to which children's and adults' models of race converge. In study 7.2, adults and children are asked to infer what the children of same-color couples and those of mixed-color couples will look like. By comparing children's reasoning about a socially relevant property (skin color) and a socially irrelevant one (hair color), study 7.2 examines whether children's expectations of the inheritability of racial features are specifically about racial identity or whether they reflect a general strategy for reasoning about the inheritance of biological properties. Study 7.3 is a control on study 7.2, repeating the same tasks but using animal stimuli. Study 7.4 examines whether the patterns of reasoning uncovered in the first three studies are evenly distributed in the population and, if they are not, what dimensions are critical to their distribution. The first three studies explore expectations about racial identity among adults and children living in a predominantly white community and attending predominantly white schools. The fourth study looks at the same expectations among black children and white children living in a highly integrated community.

Study 7.1: Mixed Parentage, Category Membership, and Resemblance

Seventeen second graders and fifteen sixth graders attending a mostly white (5% black, 17% Asian-American) private school in a midwestern university community and 43 undergraduates in an introductory anthropology class at the University of Michigan participated. The basic design was straightforward. Both child and adult subjects were shown pictures of monoracial and interracial couples and asked questions about the race of each couple's child and the degree to which the child resembled each parent. Thus, each child and each adult was given one task involving category membership and one involving physical resemblance. For each task, subjects were presented with four picture sets. Each set consisted of a color drawing of a family consisting of a man, a woman, and an infant. The infant's face was obscured by a large green dot and its body was fully clothed, so no skin was visible. Four pairs of parents were portrayed: a white man and a white woman, a black man and a black woman, a white man and a black woman, and a black man and a white woman.

The procedure differed slightly depending on the age of the subject. I found in pretesting that many second graders were not familiar with the word "race." Hence, it was not possible simply to ask them, in the category- identity task, "What race is this couple's child?" One solution would have been to use the subordinate terms "black" and "white" rather than the superordinate term "race" in the question (i.e., "Is this couple's child black, or white?"). However, I did not want to use this question, since "black" and "white" are ambiguous with respect to race and color. Ultimately I decided to use novel "racial" terms. To make the introduction of novel terms for a familiar contrast more plausible, the second graders were told a story about an island on which two kinds of people lived: hibbles and glerks. They were shown a color drawing of a white family, who were labeled glerks, and a color drawing of a black family, who were labeled hibbles.

On the category-identity task, children were shown the target pictures and asked whether the couple's child was a hibble, a glerk, or something else. Sixth graders were presented with the same target pictures and asked what was the race of each couple's baby. In the resemblance task, all children were asked to rate resemblance between parent(s) and offspring on a five-point scale. To simplify the procedure, children were asked to make their judgments in two stages. In the first stage they were asked whether the baby resembled (i) the mother more than the father, (ii) the father more than the mother, or (iii) both parents equally. If the subject chose either (i) or (ii), he or she was then asked whether the baby looked "a lot like" that parent or "a little bit like" that parent. The orders in which choices were offered and tasks performed were counterbalanced. Whereas the children were tested individually, the adults were tested in groups of about 15 and given both tasks in written form.[7] In the resemblance task, adults were asked simply to rate the child's resemblance to its parents on a five-point scale, with 2 meaning "like the father" and –2 "like the mother."

7. To reduce desirability effects, adults were asked what they thought people generally believed, even if their own beliefs were different.

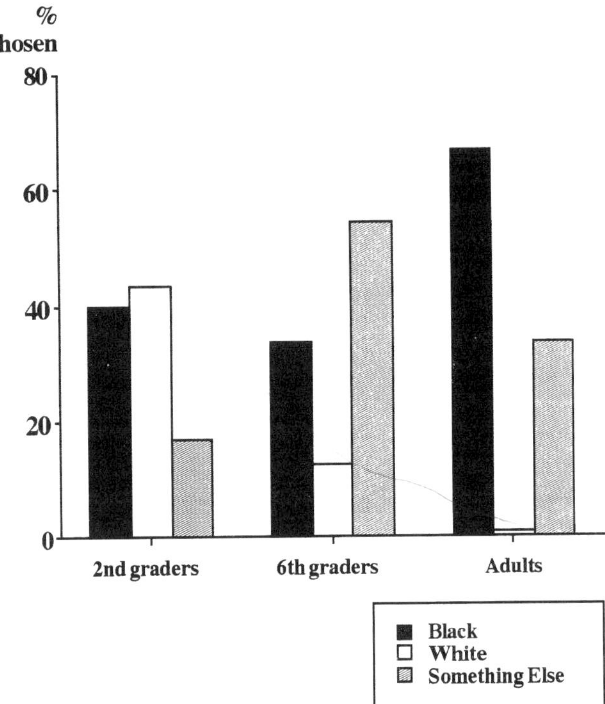

Figure 7.1
Mean percentage of times each category outcome was chosen in study of responses to mixed-race parents.

Results from Category-Identity Task
Not surprisingly, the overwhelming majority of children (90% of the second graders, 92.3% of the sixth graders) and all of the adults expected the white couple to have a white child and the black couple to have a black child. The adults' and the children's expectations about the mixed-race couples are the most interesting results. The main findings for the mixed-race couples, summarized in figure 7.1, are as follows:

Second graders showed no overall preference for white or black; however, they displayed a gender-of-parent bias, believing that a white mother–black father couple would have a white (glerk) baby and that a black mother–white father couple would have a black (hibble) baby.

Sixth graders were more likely than adults to infer that the infants would be categorically white.

Sixth graders were more likely than adults or second graders to believe that the interracial couple's infant would be something else, although the difference between sixth graders and adults was not significant.

Sixth graders thought the infant would be categorically white at a rate significantly below chance.

Adults were more likely than grade schoolers to infer that the interracial couple's infant was categorically black.

Adults said the child was black at a rate significantly above chance.

Adults' choice of "something else" was at chance. (The mixed outcome was apparently not a ready choice for most adults; of the six who referred to the child as mulatto, four misspelled the word).

On the resemblance task, most subjects regardless of age thought that a child of a same-race couple would look equally like both parents. The data for the mixed-race couples were analyzed to test for two kinds of predilection: a race bias (i.e., a tendency to infer that resemblance would be affected by the race of the parent) and a gender bias (i.e., a tendency to infer that resemblance would be affected by the gender of the parent). Subjects having a "black preference" (i.e., the expectation that the black parent contributes more to the child's physical appearance than the white parent) should have responded at a rate significantly above the scale's midpoint of zero. The responses of subjects having a "white preference" should fall reliably below the midpoint. If subjects' inferences were guided by a gender preference (for either the mother or the father), then a race-of-parent effect should emerge. Finally, if subjects believe that each parent—of whatever gender or race—contributed equally to the child's appearance, their responses should be close to the scale's midpoint. As figure 7.2 shows, the older children and the adults expected that children of mixed-race couples would resemble the black parent more than the white parent.

There is considerable historical and ethnographic evidence for the one-drop rule. This study provides the first experimental confirmation of this mark. It is important to keep in mind, however, the precise interpretation of the one-drop rule to which these data lend support. Historians and other comparative scholars have long argued that the one-drop rule is principally about *categorization*, even if it has a biological rationale. Indeed, in study 7.1 I found that adults expected an interracial couple's child to be categorically black. But I also found that adults endorsed the *biological* interpretation of the one-drop rule: they reliably expected the child of an interracial couple to resemble the black parent more than the white parent. In contrast, the grade-school children's pattern of belief is mixed. The judgments about racial-category identity by second graders and sixth graders do not accord with the one-drop rule. The second graders relied on a gender-of-parent strategy, but the sixth graders divided their choices largely between "something else" and

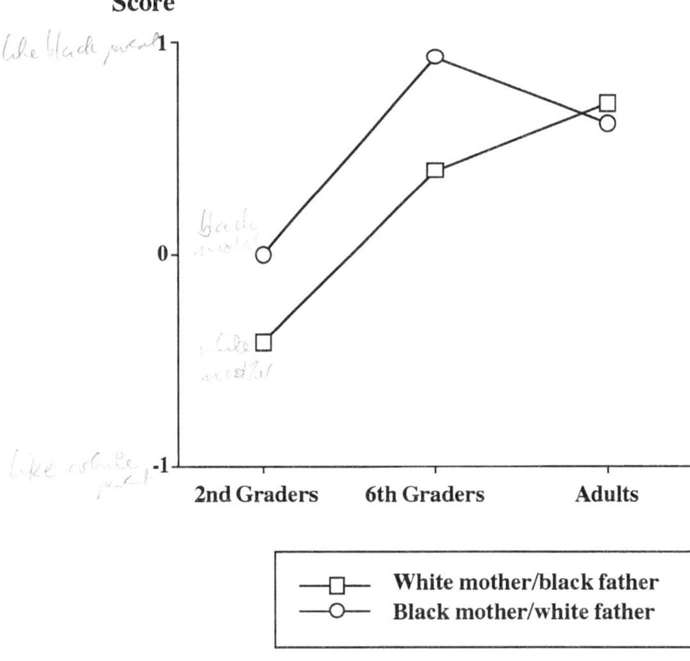

Figure 7.2
Mean scores for resemblance for each combination of mixed-race parents. (1 = closely resembles black parent, 0 = equally resembles both parents, –1 = closely resembles white parent.)

"black." On the other hand, in the resemblance task (a more direct assessment of biological beliefs, since it is a judgment of appearance rather than of category identity), the sixth graders, like the adults but unlike the second graders, reasoned in accord with the one-drop rule.

In summary: This study provides evidence for a developmental chronology in the emergence of the one-drop rule and evidence for a specific interpretation of the rule. Still, several issues are unresolved. Both older children and adults provide evidence of a physicalist interpretation of the one-drop rule, in that they believe that a mixed-race child will resemble the black parent more than the white parent. But we do not know whether these resemblance judgments are specifically about *racial* resemblance. Subjects in study 7.1 were asked to rate how closely children would resemble their parents, not how closely they would *racially* resemble them. It is possible that the subjects had in mind some other dimension of physical resemblance.

The results also do not allow us to determine whether beliefs about the inheritance of racial properties might differ from beliefs about the inheritance of nonracial properties. Race may be seen as one biological property among many. This interpretation would seem to follow from the corpus of social-psychological work on race, which makes much the same claim. Inheritance of racial properties would accordingly be governed by the processes that govern the inheritance of any and all biological properties. Alternatively, race may be conceptualized as a special property that is naturalized and controlled by biological mechanisms but not in the same way as other similar biological properties among humans and not in the same way as parallel biological properties in other species. Study 7.2 was undertaken to examine both questions directly.

Study 7.2: The Inheritance of Racial and Nonracial Features

Nineteen second graders, 17 sixth graders, and 18 adults participated in the study. The adults were given a questionnaire version of the first half of the test. The children were shown two picture sets. The first set contained the four color drawings used in study 7.1 (depicting monoracial and interracial couples) and three comparison drawings, also in color. Each comparison picture portrayed an infant from the neck up: one black, one white, and one whose skin color, hair color and texture, and facial features were intermediate between those of the black and those of the white infant. The second set contained four target pictures, each portraying a white couple whose hair color either matched or contrasted: a blond man and a blond woman, a brown-haired man and a brown-haired woman, a blond man and a brown-haired woman, and a brown-haired man and a blond woman. Each of the comparison pictures for the second set showed an infant: one with blond hair, one with brown hair, and one with intermediate hair color. Children were shown the pictures in each target set one at a time. As a child viewed each target picture, the experimenter explained that it was the picture of a mother, a father, and their baby. With the target picture in view, subjects were then shown the three comparison pictures and asked to choose which was the couple's baby. The order of presentation of the two target sets was counterbalanced. The presentation of items in each target set was randomized.

The logic of the design is simple, and is meant to answer three questions: Were children's and adults' judgments about resemblance in study 7.1 judgments about race, or were they about some other aspect of resemblance? Are children's and adults' judgments about racial inheritance the same, and if not when do they change? Are children's judgments about race specifically, or about the inheritance of physical properties generally? If children believe that the one-drop rule applies to all physical properties, then their judgments about the inheritance of hair color should agree with their judgments about the inheritance of skin color. If they believe that the one-drop rule applies specifically to

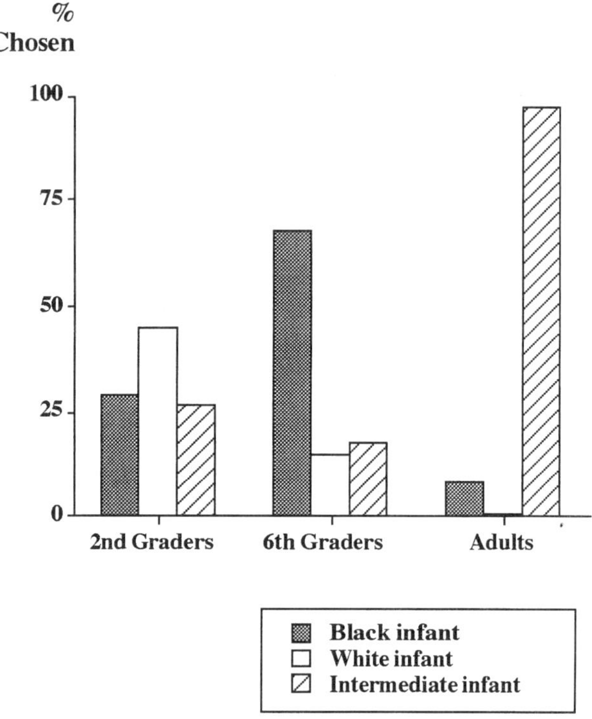

Figure 7.3
Mean percentage of times each baby was chosen in study of responses to mixed-race parents.

racially relevant properties, then their judgments about the inheritance of skin color and those about hair color should differ.

Results

Skin color All of the adults and all of the sixth graders correctly inferred that a black couple would have a black child and that a white couple would have a white child. Seventy-nine percent of the second graders also inferred that the black couple would have a black child, and 89% inferred that the white couple would have a white child. (Both findings are significantly above chance.)

The performance of primary interest involves the mixed-race couples. My analyses of these responses, summarized in figure 7.3, showed the following:

> The second graders chose the white infant more than either the sixth graders or the adults.

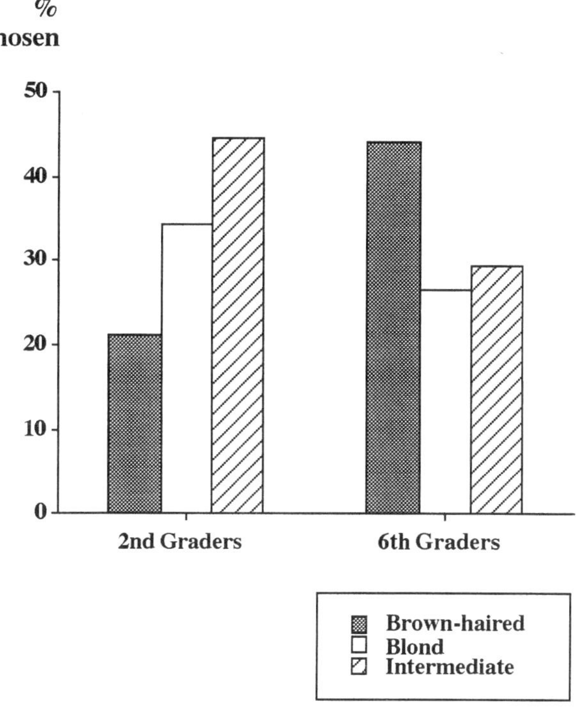

Figure 7.4
Mean percentage of times each hair-color outcome was chosen in study of responses to mixed-hair-color parents.

The second graders displayed no clear preference for any outcome.

The sixth graders chose the black infant more often than either the second graders or the adults.

The sixth graders chose the black infant significantly more often than the white or the intermediate infant.

The adults chose the intermediate infant more frequently than either the sixth graders or the second graders.

The adults chose the intermediate infant in all but one case.

Hair color For the same-hair-color items, all the sixth graders inferred that the brown-haired couple would have a brown-haired infant and that the blond couple would have a blond infant. Seventy-one percent of the second graders also inferred that the brown-haired couple would have a brown-haired infant and that the blond couple would have a blond child.

As figure 7.4 shows, in sharp contrast to their judgments about the mixed-skin-color couples, children in both age groups expected that children of mixed-hair-color unions were as likely to be blond as to be brown-haired or to have intermediate hair color. The difference in the older children's reasoning about hair color and their reasoning about skin color is clear if we compare the likelihood of the dark outcome's being chosen on the two tasks. The primary question is whether there is a general strategy for reasoning about the inheritance of color properties or a specific expectation about dark skin. The results of the hair-color task indicate that the belief is specific to the inheritance of skin color: the sixth graders expected a mixed-race couple to have a dark (i.e., black) baby over 67% of the time, whereas they expected a mixed-hair-color couple to have a dark (i.e., brown-haired) baby only 44% of the time.

These findings are important because they tell us that children do not use a single general strategy for predicting the inheritance of surface color properties. The same children who believe that dark skin dominates white skin do not believe that darker hair color dominates lighter hair colors. In short, sixth graders' inferences about the inheritability of a socially relevant physical property (skin color) are distinct from their inferences about the inheritability of a similar but socially irrelevant physical property (hair color).

Taken together, these results lend further support to the major findings of study 7.1: that during the late elementary-school years children come to reason in accord with a biological but not categorical interpretation of the one-drop rule. Both studies suggest that older children and adults interpret the rule in distinct ways: whereas adults judge principally in terms of category identity, older children judge primarily in physical terms. Study 7.2 also shows that children's judgments about physical characteristics are stronger than those of adults. From study 7.1 it was clear that both adults and older children expect an interracial child to resemble the black parent more than the white parent, indicating greater confidence in the innate potential of black essence. Study 7.2, which is a more direct assessment of subjects' beliefs about racial features, establishes that older children expect an interracial child to have black features whereas adults expect such a child to have more intermediate racial anatomy.[8]

8. In a follow-up study, Ken Springer and I found that this pattern of reasoning is robust across racial types. We repeated both the skin-color and hair-color tasks with grade-school children in Dallas. The only difference between the two studies was that in Dallas we asked children about the offspring of a Latino-white couple instead of a black-white couple. In the main, the findings were the same as those reported here. Older but not younger children reasoned in accord with a biological interpretation of the one-drop rule—that is, they inferred that the child of a mixed-race couple would have Latino racial features. In contrast, when questioned about hair color, the same children overwhelmingly believed that the mixed-hair-color couples would have a child with intermediate hair color.

Study 7.3: Inheritance of Skin Color and Hair Color in Animals

How specific are the distinct patterns of belief about property inheritance? Are they beliefs about the inheritance of physical properties in living things, or are they beliefs about the inheritance of properties in humans only? Study 7.2 lends support to the claim that children's beliefs about racial inheritance are distinct from their beliefs about the inheritance of other similar color properties. The findings, however, do not tell us whether children have distinct principles for reasoning about racial versus nonracial properties, or whether they rely on distinct principles when reasoning about skin color versus hair color. I have interpreted them as evidence of specificity in reasoning about racial as opposed to nonracial properties, and hence as informative about the acquisition of a particular cultural representation: the one-drop rule. Alternatively, the results could be interpreted as evidence of specificity in children's reasoning about skin color as opposed to hair color. We can decide between these alternatives by seeing whether children reason differently about skin color versus hair color in a species for which the distinction does not capture a socially relevant contrast, as it does for humans.

Twenty-six second graders and 20 sixth graders participated in the study. In the main task, each child saw four picture sets. As in studies 7.2 and 7.3, each set consisted of four target pictures (each set contrasting couples whose surface color was either the same or different) and three comparison pictures (depicting the offspring each couple might have). In contrast to the materials used in studies 7.2 and 7.3, these picture sets all depicted pairs of nonhuman animals of the same species: a dark pair, a light pair, a dark male–light female pair, and a light male–dark female pair. Two sets consisted of animals whose surface color derives from the color of their skin (alligators and elephants), and two sets portrayed animals whose surface color derives from the color of their fur (bears and camels). In the main task, the procedure was identical to that in study 7.2. For each picture set, each child was shown a target picture, then shown the comparison pictures, and asked to choose which was the baby of the target pair.[9]

9. To ensure that the children understood that the alligator and elephant picture sets represent animals whose surface color is due to their skin color, and that the bear and camel sets represent animals whose surface color is due to their hair color, in the control task 13 younger children were shown four pictures from the same-color set (one for each animal species) one at a time. The experimenter asked each child to identify the color of the animals in the picture. The child was then asked whether the animals were that color because of their skin color or because of their hair color. All 13 children correctly judged that the alligators' color was due to their skin and that the bears' color was due to their hair, and 12 correctly inferred that the elephants' color was due to their skin and the camels' to their hair.

Table 7.1
Mean percentage each color outcome was chosen in animal skin-color and hair-color tasks.

	Grade					
	Second			Sixth		
Outcome:	Light	Blend	Dark	Light	Blend	Dark
Skin color	33.6	32.7	33.6	20.0[a]	62.5[b]	17.5[a]
Hair color	35.6	29.8	34.6	22.5	57.5[b]	20.0[a]

a. significantly below chance at $p < 0.05$
b. significantly above chance at $p < 0.01$

Results

For the same-color pairs, as they had for human couples, children reliably inferred that a dark animal pair would have dark offspring and a light animal pair would have light offspring: 99% of the second graders' and 98% of the sixth graders' inferences were correct in this regard.

For the mixed-color pairs, children's responses varied as a function of age. The second graders chose at chance, selecting the light outcome 34.6% of the time, the dark 34.1%, and the intermediate 31.2%. The sixth graders' responses, in contrast, reliably differed from chance. Sixty percent of the time they inferred that the offspring of mixed animal pairs would be a blend of their parents' colors. In contrast, the light and dark outcomes were chosen less often than would be predicted by chance. An analysis of the responses to the skin-color-vs.-hair-color task for the mixed-pair pictures revealed that, in contrast with their inferences about human inheritability, children in both age groups showed no differences in their inferences about hair color versus skin color (see table 7.1).

In sum, younger children reasoned about the inheritability of color properties in animals much as they reasoned about the inheritability of hair color in humans. This indicates that younger children rely on a single strategy for drawing inferences across all similar properties, regardless of the species involved. Older children, in contrast to their expectations about human stimuli, believe that the offspring of animals with mixed-color parents will be intermediate in color, regardless of whether the color property is derived the animal's skin or its hair. This pattern of reasoning suggests that older children have a single undifferentiated strategy for reasoning about the inheritance of non-socially-relevant properties, whatever the species, and another strategy for reasoning about the transmission of socially relevant properties.

Study 7.4: Community, Race, and Beliefs about Inheritability

Pre-adolescence is a critical age for the reorganization of racial knowledge. In particular, during middle childhood children's racial cognitions are penetrated by cultural influences in ways that young children's cognitions are not. One possibility is that this age-related shift comes with an increase in the knowledge that children have about the cultural environment in which they live as they become more intensively immersed in it. There are a number of reasons for believing that this could be the case. For one thing, in view of the extraordinary degree of residential racial segregation in the United States (Massey 1993), younger children, who remain closer to home than older children, tend to live in a racially more segregated world. Moreover, black families (and perhaps white families) tend to provide younger children with a local buffer against pervasive currents of racism (Jackson et al. 1988). Thus, family life may draw a young child's attention away from the cultural and political correlates of race. Parents' reluctance to discuss racial matters with children would also contribute to this distancing of younger children from the dynamics of racial politics.

Arguably, then, in virtue of more direct and less mediated encounters with the structural consequences of race, with adolescence children come to have more sophisticated knowledge of the cultural rules that underlie and facilitate those consequences. This model further implies that the engagement with the system of racial thinking that occurs during middle childhood involves an engagement with an increasingly specific system of cultural thinking—because it is increasingly more concerned with racial *politics*. Such a system tends to be widely but not universally shared. Inasmuch as it is about power and relations of authority, it is also about negotiations over and contestations of particular patterns of power and authority. Holding a particular cultural ideology does not preclude being aware of other cultural ideologies. In fact, one feature of cultural beliefs is that they consciously stand in relation to some other cultural beliefs that are not held. This is particularly evident with respect to local variations in cultural ideologics (that is, differences in attribution and explanation that are part of intracultural or ethnic distinctions—the sorts that distinguish Americans of Hispanic, black, and Northern European origin).

Nineteen second grades and 20 fifth graders[10] attending an integrated (54% black) school participated in the study. The community in which the school is located is approximately 35% black and adjoins the

10. The average age of the fifth graders in this study was 11.7 years. The average ages of the sixth graders in studies 7.1, 7.2, and 7.3 were 10.7, 12.0, and 12.1 years, respectively.

Table 7.2
Mean percentage each color outcome was chosen by subjects in integrated school, as a function of age and race of subject.

	Second graders			Fifth graders		
Outcome:	Light	Blend	Dark	Light	Blend	Dark
Skin color: Animals	27.6	48.7	27.6	12.5[b]	75.0[a]	12.5[b]
Whites	27.5	52.5	27.5	15.0	67.5	17.5
Blacks	27.8	44.4	27.8	10.0	80.0	10.0
Skin color: Humans	34.2	55.2[c]	11.0[b]	15.0[b]	47.5	37.5
Whites	35.0	60.0	5.0	20.0	40.0	40.0
Blacks	33.3	50.0	16.6	10.0	55.0	35.0
Hair color: Animals	28.9	47.4	23.7	11.2[b]	75.0[a]	13.7[b]
Whites	30.0	45.0	50.0	15.0	67.5	17.5
Blacks	27.8	50.0	22.2	12.5	82.5	5.0
Hair Color: Human	23.7	23.7	52.6[c]	55.0[c]	22.5	22.5
Whites	30.0	25.0	45.0	20.0	20.0	60.0
Blacks	16.7	22.2	61.0	25.0	25.0	50.0

a. significantly above chance at $p < 0.01$
b. significantly below chance at $p < 0.01$
c. significantly above chance at $p < 0.05$

majority community from which subjects in the earlier studies were drawn. According to school records, approximately half the children tested were white and half were black. The same tasks as in studies 7.2 and 7.3 were used.

Results

For the same-race couples, the pattern of response was identical to that found in study 7.2: both second graders and fifth graders expected that the child of a same-color couple would be the same color as its parent. Second graders inferred that a brown-haired couple would have a brown-haired child and a blond couple would have a blond child 87% of the time and that a black couple would have a black child and a white couple would have a white child 92% of the time. Fifth graders judged that a brown-haired couple would have a brown-haired child and a blond couple would have a blond child 92% of the time and that a black couple would have a black child and a white couple a white child 97% of the time.

In contrast with the performance on the human-skin-color question in study 7.2, there was (as table 7.2 shows) only one age difference among children in the integrated school: fifth graders made fewer dark skin choices than second graders. Overall, the most striking feature of these children's responses is the extent to which they believed that the intermediate outcome would prevail. On all but one question, children expected that mixed couples (whether the contrast was in hair color or skin color and whether the couples were animal or human) would have offspring whose surface color was an intermediate blend of the parents' colors. The exception was the human-hair-color question: second graders believed that dark hair predominates, fifth graders that light hair dominates.

For the animal items children also correctly expected that a light pair would have a light offspring and a dark pair a dark offspring.

As with the mixed-color human items, children showed no evidence of expecting animal parents to contribute differentially to their offsprings' surface color. As in study 7.3, children's expectations on the animal items were the same whether surface color was derived from the animal's skin or from its hair. The analyses, however, did reveal reliable age differences. Younger children were more likely than older children to expect the mixed animal pairs' offspring to be like one or the other parent rather than intermediate. In contrast, older children, like the subjects in study 7.3, expected offspring of mixed animal pairs to have skin color intermediate between their parents' skin tones.

Differences in each community's pattern of judgment are clearer if we directly compare the performances of children in the nonintegrated and integrated schools on the mixed-race task. For the human questions, younger children from the integrated community chose the dark-skinned infant and the light-skinned infant less often than their majority-community counterparts. There was also a nonsignificant trend for younger minority-community children to choose the intermediate infant more often than majority-community children. Older majority-community children overwhelmingly selected the black infant in the human-skin-color question, and they were reliably higher in this choice than children living in the integrated community. For the animal questions, no significant differences between younger majority-community and integrated-community children's inferences were found. Older majority-community children chose the dark hair outcome and the dark skin outcome more than older integrated-community children.[11]

11. As we had with the earlier study, Ken Springer and I also sought to assess whether this pattern of reasoning by minority children is widespread. We repeated the same tasks used in this study with 42 Latino children in the Dallas area. We also added a task. In addition to the black-white couples, we included a set of drawings that depicted Latino-white couples. The responses of the Dallas children were much the same as those of the midwestern children. Children in both age groups in both regions tended to choose the intermediate infant for the black-white couples. Latino subjects in Dallas also tended to choose the intermediate infant for the Latino-white couples, suggesting that reasoning about the inheritability of racial features is the same regardless of the minority. The only difference between the Latino children and the children in the highly integrated midwestern school is that older Latino subjects tended to believe that the darker infant would occur more often among black-white couples than among Latino-white couples.

The results of this study also allow us to assess whether individual differences in children's reasoning reside at the level of race or at the level of community.

Previous research lends support to both possibilities. Most of this work involves variation in memory about members of one's own race relative to another race. Both children and adults find faces of members of their own racial group more memorable than faces of members of another racial group (Shepherd 1981; Katz 1973). One explanation for this phenomenon is that people underestimate the variation in the facial features of members of other races. As a consequence they demonstrate less ability to discriminate between members of another race on recognition tasks.[12] But why would the underestimation of variation increase with age? An ingroup/outgroup explanation may be useful here. The pattern of responses obtained for 11- and 12-year-olds in studies 7.1–7.3 are interpretable as an age-related decrease in attention to within-category variation in minority race individuals' skin color (and other external anatomy). In other words, it could be argued that these children anticipated a single outcome (i.e., the black baby) in circumstances that would otherwise produce greater variation. Recall that children of that age expect other kinds of color mixing (either in human hair color or in animal hair and skin color) to produce greater variation in outcome. In short, inferences about the appearance of mixed-race children can be viewed as an underestimation of the range of variation in skin color within the black community. If this is the case, then nonwhite children might expect a different outcome when asked about the offspring of racially mixed children, since their notion of outgroup (and the range of variation they underestimate) would not be the same as that of white children.

On the other hand, the community in which a child lives—regardless of the child's race—may be the critical factor in shaping that child's memory for racial variation. Feinman and Entwisle (1976) found that race-of-subject differences in performance on other-race facial recall tasks declined for children (whether they were black and white) living in an integrated community and attending an integrated school. Crucially, this decrease in the race-of-subject effect did not emerge for children attending an integrated school but *not* living in an integrated community. The idea that community rather than race of subject might be the critical dimension is plausible in view of other work showing that in minority communities subtle differences in skin color are often highly salient and meaningful (Russell et al.s 1992). Living in an integrated community, accordingly, might impel children to attend more

12. This sort of underestimation could be seen as an instance of a more general tendency to underestimate variation among outgroup members (Quattrone and Jones 1980).

closely to the way variations in skin color (and other racially relevant features) are distributed in the population.

We can test this by examining how various groups of students responded to the mixed-race questions. The distinct pattern of reasoning that children in the integrated community revealed could have one of two sources. If race of subject is the source, then we would expect to find white students using a different pattern of reasoning than blacks. If community is the source, then we would expect to find both white and black students reasoning in the same manner, and both groups reasoning differently than their majority-community counterparts. Table 7.2 also compares children's responses by race of subject. The results are striking. Black and white children from the integrated school did not differ significantly in their expectations. The crucial factor determining children's reasoning, thus, appears to be the cultural environment in which the child lives, not the child's racial status. In view of previous research, this is an unexpected finding. Studies of racial-concept formation frequently contrast the performances of children of different races; community differences are examined less often. If individuals are the appropriate units of comparison, then we would expect white children, whatever their environment, to respond similarly. If cultural environment rather than individual racial status is the appropriate unit of contrast, then whites and blacks living in a highly integrated environment should not differ in their judgments. Moreover, both groups should differ in their inductions from children living in the majority environment. In fact, differences emerged only at the community level.

Conclusions

In this chapter I have tried to show that the cultural and cognitive representations of race engage each other in a remarkable and informative way during middle childhood. By the end of grade school, children living in majority communities come to hold a version of the one-drop rule (the cultural premise, central to the North American cultural system of racial thinking, that each race possesses a distinct innnate potential). It is important to underscore how specific the juvenile version of the one-drop rule is. These children do not expect that a child with one black parent will be categorically black. Instead, they expect that a child with one black parent will have black external anatomy. Thus, their beliefs are more specific than the beliefs of adults with whom they live. But their beliefs are also specific with respect to other biological beliefs they themselves hold. These same children, for instance, do not believe that a child with one brown haired and one blond parent will have brown hair. Nor do children of the same age expect that dark hair or skin color predominates in animals. In short, older grade schoolers do not believe that all types of inheritance (distinguished in terms of the property inherited or the species in which inheritance occurs) are governed by the same principles. I have taken this as evidence that these children endorse the one-drop rule. Thus, by preadolescence a child's inferencing accords with important aspects of the predominant cultural model.

Nonetheless, this reflects neither a direct convergence toward adult knowledge nor an appropriation of more accurate knowledge. The adult belief principally involves expectations about the *category membership* of interracial children, whereas my findings indicate that children are reasoning about *physical appearance*. Crucially, these results are not attributable to simple inductions from experience, in that neither the expectations about the inheritability of skin color nor those about the inheritability of hair color correspond to the biology of the phenomenon. An older child's belief that a child with one black and one white parent will have black features is not derived from direct observation of interracial children since there is no genetic dominance for skin color (Bodmer and Cavalli-Sforza 1976). Similarly, an older child's belief that a child with one blond-haired and one brown-haired parent will have intermediate hair color is not well supported by experience, because darker hair is dominant over lighter hair (Robins 1991).

The children who participated in study 7.2 had opportunities for learning the biologically accurate pattern: the school in which the testing was conducted was primarily white, but there were several black children in each grade, and, importantly, there was one mixed-race child in each the classes from which participants were drawn. Moreover, coming to know that a person tends to have skin color intermediate between the skin colors of his or her parents does not require experience with mixed-race children. There is considerable variation in skin color within any given racial category (reflecting, among other things, fairly high and constant levels of racial admixture). Children living in a multicultural environment (as these subjects do) would thus have had much experience with children whose parents' respective skin colors vary perceptibly. Hence, these children have had many opportunities to discover what biologists have concluded, namely that offspring of parents with perceptibly different skin colors overwhelmingly tend to have a skin color that is intermediate between those of the parents. Thus, neither the older children's preference for the black infant nor the younger children's random selections in the studies discussed above are attributable to lack of input.

Older children's beliefs appear to represent a singular integration of biological and social understandings, in that these beliefs involve biological inductions based in part on social criteria. The child is thus not internalizing adult belief but appropriating it (see Rogoff 1990). The child's theory of society, apparently derived from cultural representations about both the categorical status and the biological status of interracial children, shapes biological expectations about the inheritability of human (and only human) physical properties. One explanation for this is that children are focusing on one aspect of adult knowledge—i.e., the biological interpretation of the rule. But the developmental account is actually more complex, because children distort adult knowledge: whereas adults provide evidence of a moderate expectation that interracial children resemble their black parent more than their white parent, older children show a more pronounced bias.

Children's Biological and Racial Thinking

The pattern of results obtained could be interpreted as biological reasoning dominating social inference, a possibility about which researchers from diverse traditions have speculated. The conspicuous parallels between biological and social thinking have already been discussed. As I have noted, it is often assumed that biology (whether in folk or scientific form) is a better-grounded domain, and naturalized or essentialized social reasoning is typically thought to involve a transfer of biological expectations to racial thinking. I argued in earlier chapters that this model is not well supported by what we know of the early beliefs that children develop about race. The present data reveal that the biological-to-social transfer model may be problematic for older children too. In fact, older children's social thinking appears to influence biological expectations, not vice versa. These findings also suggest that the biological domain is more internally differentiated than was previously appreciated. During the early grade-school years, children come to fold their biological understanding of humans into a unified domain of folk biology. Whereas younger children believe that humans are taxonomically and ontologically distinct from other animals, older children view humans as "one mammal among many" (Carey 1985, p. 94; see also Johnson et al. 1992). The studies described here imply that older children's (and perhaps adults') model of human biology may be internally differentiated, since throughout the grade-school years children continue to hold humans biologically apart from other species in important respects. (Both older and younger children expect that common biological processes, such as inheritance, have distinct realizations in humans and animals.)

This does not imply that the domain does not undergo conceptual reorganization during this period. The results of the hair-color and skin-color questions in studies 7.2 and 7.3 suggest that important differences exist between younger and older grade school children's racial and biological knowledge. Younger grade schoolers do not discriminate between the inheritability of socially relevant properties (i.e., skin color) and socially irrelevant ones (i.e., hair color). They do, however, distinguish between the ways such properties are inherited in humans and in animals. Though they expect the offspring of animals to resemble their mothers more than their fathers, young grade-school children expect that human infants are as likely to resemble one parent as the other (possibly because the role of human fathers is better understood). Together these findings lend support to the view that folk biology may be distinctively structured internally as well as with respect to other conceptual knowledge. That is, under certain social conditions the conceptual organization of human biology may be singular with respect to the conceptual organization of nonhuman biology.

Racial Identity and Essentialist Reasoning

A considerable literature now exists on essentialist reasoning, particularly in naive biology (Gelman et al. 1994; Gelman and Wellman 1991; Keil 1994; Medin 1989; Atran 1990). Common to this research is the characterization of essence as a nonobvious yet material substance that causes something to be the sort of thing it is. Being a certain sort of thing means having a certain physical appearance and certain behavioral qualities. The paradigm case of this comes from the commonsense model of causality and ontology that explains a creature's appearance and character in terms of underlying *species*-specific essences (e.g., in adult American folk belief DNA is presumed to be the causal agent propelling living things to develop in a biologically appropriate manner). An important aspect of this model is the presumption that all of members a category share a species essence to the same degree—e.g., that all dogs share the same amount of dog essence and all oaks the same amount of oak essence. This sort of reasoning plays an important cognitive role by allowing singular or atypical instances (e.g., three-legged albino tigers, flightless birds, or in the case of racial essence "blacks" with light skin) to be encompassed by the same explanatory model that covers typical category members. The power of such reasoning is that it explains regularities in appearance and behavior while freeing inferencing from the "errors" that are associated with similarity-based models of induction (Medin 1989). Immutability of species-specific essences (and hence their mutual incompatibility) is part of the essentialist explanation for the putative inability of members of different species to breed successfully (Mayr 1988).[13]

Other forms of commonsense reasoning recruit a notion of nonobvious essence to explain observed regularities in appearance and behavior. The notion of kinship encompasses a set of categories that comprise networks of individuals supposedly related through shared essence (Hirschfeld 1986, 1989). Although this notion parallels the idea of cate-

13. A human version of the incompatibility claim is embodied in the racist notion that miscegenation leads to biologically corrupted offspring (Davis 1991).

gory essence in many respects, the form of essentialism in kinship is relational. Essences in naive biology pick out kinds of *beings*, whereas those underlying kinship categories pick out kinds of *relationships*. That is, kinship is person-centered, depending on a set of relationships defined in terms of a specific individual rather than in terms of collectivities defined independent of each observer: a person is a brother in virtue of being *someone's* brother, a cousin in virtue of being *someone's* cousin, and so on. Because of this, the amount of shared essence between two related individuals is by definition a more-or-less property, conceptualized in terms of gradients and contingent on the degree of kin relation. Close kin resemble one another more than distant kin. Consequently, each kinship term indicates a degree of relatedness (shared essence) among the individuals covered by the term (see Schneider 1968).

Consider community differences in reasoning about racial identity in this light. Older majority-community children's inferences about the inheritability of racial properties appear to be governed by a view of essence embedded in the conceptual repertoire of naive biology. Racial-category membership confers an essence that is not varying; being categorically black entails having a "complete" black essence in that it produces typical appearances (thus, the notion of "mixed blood" is not really part of the dominant discourse on race in America). In contrast, older minority-community children's inferences about the inheritability of racial and other physical properties suggest that they view racial essence as varying, not fixed. Unlike majority-community children, these children believe that racial potentials blend, producing offspring with ambiguous external anatomical features (in fact, subjects often referred to the mixed-feature infant as a "blend"). Just as the majority-community children's notion of racial essence parallels the notion of species-specific essence found in naive biology, the minority-community children's notion of racial essence parallels the comparative notion of essence found in the naive model of kinship. Thus, the minority-community children's view simultaneously distances the concept of racial identity from the species model and identifies it with a powerful and prevalent trope for similitude. (Stack (1975) has pointed to the importance of this figure of race as kinship within the black community). In contrast, the view adopted by children in the majority community likens racial variation to an equally powerful and prevalent trope of species difference. Considerable historical and other comparative work has stressed the crucial importance the species image has played in the construction of the majority culture's view of race (Appiah 1990b; Banton 1987). This work may well overestimate the role that the species model plays in racial thinking, in assuming that all strategies for reasoning about racial categories rely on it.

Conclusion

I have focused in this book on a fundamental tension in racial thinking: that race is both a category of the mind and a category of power. Observing that race has this dual status is, of course, uncontroversial. The interesting question is: What do we make of this duality? If race is a category of both the mind and power, is it amenable to study as both a psychological and a cultural phenomenon? This too, I believe, is uncontroversial. A more substantial issue is whether the *nature* of race as a category of the mind has unique consequences for race as a category of power. And, by extension, are there consequences for the way we study race that flow from this? The answer I have offered is Yes. Race is not a category of the mind simply to the extent that, like all categories of power, it must be mentally representable. The major goal of this book has been to show that race is a category of power precisely *because* it is a peculiar category of the mind.

I began the book by repeating the frequently voiced insight that racial thinking explains power relations typically by distorting their real material basis. I am now in a position to better explain why this is. The nature of race as a category of the mind is extraordinarily well suited to distort our vision of race as a category of power. As Maurice Bloch (1974, p. 79) notes, "it is precisely through the process of making a power situation appear *a fact in the nature of the world* that traditional authority works" (emphasis added). Many have argued that in being racialized, in being naturalized, relations of power are facilitated. Since the relationship between naturalization and power is contingent, it is also widely accepted to be historically and culturally specific. In broad strokes this relationship has been approached in one of two ways. In the first, which focuses principally on material relations of power, a situation initially is conceived as one of power and then, through cultural or ideological transfusion, becomes one of race (and hence nature). In such cases, race legitimizes power relations by biologizing them. Fields's (1982) account of race as a reconciliation of contradictions in a liberal slave society is a good example. In the second, more Foucauldian tradition, power and its cultural forms are seen as inseparable. On this account they make each other up. Yanagisako and Delaney (1995, p. 19) make this argument for gender, another naturalized relation of power: "Culture is what makes the boundaries of domains seem natural, what gives ideologies power, and what makes hegemonies appear seamless. At the same time, it is what enables us to make compelling claims for connections between supposedly distinct discourses." Here power is viewed as possible only *through* culture. The consequence is much the same regardless of the interpretation. Naturalized power exists in virtue of naturalizing cultural traditions. In their absence, relations of power and ideology would be otherwise.

I have tried to show that this position is problematic for a variety of reasons. First, as already noted, if naturalization is contingent, why does naturalized thinking change so little in the face of substantial changes in either cultural formation or specific relations of power? Moreover, the view that naturalization is contingent on either culture or power implies that any cultural dimension can be naturalized in the service of power. There is little reason to believe that this is case. There are remarkably few naturalized relations of power—if we exclude gender and race, we can probably count those that recur with any frequency on one hand. It is clear that race recurs with striking regularity. Why? Surely not because race took on the mantle of naturalness simply because it serves power. Human beings did not construct racial categories simply because they provide a discursive reconciliation of relations of power and authority. Instead, I suggest, race was taken up as a category of power in part because of its unique characteristics as a *category of the mind.*

I am not suggesting that categories of the mind and categories of culture are distinct sorts of things—an epidemiology of representations would hardly be possible if they were. But it must be kept in mind that, for most historians and anthropologists, categories of culture are not understood to be psychological—and certainly not understood to be phenomena for which a psychological treatment is informative. Nor do I intend to suggest that culture has nothing to do with the naturalizing of race, that somehow it springs forth directly and unmediated from the human cognitive endowment. Race, I have repeated several times, is not a "natural" category of the mind. Human kinds are natural categories of the mind, in the sense that the mind is prepared to find them with little or no external encouragement. Moreover, I have proposed that human kinds predicated on intrinsicality are a category of the mind which human beings are prepared to hold. The notion of race is the outcome, the consequence, of this preparedness as it makes contact with contexts in which complex relations of power and authority are played out on the group level. An appreciation of this complex and contingent relationship between mind architecture and power politics follows from appreciation of the singular and recurrent way racial cognitions develop across time and across cultural contexts.

In significant measure, racial cognitions are important to relations of power less in virtue of what is directly encompassed by the race concept than in virtue of what is adducible from it. Racial cognitions, like other "natural'" concepts, function to extend knowledge and enhance reasoning far beyond what everyday experience warrants. Racial categories promote inductive inference by allowing (even encouraging) children and adults to make "educated" guesses about nonobvious aspects of human difference. Some of these inferences are conceptual (e.g., that some properties are intrinsic and others variable, or that some corporeal features are heritable but others are not); others are valuative (e.g., that members of some groups are intellectually dull, aggressive, or dirty) (Williams and Morland 1976; Katz and Zalk 1974). As with the conceptual inferences I have focused on here, young children readily, and apparently without much direct tuition, use race to project psychological and valuative attributes (Clark and Clark 1947; Porter 1971; Katz 1982). Although I have discussed this second kind of inference only in passing, it is clearly linked to relations of power and to the way these relations are mentally represented.

Previous research has almost always interpreted these attitudes, not as instantiations of ideologies of power, but as the accidental outcome of processing biases, superficial reasoning schemes, and cognitive immaturity (see, e.g., Aboud 1988; Phinney and Rotheram 1987; Holmes 1995). Conventional wisdom, rather than appreciating that race as a category of the young mind has remarkable accordance with race as a category of adult cultural power, denies both that race is a complex category of the young mind and that it is an instantiation of the category of adult cultural power. I have argued that neither of these denials is well grounded. It is the case that some of the more patent and surface-level aspects of adult racial belief (e.g., recognition of specific physical types) appear to emerge late. However, the findings I have reviewed show that many of the more intricate and to some extent obscure aspects of adult belief (including essentialist construals) appear to be in place virtually from the moment a child shows signs of being racially aware.

These findings are important because of the range of phenomena about which they inform us. In particular, they shed light on the way young children acquire and organize a complex and culturally elaborated body of knowledge. Cognitive developmentalists have almost exclusively focused attention on content areas that are both closely linked to empirical regularities in the natural world and robustly stable across disparate cultural traditions. Naive biology, folk physics, and even naive psychology are all constrained by the empirical reality that they represent. To a large degree, they are invariant from one culture and historical epoch to the next (there is, of course, controversy about whether the former accounts for the latter). Race, at least as it has been viewed by comparative scholars, is neither. It is a highly variable and culturally specific notion that creates rather than discovers the reality to which it is tethered. By treating the acquisition of racial concepts as a problem in cognitive science, I hope not only to have furthered our understanding of a specific conceptual repertoire but also to have extended cognitive theory by forcing it to engage a variety of phenomena it generally has ignored.

The notion of race is of interest for other reasons as well. The acquisition of racial concepts, I suggest, must be understood as embedded within the acquisition of a folk sociology, i.e., the development and elaboration of a naive theory of society. We know strikingly little about this process, despite the fact that humans arguably know more about other humans than about anything else. A hallmark of human existence is that it occurs in, and is mediated through, groups—groups of remarkable diversity and scope. Still, the models used to understand how humans know humans in groups are almost wholly borrowed from models meant to capture radically different phenomena, such as object perception, natural-kind classification, or self-construal. Regrettably, the willingness to reason from analogy has caused more problems than it has resolved. Object perception and human kinds have much less in common than is often accepted. Nor are human kinds simply biological categorization writ social. Nor are folk theories of sociality merely variants of folk theories of psychology. Instead, I argue, human kinds are a fundamental and unique part of our conceptual armory.

Summary of Results

It is important to keep in mind what my findings stand in contrast to. Let me begin by rehearsing the conventional wisdom on the acquisition of folk sociology. According to a widely accepted view, around $2\frac{1}{2}$ to 3 years of age children begin to show awareness of a range of human-kind differences. By the early preschool years, young children provide evidence that they can readily sort people into categories that correspond to the racial, gender, kinship, and age-grade (or generational) categories of adults around them. In the same contexts, they show the capacity to label exemplars of these categories with the appropriate terms. In these respects, young children's knowledge of social categories is much like that of adults. Numerous researchers have argued, however, that at least some of young children's social categories are fundamentally unlike those represented by adults. According to the standard view, young children's social concepts differ radically in content from those of adults. In particular, unlike adults, young children supposedly do not represent race and gender as biologically grounded or as part of an individual's intrinsic, immutable nature.

The reason for this disjunction with adult belief is that young children's social categories are supposedly constructed around physically prominent, epistemically superficial, and politically naive features (arguably a view that is driven as much by the romanticization of the innocent child as by the empirical facts). According to conventional wisdom, children form social categories because human beings are segmentable into groups that have marked physical correlates. Children use these marked physical correlates to gain purchase on a complex and variable social environment. Thus, young children know so much about social difference not because human kinds are necessarily of paramount cultural importance—researchers tend to agree that individuating characteristics, particularly those contingent on personality, are ultimately more important—but because human kinds are easy to spot.

Only to the extent that one human kind has a unique constellation of physical correlates, relative to other human kinds, does the child distinguish that kind from others. For this reason, reasoning about different kinds of kinds tends to be quite similar. For example, constancy studies show that racial, gender, and even kinship concepts are initially represented in terms of their outward and potentially varying characteristics. Not until middle childhood are the intrinsic and invariant natures of these categories grasped.

This description of development is consistent with the view that children's human-kind concepts are acquired directly, and largely passively, from the surrounding environment. Children may be motivated by an innate impulse to categorize (and possibility by an innate preference for their ingroup). Otherwise their racial and gender thinking supposedly develops through simple observation and direct interaction. To be sure, knowledge of (and attitudes about) human difference change, but the changes are a function of the general maturation process and involve direct movement toward an endpoint defined by adult behavior and belief.

I have tried to show that this story underestimates what children (and, by extension, adults) bring to the process of constructing human kind categories. The young child is at least as concerned with human groupings as with individuals and their attributes. Children display a marked and sophisticated curiosity about the organization and the constitution of the social world. This is apparent in the interest even preschool children show in the nature and the scope of human groups, particularly the qualities that link members of social groups to one another. This should not be surprising. Developing the skills for competent cultural behavior is a major task of early childhood. Achieving cultural competency, in turn, depends on recognizing what entities constitute the cultural environment. Because human groupings (i.e., collectivities of people based on gender, race, native language, or kinship status) are integral parts of nearly all social environments, acquiring knowledge of such groupings is a necessary part of the child's early development.

In treating human collectivities as individuating properties of a person rather than as kinds in which an individual can have membership, as psychologists have typically done, we are faced with a somewhat curious circumstance. We now know more about the way young children understand classes of nonhuman living kinds than we do about the way children represent and identify the relevant social entities in their environment. This is not to suggest that we lack knowledge of how human cognition about other people develops, and considerable research has examined young children's abilities to individuate persons with respect to their faces, their voices, and even their personality states. Yet we have much less understanding of the way children grasp the aggregates of persons that make up the social environment.

The importance of such understanding is readily seen. A range of competences are dependent on awareness of the groupings to which an individual belongs. Learning to use kinship terms (by learning who is and who is not a member of one's family), culturally appropriate forms of politesse (in knowing one's own and others' status-group membership), and even mastery of language itself (in which awareness of human collectivities based on gender, relative age, or degree of familiarity between speakers is necessary to selecting the appropriate syntactic or lexical form), all rest on an ability to distinguish and label human groups. Indeed, a number of researchers have found that sensitivity to differences among social groups and the ability to adjust behavior in virtue of membership in a social group emerge early (Dunn 1988; Corsaro 1979; Becker 1982; Anderson 1986, 1990). These studies, along with the ones I have presented here, demonstrate that this sort of social development does not involve attention to perceptual or raw behavioral cues but, rather, rests on an awareness of underlying currents of social organization, typically elaborated in speech.

Race and Other Intrinsic Kinds

I have tried to show that young children's attention to these nuanced aspects of social environment is animated by a curiosity about human kinds. This curiosity is shaped by a set of abstract principles that guide the child's attention toward information relevant to discovering the sorts of intrinsicalities and naturally grounded commonalities that are entrenched in his or her particular cultural environment. Hence, even 3-year-olds in the United States recognize that race is not simply a function of outward appearance and that, instead, it represents an essential aspect of a person's identity, it is something that does not change over the course of one's lifetime, and it is something that parents pass on to their children. The same abstract principles guide young children to treat different sorts of human kinds as structurally distinct. Even preschoolers reason differently about race than about other kinds. For the young child, race is more readily inherited and more relevant to identity than other aspects of outward appearance—even aspects, such as physique, that closely resemble race in their surface qualities (i.e., they are readily observable), in their structural location (i.e., they are corporeal), and in their distribution in the world (i.e., they are relatively stable across the life span and are heritable). At a minimum, then, these findings provide evidence of a more precocious development of theory-like expectations about race than earlier researchers imagined.

As important, the studies establish that children's representations are not directly derivable from those of the adults with whom they live, since not all of young children's knowledge of intrinsic human kinds maps directly onto adult beliefs. In chapter 4 we saw that 3- and 4-year-olds entertain beliefs about the nature and the scope of the social world that do *not* reflect the constellation of adult cultural beliefs that surrounds them. A substantial portion of children living in the United States believe that behavioral proclivities, specifically those associated with occupational categories, are as intrinsic, deep, and heritable as race. The fact that children develop such beliefs largely on their own does not mean that they are impervious to environmental shaping. These children also expect that a man's occupation is more likely to be passed on to his children than a woman's, a belief that presumably reflects the gender politics of modern secular societies more than a universal property of human cognition. Thus, even children who conceptualize occupation as an intrinsic kind are incorporating into their representations of human kinds knowledge that is doubtless gleaned from the prevailing environment.

Clearly, then, there are marked developmental changes in belief about human kinds during the preschool years. But these changes do not represent a shift from an inchoate, superficial understanding of racial difference toward a more adult and biologistic one. Instead, during early childhood American children come to reject one plausible cultural hypothesis about intrinsicality (that habitual behaviors are fundamentally important for grouping people into natural categories) in favor of another (that a class of physical features is fundamentally important for the task). The notion that there are intrinsic human kinds is less a discovery the child makes about the world than an expectation that is inscribed on an increasingly narrow and culturally specified range of possibilities.

Race, Biology, and Perception

Biological (or biologistic) construals of race have generally been seen as emerging late, both from a historical perspective and from an ontogenetic one. The results reviewed just above could be interpreted as suggesting that biological knowledge plays a central role in the shaping of human-kind concepts. I argue, however, that young children's concept of race is not parasitic on their concept of biology. Race is not the transfer of the folk species concept to the realm of human kinds; it is an independently emerging essentialized strategy for reasoning specifically about human collectivities. Several lines of evidence lend support to this conclusion. First, the physical affordances of the two domains are quite different. To a large extent, both young children's and adults' concepts of nonhuman living kinds appear to be tied to the perception of ecologically discrete and locally occurring species. Even if the concept of an invariant species accords poorly with science, the idea that living things fall into discrete and perceptually coherent categories makes sense from the perspective of the local folk observer. In contrast, the young child's (and the adult's) concept of race is not bound directly to visual experience. The human races (as socially defined) rarely cluster locally into biologically and morphologically discrete categories—at least not in the absence of sustained political and cultural sanctions against interbreeding. Even then, the *conviction* that racial populations are readily distinguishable in physical appearance is much more prevalent than the infrequent (and historically recent) social contexts in which abrupt differences in appearance do occur. Second, from a developmental perspective the idea that beliefs about race emerge out of encounters with physically differing populations makes little sense. Several findings discussed in the previous chapters suggest that attention to the physical correlates of race may emerge relatively late in childhood, long after a racial ontology is both highly elaborated and inferentially potent. Cultural discourse aside, there is little developmental or biological reason to believe that race is derived from the discovery of highly correlated clusters of observable features.

A basic assumption of research on the development of racial thinking in children and across historical time is that this sort of thought is about capturing difference—particularly physical, embodied difference. To the contrary, I have tried to show that racial thinking is about *the creation of difference in the face of similitude*. Children do not attend to race because of its perceptual unavoidability—in fact, as the studies I have described show, young children initially do not *see* race; they *hear* it. Children encounter a complex social world and develop strategies for rendering this complexity sensible and explicable. The strategy a child uses depends more on the task at hand than on the nature of the distal stimulus. When *parsing* a social situation (i.e., when breaking it down into constituent components) young children attend more closely to behavior and gender than to race. In contrast, when *reasoning* about difference (i.e., when using relations among constituent elements to go beyond the information given) young children rely more on race than on behavior.

Race and Culture

A major claim of this volume is that racial thinking follows from a special-purpose cognitive device in articulation with a particular cultural system. During early periods of development, the cultural system serves more to guide (by directing the child toward one hypothesis instead of another) than to deliver specific beliefs. By middle childhood the cultural system clearly plays a central role, both in defining the child's task and by providing a solution to it. Importantly, finding a solution involves more than a simple accretion of knowledge—if it did not, the role of the cognitive device would be small or even trivial. Constructing a solution involves constructing a *series* of solutions predicated on the task set forth by the cultural system but conceptualized in a way singularly defined by the cognitive device.

Take the problem of resolving ambiguous cases of racial identity in the United States. For an adult, the task and the solution turn on addressing categorical problems first defined by the political economy of slavery. Despite this, and despite the fact that children probably receive little direct instruction in how to sort out cases of ambiguous racial identity, pre-adolescents reach a quite specific solution. Unlike younger children, who conceive of the problem as the same for all species and across all similar properties, and unlike adults, who conceive of the problem as a nominal one, pre-adolescents biologize the question. They see racial ambiguity not as a categorical issue but as an embodied and biological one. This, however, does not mean that folk biology is driving folk sociology. Just the contrary. The solution pre-adolescents arrive at involves a unique theory of biology. The cultural system plays a crucial role here in specifying that ambiguity in matters racial is not permitted. The cognitive device transforms this constraint into expectations about racial essence and physical identity. It literally creates an alternative biology for racial features—a biology whose principles are unlike those governing the inheritance of similar but nonracial properties in humans or those governing the inheritance of the same but socially irrelevant properties in nonhumans.

Not only does the pattern of development evinced in the elaboration of racial cognition inform us of the way children's knowledge grows; it also provides important comparative material. These data permit informed speculation over the nature and source of the concept of race itself—a topic of considerable, and unresolved, controversy. In fact, in view of the extent to which political, economic, and social forces co-determine one another, data on the development of children's racial beliefs may be the best comparative data available on just how culturally shared and culturally varying racial thinking is. Racial thinking, I have argued, is the product of both our conceptual system and the political, economic, and cultural environment in which that system must operate. Unfortunately, the way race has traditionally been approached inhibits our understanding of the source, scope, and distribution of racial thinking. Scholars who recognize the specificity of race have overwhelmingly denied that this specificity has an interesting psychological derivation. In turn, scholars who have theorized the psychological correlates of racial thinking have overwhelmingly denied that the concept is in any way conceptually novel or unique. In short, comparativists have eschewed theories of mentation while psychologists have eschewed theories of race.

Human Kinds in Culture and Cognition

It is important to keep the notion of a conceptual device that creates and delivers knowledge of human kinds distinct from the notion of racial kinds. I do not suggest that race is an inevitable consequence of our conceptual endowment. I argue that racial thinking is derived from the operation of a human-kind-creating module, rather than being the output of a racial-kind-creating one. The reason is simple. Racial kinds are one sort among a variety of intrinsic social kinds. They are not the only intrinsic kinds that humans recognize, nor are they the only intrinsic kinds salient to the young child. As I outlined earlier, there are a myriad of human kinds that people recognize, ranging across categories based on physique, personality, occupation, gender, nationality, and so on. Among these human kinds, there are some that are construed as intrinsic—as flowing from some nonobvious commonality that all members of the kind share. Again, the range of such intrinsic kinds is quite broad, including among others gender, kinship, and race.

Intrinsic kinds are culturally quite variable. In contemporary European and American society, for example, homosexuals are thought to constitute an intrinsic kind—even to the extent that it is claimed that a preference for same-sex sex has a genetic basis. As historians have observed, however, this construal is a fairly recent development. Age grades provide another example of categories that are intrinsic in some cultures but not in others. In many Melanesian and sub-Saharan African societies, age grading provides, after gender, the most important intrinsic kind. Typically, entry into a new age grade represents a virtual rebirth—the emergence of a distinct persona, often renamed. Earlier I discussed in some detail another human kind that is intrinsic in some but not all cultures, namely occupation. In American culture this categorical affiliation is seen as incidental to a person's intrinsic nature. Occupation represents the place that a particular pattern of habitual purposeful behavior occupies in a system of delivering and exchanging services. In South Asia, however, occupation is part of a person's intrinsic nature, linked to one's identity in a deep and invariant sense, and embedded within a system of belief that motivates a wide range of behaviors and relations far removed from the mundane provision and exchange of services.

Which kinds are considered intrinsic and which are not is specified by the conceptual device and the cultural system jointly. For instance, it is not entirely accurate to say that occupation is an intrinsic kind in South Asia but not in the United States. Recall that for American 3-year-olds occupation *is* an intrinsic kind. Moreover, it is not that these children confused occupation with race. As we saw in chapter 4, children who conceived of occupation as immutable and heritable did so consistently. They did not believe that occupation was intrinsic at certain times and race at other times, or that occupation was intrinsic in certain contexts and race in others. Rather, these children apparently were representing an alternative account of the meaning of social difference. The cognitive device makes available a range of possible meanings for intrinsicality (to use a rather awkward term). The cultural environment obviously lends more credence to some and less to others. We can imagine that children raised in other social environments would provide evidence that other sorts of intrinsic kinds are more salient. For example, I presented a study in chapter 5 that contrasted children's readiness to project language differences onto racial differences with their readiness to project them onto age differences. Would children living in a culture in which age grades were more naturalized reason as my midwestern subjects did? Conceivably not.

What sets racial kinds off from other human kinds? A definitive answer may not exist—racial and other intrinsic human kinds may not necessarily be related in a categorical manner. This isn't very surprising, since racial kinds are a way of looking at a highly recurrent interpretation of human variation. But racial kinds are not natural kinds (at least, not as they have classically been conceived), and they certainly are not kinds whose existence is triggered by external reality. In what ways do racial kinds differ from other intrinsic human kinds? First, a racial kind is able to reproduce by itself. You don't need two different racial kinds to propagate. Age grades, genders, and even kinship categories are not self-reproducing in this sense. One needs two of these kinds (a male and a female, a mother and a father), typically in a relationship of sustained articulation, in order to reproduce. Indeed, racial kinds differ from other intrinsic kinds in that racial kinds are *supposed* to be self-reproducing, not only in a strict biologistic sense (you don't need members of two different intrinsic kinds to produce offspring, as you do with gender) but also in a societal sense. Unlike, say, intrinsic construals of class in seventeenth- and eighteenth-century France or caste in South Asia, races are conceptualized as distinct populations whose interrelationships are contingent, not necessary. Castes coexist in a web of mutual dependency, as do classes in their intrinsic guises. Although their members may be able to reproduce endogamously (bakers begetting bakers, nobility begetting nobility), taken together the society cannot reproduce without these various kinds' being locked together in a system of exchange and mutual responsibility. Races *may* coexist in this way, but they do not have to. Typically each race is seen as traceable to an independent population, with its own history, its own natural habitat, and so forth. Relations of interdependence between races, as the discourse of slavery and its subsequent social forms often stipulate, are historical and often are dismantleable. Even when racial hierarchies have been conceived as part of the natural order of things with respect to their relative place in hierarchies of value, their continued interdependence is not seen as a necessary part of the natural order—slaves *could* have been sent back to Africa, Jews *could* have been expelled from the Iberian peninsula, and so on.

Admittedly this set of distinctions begs more questions than it answers, but it does provide a framework in which to adequately theorize racial and other intrinsic human kinds. It also gives substance to my claim that what is widely shared across cultures is not a system of racial thinking but a system of thinking about intrinsic kinds. Comparativist scholars are doubtless correct that a disparate range of political and economic relations are racialized. Psychologists are equally correct that there is a core mode of thinking that yields racial kinds. Race is easy to think, to sustain, and to transmit, and it stabilizes readily in a broad range of cultural environments. It is these qualities that allow the notion of race to facilitate the regulation of power and authority and to transform as these relations themselves change. Racial kinds are remarkably prevalent, much more so than many scholars appreciate. This does not deny that there may be cultural formations in which racial kinds are absent. I would argue, however, that there are no cultural formations that lack intrinsic human kinds altogether.

Appendix

Experiment 7.1: Stimulus Story, Character Assignment 1

French

Il était une fois un petit garçon qui voulait faire plaisir à sa mamam pour son anniversaire. Il décida de lui offrir une belle écharpe mais il ne savait pas dans quel magasin acheter cette écharpe. Il se dirigea vers le centre commercial qui se trouvait près de chez lui. La première personne à qui il demanda un renseignement fut un grand facteur noir. "SVP, Monsieur, où se trouve le magasin qui vend des écharpes?" Le grand facteur noir réfléchit et dit: "Je sais qu'il y a un magasin, pas loin d'ici, mais je ne sais pas exactement où il se trouve. Demande à la jeune vendeuse de journaux." Le garçon s'approcha de la jeune vendeuse de journaux et lui demanda: "SVP, Madame, où se trouve le magasin qui vend des écharpes?" "Crois-tu que je n'ai que ça à faire?" répondit-elle en colère. "Je ne suis pas un bureau de renseignements. Va plutôt embêter le vieux chauffeur de taxi arabe à coté et demande-lui." Le garçon s'approcha du vieux chauffeur de taxi arabe et lui demanda: "SVP, Monsieur, où se trouve le magasin qui vend des écharpes?" Il le regarda et lui dit: "Je sais que c'est quelque part, pas loin d'ici, mais je ne sais pas exactement où il se trouve. Va demander à la grosse épicière chinoise." Le garçon s'approcha de la grosse épicière chinoise et lui demanda: "SVP, Madame, où se trouve le magasin qui vend des écharpes?" "C'est facile, jeune homme!" dit-elle en souriant, "C'est tout près d'ici, juste derrière toi, sur ta droite, à une cinquantaine de mètres. Je t'accompagne jusqu'au magasin, si tu veux." Le jeune garçon entra dans le magasin et acheta une belle écharpe rouge pour l'anniversaire de sa maman.

English

Once upon a time there was a little boy who wanted to make his mother happy on her birthday. He decided to give her a beautiful scarf but he didn't know where he could buy one. He set out for a shopping center not far from his home. The first person he asked directions from was a tall black postman. "Excuse me sir, where can I find a store that sells scarves?" The tall black postman thought for a moment and responded, "I know there's one not far from here, but I don't know exactly where it is. Ask the young saleswoman in the newspaper kiosk." The little boy went up to the young saleswoman in the newspaper kiosk and asked, "Excuse me madame, where can I find a store that sells scarves?" "Do you think I have nothing better to do than to talk with you?" she responded in anger. "I'm not an information office. Go bother the old North African taxi driver over there and ask him." The little boy went up to the old North African taxi driver and asked him, "Excuse me sir, where can I find a store that sell scarves?" He looked at the little boy and said, "I know that there is one somewhere, not far from here, but I don't know exactly where it is. Ask the fat Chinese greengrocer." The little boy went up to the fat Chinese greengrocer and asked her, "Excuse me madame, where can I find a store that sells scarves?" "Why that's easy young man" she said smiling "It's very close by, just 150 feet behind you. I can take you there if you'd like." The young boy went into the store and bought a beautiful red scarf for his mother's birthday.

References

Aboud, F. E. 1987. The development of ethnic self-identification and attitudes. In J. S. Phinney and M. J. Rotheram, eds., *Children's Ethnic Socialization*. Sage.

Aboud, F. E. 1988. *Children and Prejudice*. Blackwell.

Aboud, F. E., and Skerry, A. 1983. Self and ethnic concepts in relation to ethnic constancy. *Canadian Journal of Behavioural Science* 15, no. 1: 14–26.

Adorno, T. W., Frenkel-Brusnwick, E., Levinson, D., and Sanford, R. N. 1950. *The Authoritarian Personality*. Harper and Row.

Alba, R. 1985. *Italian Americans: Into the Twilight of Ethnicity*. Prentice-Hall.

Alejandro-Wright, M. N. 1985. The child's conception of racial classification: A socio-cognitive developmental model. In M. B. Spencer et al., eds., *Beginnings*. Erlbaum.

Alland, A. 1971. *Human Diversity*. Columbia University Press.

Allport, G. 1954. *The Nature of Prejudice*. Addison-Wesley.

Andersen, E. 1986. The acquisition of register variation by Anglo-American children. In B. Schieffelin and E. Ochs, eds., *Language Socialization across Cultures*. Cambridge University Press.

Andersen, E. 1990. *Speaking with Style: The Sociolinguistic Skills of Children*. Routledge.

Anderson, B. 1983. *Imagined Communities: Reflections on the Origin and Spread of Nationalism*. Verso.

Appiah, K. A. 1990a. Racisms. In D. T. Goldberg, ed., *Anatomy of Racism*. University of Minnesota Press.

Appiah, K. A. 1990b. Race. In F. Lentricchia and T. McLaughin, eds., *Critical Terms for Literary Study*. University of Chicago Press.

Ariès, P. 1962. *Centuries of Childhood: A Social History of Family Life*. Vintage.

Arvey, R., et al. 1994. Mainstream science on intelligence [letter to the editor]. *Wall Street Journal*, December 13, 1994.

Ashmore, R., and Del Boca, F. 1981. Conceptual approaches to stereotypes and stereotyping. In D. Hamilton, ed., *Cognitive Processes in Stereotyping and Intergroup Behavior*. Erlbaum.

Astington, J., Harris, P., and Olson, D. 1988. *Developing Theories of Mind*. Cambridge University Press.

Atran, S. 1988. Basic conceptual domains. *Mind and Language* 3: 7–16.

Atran, S. 1990. *Cognitlve Foundations of Natural History*. Cambridge University Press.

Atran, S. 1994. Core domains versus scientific theories. In L. Hirschfeld and S. Gelman, eds., *Mapping the Mind*. Cambridge University Press.

Avis, J., and Harris, P. 1991. Belief-desire reasoning among Baka children: Evidence for a universal conception of mind. *Child Development* 62: 460–467.

Aya, R. 1971. *National Liberation; Revolution in the Third World*. Free Press.

Bailey, J. M., Pillard, R. C., Neale, M. C., and Agyei, Y. 1993. Heritable factors influence sexual orientation in women. *Archives of General Psychiatry* 50, no. 3: 217–223.

Banton, M. 1978. *The Idea of Race.* Westview.

Banton, M. 1987. *Racial Theories.* Cambridge University Press.

Barkan, E. 1992. *The Retreat of Scientific Racism: Changing Concepts of Race in Britain and the United States between the World Wars.* Cambridge University Press.

Barkowitz, P., and Brigham, J. 1982. Recognition of faces: Own-race bias, incentive, and time delay. *Journal of Applied Social Psychology* 12: 255–268.

Beck, E. M., and Tolnay, S. T. 1990. The killing fields of the Deep South: The market for cotton and the lynching of blacks, 1882–1930. *American Sociological Review* 55: 526–539,

Becker, J. 1982. Children's strategic use of requests to mark and manipulate social status. In S. Kuczaj, ed., *Language Development*, volume 2. Erlbaum.

Behrend, D. A. 1990. Constraints and development: A reply to Nelson 1988. *Cognitive Development* 5: 313–330.

Bem, S. 1989. Genital knowledge and gender constancy in preschool children. *Child Development* 60: 649–620.

Berlin, B. 1972. Speculations on the growth of ethnobotanical classification and nomenclature. *Annual Review of Ecology and Systematics* 4: 259–271.

Berlin, B. 1978. Ethnobiological classification. In E. Rosch and B. Lloyd, eds., *Cognition and Categorization.* Erlbaum.

Berlin, B. 1992. *Ethnobiological Classification.* Princeton University Press.

Berlin, B., and Kay, P. 1969. *Basic Color Terms: Their Universality and Growth.* University of California Press.

Berlin, B., Breedlove, D., and Raven, P. 1973. General principles of classification and nomenclature in folk biology. *American Anthropologist* 75: 214–242.

Betancourt, H., and Lopez, S. 1993. The study of culture, ethnicity, and race in American psychology. *American Psychologist* 48: 629–637.

Biederman, I., and Shiffrar, M. M. 1987. Sexing day-old chicks: A case study and expert systems analysis of a difficult perceptual learning task. *Journal of Experimental Psychology: Learning, Memory, and Cognition* 13: 640–645.

Bigler, R., and Liben, L. 1985. Racial stereotyping and constructive memory in children. Paper presented at the Biennal Meetings of the Society for Research in Child Development, Kansas City.

Blaske, D. 1984. Occupational sex-typing by kindergarten and fourth-grade children. *Psychological Reports* 53: 795–801.

Bloch, M. 1974. Symbols, song, dance and features of articulation: Is religion an extreme form of traditional authority? *European Journal of Sociology* 15: 55–81.

Bloch, M. 1993. Domain-specificity, living kinds and symbolism. In P. Boyer, ed., *Cognitive Aspects of Religious Symbolism.* Cambridge University Press.

Bloom, P. 1994. Possible names: The role of syntax-semantics mappings in the acquisition of nominals. *Lingua* 92: 297–329.

Bodmer, W., and Cavalli-Sforza, L. 1976. *Genetics, Evolution, and Man.* Freeman.

Boster, J., Berlin, B., and O'Neill, J. 1986. The correspondence of Jivaroan to scientific ornithology. *American Anthropologist* 89: 914–920.

Bowerman, M. 1982. Reorganization and processes in lexical and syntactic development. In E. Wanner and L. Gleitman, eds., *Language Acquisition.* Cambridge University Press.

Boyer, P. 1990. *Tradition as Truth and Communication.* Cambridge University Press.

Boyer, P. 1994. *The Naturalness of Religious Ideas: A Cognitive Theory of Religion.* University of California Press.

Brace, C. L. 1964. A non-racial approach toward the understanding of human diversity. In A. Montagu, ed., *The Concept of Race*. University of Nebraska Press.

Brewer, M. 1988. A dual process model of impression formation. In T. K. Srull and R. S. Wyer, Jr., eds., *Advances in Social Cognition*, volume 1. Erlbaum.

Brewer, W. F., and Samarapungavan, A. 1991. Children's theories vs. scientific theories: Differences in reasoning or differences in knowledge? In R. Hoffman and D. Palermo, eds., *Cognition and the Symbolic Process*. Erlbaum.

Brown, A. 1990. Domain-specific principles affect learning and transfer in children. *Cognitive Science* 14: 107–133.

Bruner, J. 1990. *Acts of Meaning*. Harvard University Press.

Bulmer, R. 1967. Why is the cassowary not a bird? *Man* 2: 5–25.

Burling, R. 1993. Primate calls, human language, and nonverbal communication. *Current Anthropology* 34: 25–53.

Buss, D. M. 1994. *The Evolution of Desire: Strategies of Human Mating*. Basic Books.

Byard, P. 1981. Quantitative genetics of human skin color. *Yearbook of Physical Anthropology* 24: 123–137.

Byrne, W., and Parsons, B. 1993. Human sexual orientation: The biologic theories reappraised. *Archives of General Psychiatry* 50: 228–239.

Cahan, E., Mechling, J., Sutton-Smith, B., and White, S. 1993. The elusive historical child: ways of knowing the child of history and psychology. In G. Elder et al., eds., *Children in Time and Place*. Cambridge University Press.

Campos, J., and Sternberg, C. 1981. Perception, appraisal, and emotion: The onset of social referencing. In M. Lamb and L. Sherrod, eds., *Infants Social Cognition*. Erlbaum.

Carey, S. 1978. The child as language learner. In M. Halle, J. Bresnan, and G. A. Miller, eds., *Linguistic Theory and Psychological Reality*. MIT Press.

Carey, S. 1985. *Conceptual Development in Childhood*. MIT Press.

Carey, S. 1990. Cognitive development. In D. N. Osherson and E. E. Smith, eds., *Thinking: An Invitation to Cognitive Science*, volume 3. MIT Press.

Carey, S., and Diamond, R. 1980. Maturational determination of the developmental course of face encoding. In D. Caplan, ed., *Biological Studies of Mental Processes*. MIT Press.

Carey, S., and Gelman, R. 1991. *The Epigenesis of Mind: Essays on Biology and Cognition*. Erlbaum.

Carey, S., and Spelke, E. 1994. Domain specific knowledge and conceptual change. In L. Hirschfeld and S. Gelman, eds., *Mapping the Mind*. Cambridge University Press.

Chance, J., Turner, A., Goldstein, A. 1982. Development of differential recognition for own- and other-race faces. *Journal of Psychology* 112: 29–37.

Chase, W., and Simon, H. 1973. The mind's eye in chess. In W. Chase, ed., *Visual Information Processing*. Academic Press.

Cheney, D. L., and Seyfarth, R. M. 1990. *How Monkeys See the World: Inside the Mind of Another Species*. University of Chicago Press.

Chomsky, N. 1980a. On cognitive structures and their development: A reply to Piaget. In M. Piatelli-Palmarini, ed., *Language and Learning*. Harvard University Press.

Chomsky, N. 1980b. *Rules and Representations*. Columbia University Press.

Chomsky, N. 1986. *Knowledge of Language*. Praeger.

Chomsky, N. 1988. *Language and the Problems of Knowledge: The Managua Lectures*. MIT Press.

Clark, K, and Clark, M. 1940a. Skin color as a factor in racial identification of Negro pre-school children: A preliminary report. *Journal of Experimental Education* 8: 161–163.

Clark, K., and Clark, M. 1940b. Skin color as a factor in racial identification of Negro preschool children. *Journal of Social Psychology* 11: 159–169.

Clark, K., and Clark, M. 1947. Racial identification and preferences in Negro children. In T. Newcombe and E. Hartley, eds., *Readings in Social Psychology*. Holt.

Cole, M. 1990. Cultural psychology: A once and future discipline? In J. J. Berman, ed., *Nebraska Symposium on Motivation, 1989: Cross-Cultural Perspectives* 3. University of Nebraska Press.

Cordua, G., McGraw, K., and Drabman, R. 1979. Doctor or nurse: Children's perception of sex typed occupations. *Child Development* 50: 590–593.

Corenblum, B., and Wilson, A. E. 1982. Ethnic preference and identification among Canadian Indian and White children: replication and extension. *Canadian Journal of Behavioral Science* 14, no. 1: 50–59.

Corsaro, W. 1979. Young children's conception of status and role. *Sociology of Education* 5: 46–59.

Corsaro, W. 1986. Routines in peer culture. In J. Cook-Gumperz et al., eds., *Children's Worlds and Children's Language*. Mouton de Gruyter.

Corsaro, W., and Eder, D. 1990. Children's peer cultures. *Annual Review of Sociology* 16: 197–220.

Cosmides, L. 1989. The logic of social exchange: Has natural selection shaped how humans reason? Studies with the Wason selection task. *Cognition* 31: 187–276.

Cosmides, L., and Tooby, J. 1989. Evolutionary psychology and the generation of culture. Part II: A computational theory of social exchange. *Ethology and Sociobiology* 10: 51–97.

Cosmides, L., and Tooby, J. 1994. Origins of domain-specificity: The evolution of functional organization. In L. Hirschfeld and S. Gelman, eds., *Mapping the Mind*. Cambridge University Press.

Crocker, J. 1977. My brother the parrot. In J. Sapir and J. Crocker, eds., *The Social Use of Metaphor*. University of Pennsylvania Press.

Cross, W. 1985. Black identity: Discovering the distinction between personal identity and reference group orientation. In M. B. Spencer et al., eds., *Beginnings*. Erlbaum.

Cross, W. 1991. *Shades of Black: Diversity in African-American Identity*. Temple University Press.

Curtin, P. 1964. *The Image of Africa: British Ideas and Action, 1780–1880*. University of Wisconsin Press.

Daniel, E. 1984. *Fluid Signs: Being a Person the Tamil Way*. University of California Press.

Davey, A. 1983. *Learning to Be Prejudiced: Growing Up in Multi-Ethnic Britain*. Edward Arnold.

Davey, A., and Norburn, M. 1980. Ethnic awareness and ethnic differentiation amongst primary school children. *New Community* 8: 51–60.

Davis, F. 1991. *Who Is Black: One Nation's Definition*. Pennsylvania State University Press.

DeCasper, A., and Fifer, W. 1980. Of human bonding: newborns prefer their mothers' voices. *Science* 208: 1174–1176.

Degler, C. 1971. *Neither Black nor White: Slavery and Race Relations in Brazil and the United States*. Macmillan.

Degler, C. 1991. *In Search of Human Nature: The Decline and Revival of Darwinism in American Social Thought*. Oxford University Press.

deMause, L. 1974. The evolution of childhood. *History of Childhood Quarterly* 1: 503–575.

Denhière, G. 1984. Il y a bien longtemps. . . . Aspects de la genese de la comprehension et de la memorisation de recits. In M. Moscato and J. Pieraut-Le Bonniec, eds., *Ontogenese de la processus psychologiques*. Presses Universitaire de Rouen.

Denhière, G. 1988. Story comprehension and memorization by children: The role of input-, conservation-, and output-processes. In F. Weinert and M. Perlmutter, eds., *Memory Development: Universal Changes and Individual Differences*. Erlbaum.

Denhière, G., and Le Ny, J. 1980. Relative importance of meaningful units in comprehension and recall of narratives by children and adults. *Poetics* 9.

Dennett, D. 1976. Conditions on personhood. In A. Rorty, ed., *The Identities of Persons*. University Of California Press.

Dennett, D. 1995. *Darwin's Dangerous Idea: Evolution and the Meanings of Life*. Simon and Schuster.

Dole, G. 1967. Tribe as the autonomous unit. In *Essays on the Problem of Tribe*. Seattle: American Ethnological Society.

Domìnguez, V. 1986. *White by Definition: Social Classification in Creole Louisiana*. Rutgers University Press.

Dougherty, J. 1978. Salience and relativity in classification. *American Ethnologist* 5: 66–80.

Doyle, A. 1983. Friends, acquaintances, and strangers: The influence of familiarity and ethnolinguistic background on social interaction. In K. Rubin and H. Ross, eds., *Peer Relationships and Social Skills in Childhood*. Springer-Verlag.

Doyle, A., Beaudet, J., and Aboud, F. 1988. Developmental patterns in the flexibility of children's racial attitudes. *Journal of Cross-Cultural Psychology* 9: 3–18

Doyle, A., Rappard, P., and Connolly, J. 1980. Two solitudes in the preschool classroom. *Canadian Journal of Behavioral Science* 12: 221–232.

Dumont, L. 1970. *Homo hierarchicus*: An Essay On The Caste System. University of Chicago Press.

Dunn, J. 1988. *The Beginnings of Social Understanding*. Blackwell.

Dupré, J. 1987. Human kinds. In J. Dupré, ed., *The Latest on the Best: Essays on Evolution and Optimality*. MIT Press.

Durrett, M. E., and Davy, A. J. 1979. Racial awareness in young Mexican-American, Negro and Anglo children. *Young Children* 26: 16–24.

Eder, R. 1989. The emergent personologist: The structure and content of $3\frac{1}{2}$, $5\frac{1}{2}$, and $7\frac{1}{2}$ year-olds' concepts of themselves and other persons. *Child Development* 60: 1218–1228.

Eder, R. 1990. Uncovering young children's psychological selves: Individual and developmental differences. *Child Development* 61: 849–863.

Elder, G. H. Jr., Modell, J., and Parke, R. D. 1993. *Children in Time and Place: Developmental and Historical Insights*. Cambridge University Press.

Emmerich, W., Goldman, K., Kirsch, B., and Sharabany, R. 1977. Evidence for a transitional phase in the development of gender constancy. *Child Development* 48: 930–936.

Evans, E. M. 1994. God or Darwin? The Development of Beliefs About the Origin of the Species. Doctoral dissertation, University of Michigan.

Eysenck, H., and Kamin, L. 1981. *The Intelligence Controversy*. Wiley.

Fagot, B., Leinbach, M., and Hagan, R. 1986. Gender labeling and the adoption of sex-typed behaviors. *Developmental Psychology* 22: 440–443.

Fairchild, C. 1984. *Domestic Enemies: Servants and their Masters in Old Regime France*. Johns Hopkins University Press.

Fanon, F. 1968. *Black Skin, White Masks*. MacGibbon and Kee.

Feinman, S., and Entwisle, D. 1976. Children's ability to recognize other children's faces. *Child Development* 47: 506–510.

Fields, B. J. 1982. Ideology and Race in American History. In J. Konsserf and S. McPherson, eds., *Region, Race and Reconstruction*. Oxford University Press.

Fields, B. J. 1990. Slavery, race and ideology in the United States of America. *New Left Review* 181: 95–118.

Finkelstein, N., and Haskins, R. 1983. Kindergarten children prefer same-color peers. *Child Development* 54.

Fiske, S. T., and Neuberg, S. L. 1990. A continuum of impression formation, from category based to individuating processes: Influences of information and motivation on attention on attention and interpretation. *Advances in Experimental Social Psychology* 23: 1–74.

Fiske, S., and Taylor, S. 1991. *Social Cognition*. McGraw-Hill.

Frankenberg, R. 1993. *White Women, Race Matters: The Social Construction of Whiteness.* University Of Minnesota Press.

Fredrickson, G. M. 1988. *The Arrogance of Race: Historical Perspectives on Slavery, Racism, and Social Inequality.* Wesleyan University Press.

Fried, M. 1975. *The Notion of Tribe*. Cummings.

Fuss, D. 1989. *Essentially Speaking: Feminism, Nature, and Difference*. Routledge.

Gallistel, C. 1990. *The Organization of Learning*. MIT Press.

Gallistel, C., Brown, A., Carey, S., Gelman, R., and Keil, F. 1991. Lessons from animal learning for the study of human development. In S. Carey and R. Gelman, eds., *The Epigenesis of Mind: Essays on Biology and Cognition*. Erlbaum.

Gardner, D., Harris, P., Ohmoto, M, and Hamazaki, T. 1988. Japanese children's understanding of the distinction between real and apparent emotions. *International Journal of Behavioral Development* 11: 203–218.

Garret, C., Ein, P., and Tremaine, L. 1977. The development of gender stereotyping of adult occupation in elementary school children. *Child Development* 48: 507–512.

Gates, H. L. 1993. Backlash? *New Yorker*, May 17.

Geertz, C. 1973. *Interpretation of Cultures*. Basic Books

Gelman, R. 1990. Structural constraints on cognitive development. *Cognitive Science* 14: 3–10.

Gelman, R., and Brenneman, K. 1994. First principles can support both universal and culture-specific learning about number and music. In L. A. Hirschfeld and S. A. Gelman, eds., *Mapping the Mind*. Cambridge University Press.

Gelman, R., and Gallistel, R. 1978. *The Child's Understanding of Number* Harvard University Press.

Gelman, R., Spelke, E., and Meck, E. 1983. What preschoolers know about animate and inanimate objects. In D. Rogers and J. Sloboda, eds., *The Acquisition of Symbolic Skills*. Plenum.

Gelman, S. 1988. The development of induction within natural kind and artifact categories. *Cognitive Psychology* 20: 65–96.

Gelman, S. 1989. Children's use of categories to guide biological inferences. *Human Development* 32: 65–71.

Gelman, S., Coley, J., and Gottfried, G. 1994. Essentialist beliefs in children: The acquisition of concepts and theories. In L. Hirschfeld and S. Gelman, *Mapping the Mind*. Cambridge University Press.

Gelman, S., Collman, P., and Maccoby, E. 1986. Inferring properties from categories versus inferring categories from properties: The case of gender. *Child Development* 57: 396–404.

Gelman, S., and Markman, E. 1986. Categories and induction in young children. *Cognition* 23: 183–209.

Gelman, S., and Markman, E. 1987. Young children's inductions from natural kinds: The role of categories and appearances. *Child Development* 58: 1532–1541.

Gelman, S., and Wellman, H. 1991. Insides and essences: Early understandings of the non-obvious. *Cognition* 38: 213–244.

Gettys, L., and Cann, A. 1981. Children's perceptions of occupational sex stereotypes. *Sex Roles* 7: 301–308.

Gill, D. Mayor, B., and Blair, M. 1992. *Racism and Education*. Sage.

Gill, D., and Levidow, L. 1987. *Anti-Racist Science Teaching*. Free Association Press.

Gleitman, L. 1986. Biological dispositions to learn language. In W. Demopoulous and A. Marras, eds., *Langauge Learning and Concept Acquisition: Foundational Issues*. Ablex.
Gobineau, A. 1970/1853–55. *Essay on the Inequality of Human Races*. H. Fertig.
Goldberg, T. 1993. *Racist Culture: Philosophy and the Politics of Meaning*. Blackwell.
Goldstein, A., and Chance, J. 1981. Laboratory studies of face recognition. In G. Davies et al., eds., *Perceiving and Remembering Faces*. Academic Press.
Goodman, M. E. 1970. *The Culture of Childhood: Child's-Eye Views of Society and Culture*. Teachers College Press.
Goodman, N. 1972. Seven strictures on similarity. In N. Goodman, ed., *Problems and Project*. Bobbs-Merrill.
Gopnik, A., and Wellman, H. 1994. The theory theory. In L. Hirschfeld and S. Gelman, eds., *Mapping the Mind*. Cambridge University Press.
Gordon, L. 1990. Family violence, feminism, and social control. In L. Gordon, ed., *Women, the State, and Welfare*. University of Wisconsin Press.
Gordon, L. 1994. *Pitied But Not Entitled: Single Mothers and the History of Welfare*. Free Press.
Gossett, T. F. 1963. *Race: The History of an Idea in America*. Schocken.
Gould, S. 1981. *The Mismeasure of Man*. Norton.
Greenfield, P. 1991. Language, tools and brain: The ontogeny and phylogeny of hierarchically organized sequential behavior. *Behavioral and Brain Sciences* 14: 531–995.
Grosjean, F. 1982. *Life with Two Languages: An Introduction to Bilingualism*. Harvard University Press.
Guardo, C., and Bohan, J. 1971. Development of a sense of self-identity in children. *Child Development* 42: 1909–1921.
Guillaumin, C. 1980. The idea of race and its elevation to autonomous scientific and legal status. In *Sociological theories: Race and Colonialism*. UNESCO.
Hacking, I. 1995. The looping effect of human kinds. In D. Sperber et al., eds., *Causal Cognition*. Clarendon.
Hahn, R., Mulinare, J., and Teutsch, S. 1992. Inconsistencies in coding of race and ethnicity between birth and death in US infants: A new look at infant mortality, 1983 through 1985. *Journal of the American Medical Association* 267: 259–263.
Hahn, R., and Stroup, D. 1994. Race and ethnicity in public health surviellance: Criteria for the scientific use of social categories. *Public Health Reports* 109: 7–15.
Hall, S. 1980. Race, articulation and societies structured in dominance. In C. Guillaumin, ed., *Sociological Theorie: Race and Colonialism*. UNESCO.
Hallpike, C. 1979. *The Foundations of Primitive Thought*. Oxford University Press.
Hamilton, D. 1981. Illusory correlation as a basis for stereotyping. In D. Hamilton, ed., *Cognitive Processes in Stereotyping and Intergroup Behavior*. Erlbaum.
Hamilton, D. L., and Gifford, R. K. 1976. Illusory correlation in interpersonal perception: A cognitive basis of stereotypic judgements. *Journal of Experimental Social Psychology* 12: 392–407.
Hamilton, D., and Trolier, T. 1986. Stereotypes and stereotyping: An overview of the cognitive approach. In J. Dovidio and S. Gaertner, eds., *Prejudice, Discrimination, and Racism*. Academic Press.
Harris, M. 1964. *Patterns of Race in the Americas*. Walker.
Harris, P. 1994. Thinking by children and scientists: False analogies and neglected similarities. In L. Hirschfeld and S. Gelman, eds., *Mapping the Mind*. Cambridge University Press.
Hatano, G., and Inagaki, K. In press. Cognitive and cultural factors in the acquisition of intuitive biology. In D. R. Olson, ed., *Handbook of Psychology in Education*. Blackwell.

Haynes-Bautista, D. 1980. Identifying "Hispanic" populations: The influence of research methodology upon public policy. *American Journal of Public Health* 70, no. 4: 353–356.

Heath, S. 1982. What no bedtime story means: Narrative skills at home and school. *Language in Society* 11: 49–76.

Heider, E., and Oliver, D. 1972. The structure of the color space in naming and memory for two languages. *Cognitive Psychology* 3: 337–354.

Herrnstein, R. J. 1979. Acquisition, generalization, and discrimination reversal of a natural concept. *Journal of Experimental Psychology: Animal Behavior Processes* 5 116–129.

Herrnstein, R. J., and Murray, C. 1994. *The Bell Curve: Intelligence and Class Structure in American Life.* Free Press.

Hewstone, M., Hantzi, A., and Johnston, L. 1991. Social categorization and person memory: The pervasiveness of race as an organizing principle. *European Journal of Social Psychology* 21: 517–528.

Higham, J. 1955. *Strangers in the Land; Patterns of American Nativism, 1860–1925.* Rutgers University Press.

Hirschfeld, L. 1986. Kinship and cognition: Genealogy and the meaning of kinship terms. *Current Anthropology* 27: 217–242.

Hirschfeld, L. 1988. On acquiring social categories: Cognitive development and anthropological wisdom. *Man* 23: 611–38.

Hirschfeld, L. 1989a. Discovering linguistic differences: domain specificity and the young child's awareness of multiple languages. *Human Development* 32: 223–236.

Hirschfeld, L. 1989b. Rethinking the acquisition of kinship terms. *International Journal of Behavioral Development* 12: 541–568.

Hirschfeld, L. 1993. Discovering social difference: The role of appearance in the development of racial awareness. *Cognitive Psychology* 25: 317–350.

Hirschfeld, L. 1994. Is the acquisition of social categories based on domain-specific competence or on knowledge transfer? In L. Hirschfeld and S. Gelman, eds., *Mapping the Mind.* Cambridge University Press.

Hirschfeld, L. 1995a. Anthropology, psychology, and the meanings of social causality. In D. Sperber et al., eds., *Causal Cognition.* Oxford University Press.

Hirschfeld, L. 1995b. Do children have a theory of race? *Cognition* 54: 209–252.

Hirschfeld, L. 1995c. The inheritability of identity: Children's understanding of the innate potential of race. *Child Development* 66. 1418–1437.

Hirschfeld, L., and Gelman, S. 1991. Metalinguistic and metasocial understanding in preschoolers. Presented at meeting of Society for Research in Child Development, Seattle.

Hirschfeld, L., and Gelman, S. 1994a. Toward a typography of the mind: an introduction to domain-specificity. In L. Hirschfeld and S. Gelman, eds., *Mapping the Mind.* Cambridge University Press.

Hirschfeld, L., and Gelman, S. 1994b. *Mapping the Mind: Domain Specificity in Cognition and Culture.* Cambridge University Press.

Hirszfeld, L., and Hirszfeld, H. 1919. Serological differences between the blood of different races: The result of researches on the Macedonian front. *Lancet* 2: 675–679.

Hoffman, M. 1981. Perspectives on the difference between understanding people and understanding things: The role of affect. In J. Flavell and L. Ross, eds., *Social Cognitive Developments.* Cambridge University Press.

Holmes, R. 1995. *How Young Children Perceive Race.* Sage.

Horowitz, R. 1939. Racial aspects of self-identification in nursery school children. *Journal of Psychology* 7: 91–99.

Hughes, W. 1975. Skin color identification and preference among children in Sweden and America: A comparative analysis. Department of Educational Research, School of Education, Uppsala, Sweden.

Hull, D. 1992. Biological species: an inductivists' nightmare. In M. Douglas and D. Hull, eds., *How Classification Works.* Edinburgh University Press.

Hunsberger, B. 1978. Racial awareness and preference of White and Indian Canadian children. *Canadian Journal of Behaviour Science* 10, no. 2: 176–180.

Inagaki, K. 1990. Young children's everyday biology as the basis for learning school biology. *Bulletin of the Faculty of Education, Chiba University* 38: 177–84.

Inagaki, K., and Hatano, G. 1987. Young children's spontaneous personification and analogy. *Child Development* 58: 1013–20.

Inagaki, K., and Hatano, G. 1988. Young children's understanding of the mind-body distinction. Paper presented at the meetings of American Educational Research Association, New Orleans.

Jackendoff, R. 1992. *Language of the Mind: Essays on Mental Representation.* MIT Press.

Jackson, J., McCullough, W., Gurin, G. 1988. Family, socialization environment, and identity development in Black Americans. In H. P. McAdoo, ed., *Black Families.* Sage.

Jahoda, G. 1963. The development of children's ideas about country and nationality. *British Journal of Educational Psychology* 33: 47–60, 142–153.

Johnson, K., Mervis, C., and Boster, J. 1992. Developmental changes within the structure of the mammal domain. *Developmental Psychology* 28: 74–83.

Jones, E., and Nisbett, R. 1972. The actor and the observer: Divergent perceptions of the causes of behavior. In E. Jones et al., eds., *Attribution.* General Learning Press.

Jones, J. 1991. Psychological models of race: What have they been and what should they be? In J. D. Goodchilds, ed., *Psychological Perspectives on Human Diversity in America.* American Psychological Association.

Jordan, W. D. 1968. *White Over Black: American Attitudes Toward the Negro, 1550–1812.* Norton.

Kaiser, M. K., Proffitt, D. R., and Anderson, K. 1985. Judgements of natural and anomalous trajectories in the presence and absence of motion. *Journal of Experimental Psychology: Learning, Memory, and Cognition* 11, no. 1 –4: 795–803.

Kalmijn, M. 1993. Trends in black/white intermarriage. *Social Forces* 72: 119–146.

Karmiloff-Smith, A. 1979. *A Functional Approach to Child Language: A Study of Determiners and Reference.* Cambridge University Press.

Karmiloff-Smith, A., and Inhelder, B. 1975. If you want to get ahead, get a theory. *Cognition* 3: 195–211.

Katz, P. 1973. Perception of racial cues in preschool children: A new look. *Developmental Psychology* 8: 295–299.

Katz, P. 1982. Development of children's racial awareness and intergroup attitudes. In L. Katz, ed., *Current Topics in Early Childhood Education*, volume 4. Ablex.

Katz, P. 1983. Developmental foundations of gender and racial attitudes. In R. L. Leahy, ed., *The Child's Construction of Social Inequality.* Academic Press.

Katz, P., Sohn, M., and Zalk, S. 1975. Perceptual concomitants of racial attitudes in urban grade-school children. *Developmental Psychology* 11: 135–144.

Katz, P., and Zalk, S. 1974. Doll preferences: an index of racial attitudes? *Journal of Educational Psychology* 66: 663–668.

Kempton, W., and Kay, P. 1984. What is the Sapir-Whorf hypothesis? *American Anthropologist* 86: 65–79.

Keil, F. 1979. *Semantic and Conceptual Development: An Ontological Perspective.* Harvard University Press.

Keil, F. 1981. Constraints on knowledge and cognitive development. *Psychological Review* 88: 197–227.

Keil, F. 1989. *Concepts, Kinds, and Cognitive Development*. MIT Press.

Keil, F. 1994. The birth and nurturance of concepts by domains: The origins of concepts of living things. In L. Hirschfeld and S. Gelman, eds., *Mapping the Mind*. Cambridge University Press.

Kessen, W. 1993. A developmentalist's reflections. In G. Elder et al., eds., *Children in Time and Place*. Cambridge University Press.

Klineberg, O. 1935. *Race Differences*. Harper.

Klineberg, O. 1975. Race and psychology: The problem of genetic differences. In L. Kuper, ed., *Race, Science and Society*. UNESCO Press.

Kohlberg, L. 1966. A cognitive-developmental analysis of children's sex-role concepts and attitudes. In E. Maccoby, ed., *The Development of Sex Differences*. Stanford University Press.

Kuczaj, S. 1989. Commentary. *Human Development* 32: 237–240.

Kuczaj, S. A., and Harbaugh, B. 1980. What children think about the speaking capabilities of other persons and things. In S. Kuczaj, ed., *Language Development*,volume 2. Erlbaum.

Kuhl, P. 1985. Categorization of speech by infants. In J. Mehler and R. Fox, eds., *Neonate Cognition*. Erlbaum.

Lakoff, G. 1987. *Women, Fire, and Dangerous Things: What Categories Reveal About the Mind*. University of Chicago Press.

Lakoff, G., and Kövescses, Z. 1987. The cognitive model of anger inherent in American English. In D. Holland and N. Quinn, eds., *Cultural Models in Language and Thought*. Cambridge University Press.

Lambert, W., and Tachuchi, Y. 1956. Ethnic cleavage among young children. *Journal of Abnormal and Social Psychology* 53.

Langlois, J., and Roggman, L. 1990. Attractive faces are only average. *Psychological Science* 1, no. 2: 115–121.

Latter, B. 1980. Genetic differences within and between populations of the major human subgroups. *American Naturalist* 116: 220–237.

Leach, E. 1964. Anthropological aspects of language: Animal categories and verbal abuse. In E. Lennenberg, ed., *New Directions in the Study of Language*. MIT Press.

Lemaine, G., Santolini, A., Bonnet, P., and Ben Brika, J. 1985. Préferences raciales, identité et soi idéal chez les enfants de 5 à 11 ans. *Bulletin de Psychologie* 39: 129–157.

Lerner, R. 1969. The development of stereotyped expectancies of body build-behavior relations. *Child Development* 40: 137–141.

Lerner, R. 1973. The development of personal space schemata toward body build. *Journal of Psychology* 84: 229–235.

Lerner, R., and Schroeder, C. 1971. Physique identification, preference, and aversion in kindergarten children. *Developmental Psychology* 5: 538

Lesgold, A. M., Rubinson, H., Feltovich, P., Glaser, R., Klopfer, D., and Wang, Y. 1988. Expertise in a complex skill: Diagnosing x-ray pictures. In M. Chi et al., eds., *The Nature of Expertise*. Erlbaum.

Leslie, A. 1994. ToMM, ToBy, and agency: Core architecture and domain specificity. In L. Hirschfeld and S. Gelman, eds., *Mapping the Mind*. Cambridge University Press.

Lévi-Strauss, C. 1962. *Totemism*. Beacon.

LeVine, R., and Campbell, D. 1972. *Ethnocentrism: Theories of Conflict, Ethnic Attitudes, and Group Behavior*. Wiley.

Lewontin, R. 1972. The apportionment of human diversity. *Evolutionary Biology* 25: 276–280.

Lewontin, R. 1987. Are the races different? In D. Gill and L. Levidow, eds., *Anti-Racist Science Teaching*. Free Association Books.

Lindholm, K., and Padilla, A. 1977. Language mixing in bilingual children. *Child Language* 5: 327–335.

Lindsay, D, Jack, P., Christian, M. 1991. Other-race face perception. *Journal of Applied Psychology* 76: 587–589.

Loehlin, J., Vandenberg, S., and Osborne, R. 1973. Blood group genes and Negro-white ability differences. *Behavior Genetics* 3: 257–270.

López, A., Gutheil, G., Gelman, S., and Smith, E. 1992. The development of category based induction. *Child Development* 63: 1070–1090.

Lucy, J., and Shweder, R. 1979. Whorf and his critics: Linguistic and nonlinguistic influences on color memory. *American Anthropologist* 81: 581–615.

Lucy, J., and Shweder, R. 1988. The effect of incidental conversation on memory for focal colors. *American Anthropologist* 90: 923–931.

Lutz, C. 1988. *Unnatural Emotions: Everyday Sentiments on a Micronesian Atoll and Their Challenge to Western Theory*. University of Chicago Press.

Lynn, M., Shavitt, S., and Ostrom, T. 1985. Effects of pictures on the organization and recall of social information. *Journal of Personality and Social Psychology* 49: 1160–1168

MacWhinney, B. and Snow, C. 1985. The child language data exchange system. *Journal of Child Language* 12: 271–296.

MacWhinney, B. and Snow, C. 1990. The child language data exchange system: an update. *Journal of Child Language* 17: 457–472.

Mandler, J. 1985. *Stories, Scripts, and Scenes: Aspects of Schema theory*. Erlbaum.

Mandler, J. 1992. How to build a baby: II. Conceptual primitives. *Psychological Review* 99: 587–604.

Mandler, J., Bauer, P., and McDonough, L. 1991. Separating the sheep from the goats: Differentiating global categories. *Cognitive Psychology* 23: 263–298.

Mannoni, D. 1964. *Prospero and Caliban: The Psychology of Colonialism*. Praeger.

Marcus, G. E., and Fischer, M. J. 1986. *Anthropology as Cultural Critique: An Experimental Moment in the Human Sciences*. University of Chicago Press.

Marks, J. 1995. *Human Biodiversity: Genes, Race, and History*. Aldine de Gruter.

Markus, H., and Kitayama, S. 1991. Culture and self: implications for cognition, emotion, and motivation. *Psychological Review* 98: 224–253.

Markus, H. R., and Kityama, S. 1994. A collective fear of the collective: Implications for selves and theories of selves. *Journal of Personality and Social Psychology* 20, no. 5: 568–579.

Marr, D. 1982. *Vision: A Computational Investigation Into the Human Representation and Processing of Visual Information*. San Francisco: Freeman.

Martinez-Alier, V. 1989. *Marriage, Class and Colour in Nineteenth-Century Cuba: A Study of Racial Attitudes and Sexual Values in a Slave Society*. University of Michigan Press.

Marvick, E. 1974. Nature versus nurture: patterns and trends in seventeenth-century French child-rearing. In L. deMause, ed., *The History of Childhood*. Psychohistory Press.

Massey, D. 1993. *American Apartheid: Segregation and the Making of the Underclass*. Harvard University Press.

Mayr, E. 1988. *Toward a New Philosophy of Biology: Observations of an Evolutionist*. Harvard University Press.

McCandless, B., and Hoyt, J. 1961. Sex, ethnicity and play preferences of preschool children. *Journal of Abnormal Social Psychology* 62: 683–685.

McCarthy, C., and Crichlow, W. 1993. *Race Identity and Representation in Education*. Routledge.

McCauley, C., Stitt, C., and Segal, M. 1980. Stereotyping: From prejudice to prediction. *Psychological Bulletin* 87: 195–215.

McCloskey, M., Caramazza, A., and Green, B. 1980. Curvilinear motion in the absence of external forces: naive beliefs about the motion of objects. *Science* 210: 1139–1141.

McConaghy, N. 1994. Biologic theories of sexual orientation. *Archives of General Psychiatry* 51: 431–432.

Mead, M. 1932. An investigation of the thought of primitive children with special reference to animism. *Journal of the Royal Anthropological Institute* 62: 173–190.

Medin, D. 1989. Concepts and conceptual structure. *American Psychologist* 45: 1469–1481.

Medin, D. L., and Shoben, E. J. 1988. Context and structure in conceptual combination. *Cognitive Psychology* 20: 158–190.

Mehler, J., Jusczyk, P., Lambertz, G., Halsted, N., Bertoncini, J., and Amiel-Tison, C. 1988. A precursor of language acquisition in young infants. *Cognition* 29: 143–178.

Memmi, A. 1965. *The Colonizer and the Colonized.* Orion Press.

Miller, P., and Aloise, P. 1989. Young children's understanding of the psychological causes of behavior: A review. *Child Development* 60: 257–285

Milner, D. 1984. The development of ethnic attitudes. In H. Tajfel, ed., *The Social Dimension.* Cambridge University Press.

Moghaddam, F., Taylor, D., and Wright, S. 1993. *Social Psychology in Cross-Cultural Perspective.* Freeman

Molnar, S. 1992. *Human Variation: Races, Types, and Ethnic Groups.* Prentice- Hall.

Morgan, E. 1975. *American Slavery, American Freedom: The Ordeal of Colonial Virginia.* Norton.

Morland, J. K. 1969. Race awareness among American and Hong Kong Chinese children. *American Journal of Sociology* 75: 360–374.

Mosse, G. 1978. *Toward the Final Solution: A History of European Racism.* H. Fertig.

Murphy, G., and Medin, D. 1985. The role of theories in conceptual coherence. *Psychological Review* 92: 289–316.

Myrdal, G. 1944. *An American Dilemma; The Negro Problem and Modern Democracy.* Harper.

Nei, M., and Roychoudhury, A. 1983. Genetic relationship and evolution of the human races. *Evolutionary Biology* 14: 1–59.

Nelson, K. 1988. Constraints on word learning? *Cognitive Development* 3: 221–246.

Nisbett, R. 1993. Violence and U.S. regional culture. *American Psychologist* 48: 441–449.

Novick, L. 1988. Analogical transfer, problem similarity, and expertise. *Journal of Experimental Psychology: Learning, Memory, and Cognition* 14: 510–520.

Ogbu, J. U. 1990. Cultural mode, identity, and literacy. In J. W. Stigler et al., eds., *Cultural Psychology.* Cambridge University Press.

Omi, M., and Winant, H. 1994. *Racial Formation in the United States: From the 1960s to the 1990s.* Routledge.

Osherson, D., Smith, E., Wilkie, O., López, A., and Shafir, E. 1990. Category-based induction. *Psychological Review* 90: 339–363.

Phinney, J., and Rotheram, M. 1987. *Children's Ethnic Socialization.* Sage.

Piaget, J. 1951. *Judgment and Reasoning in the Child.* K. Paul, Rench, Trubner.

Piaget, J. 1967. *Etudes sur la logique de l'enfant. Tome II: Le jugement et le raisonnement chez l'enfant.* Delachaux et Niestlé.

Piaget, J., and Weil, A-M. 1951. The development in children of the idea of homeland and of relations with other countries. *International Social Science Bulletin* 3: 561–578.

Pinker, S. and Bloom, P. 1990. Natural language and natural selection. *Behavioral and Brain Sciences* 12: 707–784.

Plummer, K. 1981. *The Making of the Modern Homosexual.* Barnes and Noble.

Pope Edwards, C. 1984. The age group labels and categories of preschool children. *Child Development* 55: 440–452.

Popenoe, R. 1994. Racism in the Shara desert: skin color, caste, and paternity among Arab-Berber Moors. Paper delivered at the annual meeting of the American Ethnological Society, Santa Monica.

Porter, J. 1971. *Black Child, White Child: The Development of Racial Attitudes*. Harvard University Press.

Poulsen, D., Kintsch, E., Kintsch, W., and Premack, D. 1979. Children's comprehension and memory for stories. *Journal of Experimental Child Psychology* 28.

Premack, D. 1990. The infant's theory of self-propelled objects. *Cognition* 36: 1–16.

Premack, D. 1994. Moral belief: Form versus content. In L. Hirschfeld and S. Gelman, eds., *Mapping the Mind*. Cambridge University Press.

Proshansky, H. 1966. The development of intergroup attitudes. In L. Hoffman, ed., *Review of Child Development*, volume 2. Russell Sage Foundation.

Pryor, J., and Ostom, T. 1981.The cognitive organization of social information: a convergence operations approach. *Journal of Personality and Social Psychology* 41: 628–641.

Putnam, H. 1975. The meaning of "meaning". In H. Putnam, ed., *Mind, Language and Reality: Philosophical Papers*, volume 2. Cambridge University Press.

Quattrone, G., and Jones, E. 1980. The perception of variability within ingroups and outgroups: Implications for the Law of Small Numbers. *Journal of Personality and Social Psychology* 38: 141–152.

Quine, W. V. O. 1960. *Word and Object*. MIT Press.

Radke, M. Trager, H., and Davis, H. 1949. Social perceptions and attitudes in children. *Genetic Psychology Monographs* 40: 327–447.

Ramsey, P. 1987. Young children's thinking about ethnic differences. In J. Phinney and M. Rotheram, eds., *Children's Ethnic Socialization*. Sage.

Redlinger, W., and Park, T. 1980. Language mixing in young bilinguals. *Journal of Child Language* 7: 337–352.

Resnick, L. 1994. Situated rationalism: biological and social preparation for learning. In L. Hirschfeld and S. Gelman, eds., *Mapping the Mind*. Cambridge University Press.

Rips, L. J. 1989. Similarity, typicality, and categorization. In S. Vosniadou and A. Ortony, eds., *Similarity and Analogical Reasoning*. Cambridge University Press.

Robins, A. 1991. *Biological Perspectives on Human Pigmentation*. Cambridge University Press.

Roediger, D. 1991. *The Wages of Whiteness: Race and the Making of the American Working Class*. Verso.

Roediger, D. 1994. *Towards the Abolition of Whiteness: Essays on Race, Politics, and Working Class History*. Verso.

Rogoff, B. 1990. *Apprenticeship in Thinking: Cognitive Development in Social Context*. Oxford University Press.

Rogoff, B., and Lave, J. 1984. *Everyday Cognition: Its Development in Social Context*. Harvard University Press.

Rosch, E., and Mervis, C. 1975. Family resemblances: Studies in the internal structure of natural categories. *Cognitive Psychology* 8: 382–439.

Rosch, E., Mervis, C., Gray, W., Johnson, D., and Boyes-Braem, P. 1976. Basic objects in natural categories. *Cognitive Psychology* 8: 382–439.

Rosenberg, M. 1979. *Conceiving the Self*. Basic Books.

Rosengren, K., Gelman, S., Kalish, C., and McCormick, M. 1991. As time goes by: Children's early understanding of growth in animals. *Child Development* 62: 1302–1320.

Ross, L. 1981. The "intuitive scientists" formulation and its developmental implications. In J. Flavell and L. Ross, eds., *Social Cognitive Development*. Cambridge University Press.

Rothbart, M. 1981. Memory processes and social beliefs. In D. Hamilton, ed., *Cognitive Processes in Stereotyping and Intergroup Behavior*. Erlbaum.

Rothbart, M., and Taylor, M. 1990. Category labels and social reality: Do we view social categories as natural kinds? In G. Semin and K. Fiedler, eds., *Language and Social Cognition*. Sage.

Rozin, P., and Schull, J. 1988. The adaptive-evolutionary point of view in experimental psychology. In R. Atkinson et al., eds., *Steven's Handbook of Experimental Psychology*. Wiley.

Russell, B. 1948. *Human Knowledge, Its Scope and Limits*. Simon and Schuster.

Russell, K., Wilson, M., and Hall, R. 1992. *The Color Complex: The Politics of Skin Color among African Americans*. Harcourt Brace Jovanovich.

Sartre, J.-P. 1948. *Anti-Semite and Jew*. Schocken.

Scarr, S. 1988. Race and gender as psychological variables. *American Psychologist* 43: 56–59.

Scarr, S., Pakstis, A., Katz, S., and Barker, W. 1977. Absence of a relationship between degree of white ancestry and intellectual skills within a black population. *Human Genetics* 39: 69–89.

Schneider, D. 1968. *American Kinship: A Cultural Account*. Prentice-Hall.

Schofield, J. 1989. *Black and White in School: Trust, Tension or Tolerance?* Teachers College Press.

Schwartz, S. P. 1979. Natural kind terms. *Cognition* 7: 301–315.

Semaj, L. 1980. The development of racial evaluation and preference: a cognitive approach. *Journal of Black Psychology* 6: 59–79.

Shanklin, E. 1994. *Anthropology and Race*. Wadsworth.

Shell, M. 1993. *Children of the Earth: Literature, Politics, and Nationhood*. Oxford University Press.

Shepherd, J. 1981. Social factors in face recognition. In G. Davies et al., eds., *Perceiving and Remembering Faces*. Academic Press.

Sherif, M., and Sherif, C. 1969. *Social Psychology*. Harper and Row.

Shultz, T. 1982. Causal reasoning in the social and nonsocial realms. *Canadian Journal of Behavioral Sciences* 14: 307–322.

Shweder, R. 1982. On savages and other children. *American Anthropologist* 84: 354–366.

Singleton, L., and Asher, S. 1979. Racial integration and children's peer preferences: An investigation of developmental and cohort differences. *Child Development* 50, no. 4: 936–941.

Slaby, R., and Frey, K. 1975. Development of gender constancy and selective attention to same-sex models. *Child Development* 46: 849–856.

Slobin, D. 1978. A case study of early language awareness. In S. A. Sinclair et al., eds., *The Child's Conception of Language*. Springer-Verlag.

Smedley, A. 1993. *Race in North America: Origin and Evolution of a Worldview*. Westview.

Smith, C. 1979. Children's understanding of natural language hierarchies. *Journal of Experimental Child Psychology* 27: 437–458.

Smith, E. E., and Medin, D. L. 1981. *Categories and Concepts*. Harvard University Press.

Snyder, L. 1947. The principles of gene distribution in human populations. *Yale Journal of Biological Medicine* 19: 817–833.

Sollors, W. 1986. *Beyond Ethnicity: Consent and Descent in American Culture*. Oxford University Press.

Solomon, G., Johnson, S., Zaitchik, D., and Carey, S. In press. Like father, like son: Young children's understanding of how and why offspring resemble their parents. *Child Development*.

Sorce, J. 1979. The role of physiognomy in the development of racial awareness. *Journal of Genetic Psychology* 134: 33–41.

Spelke, E. S. 1990. Principles of object perception. *Cognitive Science* 14: 29–56.

Spelke, E., and Gelman, R. 1981. The development of thoughts about animate and inanimate objects: Implications for research on social cognition. In J. Flavell and L. Ross, eds., *Social Cognitive Development*. Cambridge University Press.

Sperber, D. 1974. Contre certains a priori anthropologiques. In E. Morin and M. Piatelli-Palmarini, eds., *L' Unite de l'homme*. Le Seuil.

Sperber, D. 1975a. *Rethinking Symbolism*. Cambridge University Press.

Sperber, D. 1975b. Pourquoi les animaux parfaits, les hybrides et les monstres sont-ils bon à penser symboliquement?. *L'Homme* 15: 5–24.

Sperber, D. 1985. Anthropology and psychology: Towards an epidemiology of representations. *Man* 20: 73–89.

Sperber, D. 1990. The epidemiology of beliefs. In C. Fraser and G. Gaskell, eds., *The Social Psychological Study of Widespread Beliefs*. Clarendon.

Sperber, D. 1994. The modularity of thought and the epidemiology of representations. In L. A. Hirschfeld and S. A. Gelman, eds., *Mapping the Mind*. Cambridge University Press.

Springer, K. 1992. Children's awareness of the biological implications of kinship. *Child Development* 63: 950–959.

Springer, K. 1994. Do children believe mothers or fathers contribute more to inheritance? Poster presented at the 13th biennial meeting of the International Society for the Study of Behavioral Development, Amsterdam.

Springer, K. 1995. The role of factual knowledge in a naive theory of biology. Presented at meeting of Society for Research in Child Development, Indianapolis.

Springer, K., and Keil, F. 1989. On the development of biologically specific beliefs: The case of inheritance. *Child Development* 60: 637–648.

Springer, K., and Keil, F. 1991. Early differentiation of causal mechanisms appropriate to biological and nonbiological kinds. *Child Development* 62: 767–781.

Stack, C. 1975. *All Our Kin: Strategies for Survival in a Black Community*. Harper and Row.

Starr, P. 1987. Social categories and claim in the liberal state. In M. Douglas and D. Hull, eds., *How Classification Works*. Edinburgh University Press.

Stein, N., and Glenn, C. 1979. An analysis of story comprehension in elementary school children. In R. Freedle, ed., *New Directions in Discourse Processing*, volume 2. Ablex.

Steiner, I. 1974. Whatever happened to the group in social psychology? *Journal of Experimental Social Psychology* 10: 94–108.

Stepan, N. 1985. Biological degeneration: races and proper places. In J. E. Chamberlin and S. Gilman, eds., *The Dark Side of Progress*. Columbia University Press.

Stevenson, H., and Stevenson, N. 1960. Social interaction in an interracial nursery school. *Genetic Psychology Monographs* 61: 37–75.

Stoler, A. 1992. Sexual affronts and racial frontiers: European identities and the cultural politics of exclusions in colonial Southeast Asia. *Comparative Study in Society and History* 34: 514–551.

Stoler, A. 1995. *Race and the Education of Desire: Foucault's History of Sexuality and the Colonial Order of Things*. Duke University Press.

Strauss, S., and Shilony, T. 1994. Teacher's models of children's minds and learning. In L. A. Hirschfeld and S. A. Gelman, eds., *Mapping the Mind*. Cambridge University Press.

Stross, B. 1972. Verbal processes in Tzeltal speech socialization. *Anthropological Linguistics* 14: 1–13.

Stross, B. 1973. Acquisition of botanical terminology by Tzeltal children. In M. Edmonson, ed., *Meaning in Mayan Languages*. Mouton.

Sugarman, S. 1983. *Children's Early Thought*. Cambridge University Press.

Symons, D. 1979. *The Evolution of Human Sexuality*. Oxford University Press.

Tajfel, H. 1981. *Human Groups and Social Categories*. Cambridge University Press.

Takaki, R. 1992. *The Tempest* in the wilderness: The racialization of slavery. *Journal of American History* 79: 892–912.

Tambiah, S. 1969. Animals are good to think and good to prohibit. *Ethnology* 8, no. 4: 422–459.

Taylor, M., and Gelman, S. 1993. Children's gender- and age-based categorization in similarity and induction tasks. *Social Development* 2: 104–121.

Taylor, S., Fiske, S., Etcoff, N., and Ruderman, A. 1978. The categorical and contextual bases of person memory and stereotyping. *Journal of Personality and Social Psychology* 36: 778–793.

Taylor, S. 1981. A categorization approach to stereotyping. In D. Hamilton, ed., *Cognitive processes in Stereotyping and Intergroup Behavior*. Erlbaum.

Thornton, M., Chatters, L., Taylor, R., and Allen, W. 1990. Sociodemographic and environmental correlates of racial socialization by Black parents. *Child Development* 61: 401–409.

Tooby, J., and Cosmides, L. 1992. The psychological foundations of culture. In J. Barkow et al., eds., *The Adapted Mind*. Oxford University Press.

Trehub, S. 1976. The discrimination of foreign speech contrasts by infants and adults. *Child Development* 47: 66–76.

Troyna, B. 1993. *Racism and Education*. Open University Press.

Troyna, B., and Hatcher, R. 1992. *Racism in Children's Lives: A Study of Mainly-White Primary Schools*. Routledge.

Turiel, E. 1983. Interaction and development in social cognition. In E. T. Higgins et al., eds., *Social Cognition and Social Development*. Cambridge University Press.

Turner, T. 1989. 'We are parrots,' 'Twins are bird': Play of tropes as operational structure. In J. Fernadez, ed., *Beyond Metaphor*. Stanford University Press.

van den Berghe, P. 1981. *The Ethnic Phenomenon*. Elsevier.

van den Boogaart, E. 1980. Colour prejudice and the yardstick of civility: The initial Dutch confrontation with black Africans, 1590–1635. In *Sociological Theories*. UNESCO.

Vaughan, G. M. 1963. Concept formation and the development of ethnic awareness. *Journal of Genetic Psychology* 103: 93–103.

Vaughan, G. M. 1987. A social psychological model of ethnic identity. In J. Phinney and M. Rotheram, eds., *Children's Ethnic Socialization*. Sage.

Vihman, M. 1985. Language differentiation by the bilingual infant. *Journal of Child Language* 12: 297–324.

Volterra, V., and Taeschner, R. 1978. The acquisition and development of language by bilingual children. *Journal of Child Language* 5: 311–326.

Vygotsky, L. 1978. *Mind in Society*. Harvard University Press.

Waters, M. 1990. *Ethnic Options: Choosing Identities in America*. University of California Press.

Watson-Gegeo, A., and Gegeo, D. 1986) Calling-out and repeating routines in Kwara'ae children's language socialization. In B. Schieffelin and E. Ochs, eds., *Language Socialization across Cultures*. Cambridge University Press.

Waxman, S. 1991. Convergences between semantic and conceptual organization in the preschool years. In S. Gelman and J. Byrnes, eds., *Perspectives on Language and Thought*. Cambridge University Press.

Wellman, H. 1990. *The Child's Theory of Mind*. MIT Press.

Wellman, H., and Gelman, S. 1992. Cognitive development: Foundational theories of core domains. *AnnuaL Review of Psychology* 43: 337–375.

Werker, J. 1989. Becoming a native speaker. *American Scientist* 77: 54–59.

Wertsch, J. 1985. *Culture, Communication and Cognition: Vygotskian Perspectives*. Cambridge University Press.

White, L. 1994. Alien nation: The hidden obsession of UFO literature. *Transition* 63: 24–33.

Whitehead, H. 1981. The bow and the burden strap: a new look at institutionalized homosexuality in native North America. In S. Ortner and H. Whitehead, eds., *Sexual Meanings*. Cambridge University Press.

Williams, J. 1980. *New People: Miscegenation and Mulattoes in the United States*. Free Press.

Williams, J. E., and Morland, J. K. 1976. *Race, Color, and the Young Child*. University of North Carolina Press.

Winant, H. 1994. *Racial Conditions: Politics, Theory, Comparisons*. University of Minnesota Press.

Wiser, M., and Carey, S. 1983. When heat and temperature were one. In D. Gentner and A. Stevens, eds., *Mental Models*. Erlbaum.

Witowski, S., Brown, C., and Chase, P. 1981. Where do trees come from? *Man* 16: 1–14.

Wright, L. 1994. Annals of politics: one drop of blood. *New Yorker*, July 25.

Wyer, R., and Martin, L. 1986. Person memory: The role of traits, group stereotypes, and specific behaviors in the cognitive representation of persons. *Journal of Personality and Social Psychology* 50: 661–675.

Yanagisako, S., and Delaney, C. 1995. Naturalizing power. In S. Yanagisako and C. Delaney, eds., *Naturalizing Power*. Routledge.

Yuill, N. 1992. Children's conception of personality traits. *Human Development* 35: 265–279.

Zinser, O., Rich, M., and Bailey, R. 1981. Sharing behavior and racial preference in children. *Motivation and Emotion* 5: 179–187.

Zuckerman, M. 1990. Some dubious premises in research and theory on racial differences: Scientific, social, and ethnical issues. *American Psychologist* 45: 1297–1303

Index